Performing Democracy in Iraq and South Africa

Performing Democracy in Iraq and South Africa

Gender, Media, and Resistance

Kimberly Wedeven Segall

SYRACUSE UNIVERSITY PRESS

First Paperback Edition 2016
16 17 18 19 20 21   6 5 4 3 2 1

Chapters 1 and 6 were originally published in a slightly different form as "Story and Song in Iraq and South Africa: From Individual to Collective Mourning Performances," *Comparative Studies of South Asia, Africa, and the Middle East* 25, no. 1 (2005): 138–51. Reprinted by permission of the author and the publisher.

Chapter 5 was originally published in a slightly different form as "Melancholy Ties: Intergenerational Loss and Exile in *Persepolis*," *Comparative Studies of South Asia, Africa, and the Middle East* 28, no. 1 (2008): 38–49. Reprinted by permission of the author and the publisher.

∞ The paper used in this publication meets the minimum requirements of the American National Standard for Information Sciences—Permanence of Paper for Printed Library Materials, ANSI Z39.48-1992.

For a listing of books published and distributed by Syracuse University Press, visit our website at http://www.syracuseuniversitypress.syr.edu.

ISBN: 978-0-8156-3343-3 (cloth)   978-0-8156-3474-4 (paperback)
978-0-8156-5256-4 (e-book)

Library of Congress has catalogued the cloth edition as follows:
Segall, Kimberly Wedeven.
    Performing democracy in Iraq and South Africa : gender, media, and resistance / Kimberly Wedeven Segall.
        pages cm
    Includes bibliographical references and index.
    ISBN 978-0-8156-3343-3 (cloth. : alk. paper) 1. Democracy—Social aspects—Iraq. 2. Democracy—Social aspects—South Africa.   3. Performance—Political aspects— Iraq.   4. Performance—Political aspects—South Africa.   5. Mass media—Political aspects—Iraq.   6. Mass media—Political aspects—South Africa.   I. Title.
    JQ1849.A91S44 2013
    320.9567—dc23   2013029840

Manufactured in the United States of America

A single flower—
breaks winter's grasp

Kimberly Wedeven Segall teaches courses accredited for women's studies, global development, and reconciliation studies at Seattle Pacific University, where she is professor of English. Over the past twenty years she has lived, worked, and conducted research in the Middle East and Africa, publishing numerous articles on how national identities are connected to the politics of loss and healing in *Comparative Studies of South Asia, Africa, and the Middle East, Public Culture,* and *Research in African Literatures.* As an activist and volunteer, she has worked with refugees, political prisoners, and guerrilla fighters. Her research on cultural forms includes these diverse voices, such as the militant and the street poet, the blog writer and the performance artist, tracing out a journey through Arab and African Springs. Her expertise in gender, culture, and performance studies has been recognized in her publications, and her placement as affiliate faculty of Gender, Women, and Sexuality Studies at the University of Washington. As study abroad director, she leads programs to South Africa and Morocco.

Contents

Illustrations

Preface

Because the journey of a researcher is never a straight path, any analysis of performed politics is also a map of one's own personal biography and political interests. Writing about gender, media, and innovative forms of political voicing—what I call the "forgotten spring"—reflects my experience at several sites. But for me, the forgotten "forgotten spring" happened in Kurdistan, over twenty years ago. Living in Iraq in 1993, I discovered that the Kurds had been largely forgotten by Western politics and media. The articles in *The New York Times*, for instance, mostly focused on the Turkish war against its Kurds from 1993 to 1995.[1] There were no headlines about the young democracy formed within Iraqi Kurdistan. In fact, the ethnic cleansing through chemical weapons was rarely remembered, the newly formed northern democracy was not recognized by Western politicians, and they were in a nationless, sanctioned, no-fly zone. During this year, I worked with guerrilla fighters—labeled at different times by the United States as "terrorists" or "freedom fighters"—who used stories and songs to transition from alienation to expression. At this time, I also volunteered with a Swiss relief agency, delivering bags of food to widows, listening to their stories unfold amidst the rubble of their houses destroyed by Saddam's tanks. These women of the *Anfal*—the period of ethnic cleansing—survived in tents, caves, and houses full of hungry children. Writing down stories told to me by survivors, I learned of government arrests, disappearances, chemical weapon attacks, and an obliteration of civilian populations. And I recorded their songs of lament and protest that emanated from radios, televisions, videos, and ceremonies.

After traveling to the Iraq-Iran border to a makeshift clinic supported by Doctors Without Borders, I saw children, who had been tending their family's sheep, being fitted for prosthetics—young landmine victims. At that point, I decided that more needed to be done. While I had taught an English language course—where the participants (mainly political leaders, like the sheik's son) were all male—I wanted to learn the stories of working women. Since most teachers are female, I created a conversation class for English teachers, mainly women. During this time, the Kurdish government had established a democracy, but given that it received no political recognition and was crippled by sanctions, tensions over controlling the borders, especially the illicit oil trafficking, led to conflict between two Kurdish political groups. I witnessed a split gendered response to violence, demonstrated by protests of public shame (*Haram!*) by women. After the near ethnic genocide by Saddam Hussein's regime, they were furious that "we are attacking each other." From this wartime experience, I have learned that political voicing is multitongued and gendered, not a homogenous act.

Living for a year in a civil war region—the so-called no-fly zone—has changed my perspective. Through the Kurdish civil war and sanctions, I heard stories from friends who had suffered through four consecutive wars: the Iran-Iraq War, then the ethnic cleansing of the *Anfal*, followed shortly by the Gulf War, and then the civil war. My husband and I were adopted into two Kurdish families who belonged to two different political parties. Part of the year, we lived with Kaka Muhammad and his two wives; then we were adopted by the Gozeh family. They had assigned bodyguards to us because we were aid workers. After the all-night bombings and shootings in our town, half of my students did not come to class, which was located in a building owned by one of the political parties, and I stopped teaching English. While conflict is not uncommon in newborn democracies, without economic or political support the Kurdish Spring was not only forgotten, but the lack of recognition also contributed to its collapse.

We lived in a war zone, and we also had to cross through a Turkish militarized zone, since there was no mail or international telephone service in Iraq. Once when traveling from Istanbul to the Iraqi border, the public bus was stopped by the Turkish military; for there was a war over territory, cultural rights, and water, waged against the Kurds in Turkey. After checking each person's identity cards, the Turkish soldiers lined up the men outside. Twenty minutes later, they took my husband into the station for questioning, and then placed him in a jail cell. When he didn't return, I decided to face the police. Walking off the bus, despite the Kurdish women's repeated admonitions to stay seated and to avoid arrest, I entered the military station to negotiate with the chief officer, who eventually released my husband from his cell. When we finally arrived at the border, two Amnesty International workers, waiting for a plane, described how they had been threatened by Turkish officers. The military had fired shots into the air, stating that if the two women from Amnesty did not get on the next plane, the next shots wouldn't miss. Continuing across the border, we were stamped out of Turkey with an exit visa, but not stamped into any political territory, since this Kurdish border was not connected to the state government of Iraq and did not have an Iraqi entrance visa. Yet this sanctioned area was imaginatively claimed with a large sign: "Welcome to Kurdistan." Even while crossing the restricted boundaries of transnational lines, I have witnessed sentimental citizenship, in the midst of great contestation, seeping through the minute capillaries of people and their creative publicity, the groundwater of young democratic movements.

When writing about creative forms of democratic expression, any record of protests also contains a certain point of view. My culture has shaped my sense of myself as a Western female. From the start, close friendships with Kurdish women—not only powerful mothers, but also political activists—influenced my views. My perceptions have been challenged by women who fought as guerrilla fighters or who have considerable domestic power. Also in Iraq, I took on a third gender, shifting realms where my husband could not. Shifting to male and female spaces, I sat with men discussing politics, then helped in the kitchen. Neither fully male, nor female, I was a third body—*mamosta*. After recording these stories and songs—not just spoken in communities but also broadcast through local television and radio stations—I started researching combinations of media, memory, and local expression, leading to this study of protest forms.

But, initially, when I left these war zones, it felt like a betrayal, since my Kurdish friends did not have passports. Despite the escalating violence, they could not leave. Before loading my last bag into the taxi, I hugged each member of the family that had taken us in and taught us the history of this region. "Don't forget us," Asad Gozeh urged, "Don't forget the Kurds." After we left, the civil war further escalated; the Second Gulf War, historically speaking, was not far behind; and after 2011, massive civilian displacements to Syria are further uprooted in the Arab Spring. In *Performing Democracy in Iraq and South Africa*, I have tried to keep my promise. Even as the impetus of this book began over twenty years ago, I have continued to work in various regions with guerrilla fighters, refugees, and political prisoners. Given the closed borders of war, my work has continued in cultural studies, in witnessing forums with refugees, in political performances with survivors of torture. Also this past decade I have crossed other borders through study abroad—building houses in million-person ghettos in Khayelitsha and working on reconciliation projects in Meknes; 120 students have traveled with me to North Africa and South Africa. Throughout this time, my ideas of protest, violence, and healing—first witnessed in the forgotten Kurdish democracy—have inflected my concept of "springtime." On this journey, I gratefully acknowledge cultural guides—Khawla Hadi, Marwa al-Mtowaq, Monwabisi Maqogi, and Asad Gozeh; academic guides—Luke Reinsma, Margaret Thompson Drewal, and Susan VanZanten; and my closest companions—William and Anika Segall. Throughout this path, my reflections on creative expressions of democratic culture—the heartland of *Performing Democracy*—address contemporary issues even as it recounts my own two-decade research journey into Arab and African Springs.

Introduction

The stubborn voice—
the one that blogs.
                    —Riverbend, *Baghdad Burning*, 2005

A newsflash shows a woman, beaten by police during mass protests, then the image fades out, leaving us with scenes of violence, gender, and democratic transition. But are we missing pieces? After working as an activist and volunteer in Middle Eastern and African communities over the past two decades, and based on my research as a scholar of cultural studies, I have noticed other diverse stories. For instance, when Marwa al-Mtowaq wrapped her national flag around herself, she smiled for the camera. This photo, posted on Facebook, enacted her excitement for a newborn democracy. But after several traumatic experiences, including fleeing as an exile into Saudi Arabia, Marwa's identity is not simple. Her rather militant claims for nationalism—not a Shiite image, but rather based in part on her reaction to mass media—astound her parents: an intergenerational gap. In a very distinct community, a group of Xhosa women who have fought as militants and been tortured as political dissidents voice protests over reparation emanating from the township; their stories are televised at a state commission, then restaged as a public performance. And far away, Fadwa Laroui protested against the state dictatorship. Not in some political march; rather, she went to the courts, she went to the police, she protested against the destruction of her shack, where she lived as a single mother with her children. When the state government ignored her claims, denied her petition for low-income housing, Fadwa lit herself on fire in front of the police station—a desperate suicide expressing the deepest desire for a new nation that granted justice to the poor. The fiery resistance was filmed, igniting protest as it spread on YouTube sites, then merged into popular blogs.[1] Beyond the newsflash, these women—one wrapped in a flag, one group televised, one enveloped in flames—perform democratic desire with diverse claims.

In this study of blogs and other performed protests, why do these stories, which fill the pages of this book, matter? These stories, circulated in popular culture but not captured by the Western press, add nuanced ideas of political identities in young democracies. And just as news media map out regions in Africa and the Middle East, so too these stories at times cross global lines, an alternate circuit of creative forms. Locating these stories in historical venues, I analyze how circulating forms, integrating creative media in blogs, plays, songs, and poetry, record transitional violence in emergent and young democracies, and I consider how these expressions, often as protest performances, attempt to cope with violence and imagine transition, after atrocity, years of dictatorship, disappearances, or upheaval. Within these popular and artistic forms, there are historical memories that entwine with economic, religious, generational, and gendered affinities—hybrid sites, forgotten springs. Given recent media attention to street culture and popular venues, my idea of "performing democracy" both challenges and extends the framework of protest presented by global media. With great excitement, I trace how blogs that witness street protests and other forms of performed resistance are important creative acts, voicing diverse political identities in a young democracy. At the same time, this book problematizes the way in which media frame culture and politicized terms.

What we are witnessing is not necessarily a renaissance of culture, since these societies have long resisted oppression, and cultural forms have always been working out loss; in fact, any performance of an economic dream can resist state power. Much is forgotten by the blinding flash of the media lens, as in the coverage of the Middle East and Africa: the quick shot of the "Arab Spring," of Religious Spring, or even of the "miracle" of transition in South Africa, whose young democracy still feels the apartheid tremors of violence and racist economics. While Western media spotlight protest, rightly claiming the importance of political voicing, the swinging lens from political spring to winter ignores creative resistance and simplifies history—with its ebb and flow of traumatic experiences and economic challenges—which carves *sacred spaces* into communities. Because traumatic histories, similar to painful personal experiences, can have a silencing effect, this book claims that any form of protest is, at once, a political voicing of past injustice, even as a survivor's claim of self after unbearable loss can enact personal agency or a claim of communal bonds. Instead of the newsflash that forgets the subtlety of emergent democratic identifications, spoken amidst contestation and gendered territories, can we not spare a glance, a moment to consider the imaginative ways that individuals name themselves, after decades of trauma and their own resistance, in creative forms—in effect, *performing democracy*.

In my larger attempt to expand on this contemporary paradigm of political bloom, I add three correctives. Cultural forms associated with protest (not to be over-valorized as political tidal waves, nor only noticed for their subtle economic and political tides) should also be considered as important signs to illuminate what is less noticed: *gender locations, social contestation* (often rising from traumatic sites of history), and *artistic revision* (attempts to imagine collective bonds after atrocity). To be sure, I am not claiming that popular speech acts guarantee a democratic revolution, nor do popular expressions wipe out the aftermath of atrocity. But these verbalizations are healing venues, if we consider how repressive regimes, characterized by elite economic privileging after decades of colonization and upheaval, and by imprisonment and torture, have stifled so many voices. So while acknowledging the ongoing resistance of cultural forms, which are always shifting, and clarifying that media art illuminates social dynamics but, of course, cannot claim to change political tides, I appreciate how the idea of the miracle of South Africa or the hope of the Arab Spring also captures the excitement about these ever-changing, alternative spaces of communication and reception, such as blogs, televised commissions, protest performances of media images, or even broadcasts of songs, like radio hip-hop or rap. What is *original* is the public participation in emerging cultural forms, and the divergent case studies in this book pay attention to authorship and audience as new Internet forms, televised testimonies, and creative media arts have provided more opportunities for wider involvement.

Since my case studies cross regions into areas of extreme political transition, what needs to be clear from the start is that this book is not a political mapping, but rather a study of cultural forms—traveling across time and regions from Arab to African Springs. My obsession with cultural forms that speak in the midst of regimes and after periods of atrocity, and my particular fascination with women's innovative incorporations of media and culture, may not be the same path that other scholars select. Indeed, given my own work facilitating performances and volunteering in communities—a practitioner who has lived in Iraq and South Africa—it is not a route that many would take. But even as research is inevitably informed by experience, this book, first and foremost, is a research study of how popular and artistic expressions engage media, extending the locution and location of a cultural spring, accentuating alternative sites and transitional stages, telling stories omitted by the press.

Before embarking on this study of media and cultural springs, it is important to understand the mass media context. While Western media tracked a groundswell of protest as an "Arab Spring," the press forgot that the original use of this term was highly controversial. In 2005, the media connected the Bush doctrine and the invasion of Iraq as a force that would usher in an "Arab Spring" of democracy to the region. In *The Washington Post*, for example, Charles Krauthammer argued, "all this regional mischief-making is critical because we are at the dawn of an Arab Spring—the first bloom of democracy in Iraq, Lebanon, Egypt, Palestine."[2] Although forgetting to mention the crushed spring in Iran, when the United States and Britain helped overthrow the democratic government of Mossadeq in 1953, he continued, condemning certain groups as the "axis of evil" that will try to "squash this Arab Spring." But the first springing of democracy, after the Gulf War, was not recognized by the American government, even if, in 2005, Hezbollah won elections, and Palestinians in 2006 voted against the current authority, the al-Fatah party, given their discontent with the endlessness of Israeli occupation. Not surprisingly, the rhetoric of the Arab Spring completely died out when the invasion of Iraq and lack of postwar planning led to an anti-occupation reaction and civil war. Nor did it emerge after the young democracy's stabilization in Iraq in 2008, when President Maliki (a Shiite Iraqi) battled another Shiite group, the Mahdi army, which had become a violent force of civil unrest. In 2011, the Arab Spring was in the air once again, only after Egypt's protest. But now the political term has a changed meaning: "Arab Spring" refers to local political protests. For instance, in 2012 in Iraq, the term "spring" refers to grassroots protest with demands for more economic opportunities and a limited term for the president. But with quick-tempered impatience, journals and books begin questioning what comes next after the Arab Spring.[3]

But mass media do track "Arab Spring" as a traveling term: the press inroads this movement of 2011 across North Africa—Tunisia and Egypt—and then tracks it across the Middle East—from Iraq, Syria, Iran, and Libya—and then into West Africa. Similarly, this book extends the conversation on creative expressions of political desire across geopolitical lines. Organized around the primary moment of violence—a claim of a Western democracy, which was completely redefined less than ten years later—this book questions what other ways the concept of populist springtime has been forgotten. What groups are dismissed, labeled, or excluded by the Western press from this idea of democratic desire? How does this idea also apply to Muslim communities in Africa? What altered meanings are found in a South African Spring? What religious identifications—as in maternal bonds of Shiite heroism, female *sangoma* healers, or even social witch hunts that target women—are enacted in these young democracies? Are these popular expressions also gendered sites of political desire? During this time period when we think of popular media art as a political voicing, I propose that we use this learning moment to make sense of creative activism, a catalytic reimagining of Arab and African Springs.

Fostering a renewed vision of how public protests perform political identifications in emergent democracies is a timely and critical intervention. Indeed, this book questions how we can understand non-Western democracies after the mediated depictions of the Islamic and African world after 9/11. While images of women, abused by police, flash via the news coverage of protest, without detailing their stories, there was a distinct, earlier circulation of sexual politics. Kelly Oliver interrogates how coverage of sexual violence and torture by female soldiers captivated the "public imagination" with its "pornographic" power of dominant women and their victims, while the post-9/11 deaths of female soldiers "receive little attention."[4] Media provides a way of seeing, Oliver adds, restricting the view of corpses of soldiers and civilians, and stimulating live-time coverage of war, with journalists peering from their helmets, preventing us any "critical" perception of others; indeed, the spectacle of embedded media creates "willful ignorance" about our shared world connection, since we cringe with the journalist, denying the responsibility of "witnessing" the violence.[5] At first the press largely reported the "script" of the administration after 9/11, claim the authors of *When the Press Fails*, until the "policy misadventure spiraled into insurgency"; but also, alternate frames after 9/11 were not "culturally resonant," suggests Robert Entman, since the "preferred framing" of the White House was more compatible to the dominant thinking in the United States.[6] Not only are alternative cultural interpretations ignored, but Western media are accused of forgetting the subtleties of religion and politics—as in the 2009 critique, *Blind Spot: When Journalists Don't Get Religion.*[7] Michael Rubin argues that Western presses report violence and political conflict, but completely miss any "disagreements [that] involve doctrinal disputes within sects, rather than fighting between sects or religions." The end result is that Western presses "often get . . . the Middle East wrong."[8] Thus, political movements suffer the Western media's glaring spotlight with its blind spots, even as they endure, at other points, the black holes of media neglect.

But what happens next? Soon after the press highlighted the excitement of springtime, there was a call for democracy through "Arab Mandelas."[9] While South Africa's transition to democracy avoided civil war, the transitional violence and the process of populist voicing after elections, a historical protest of the past via the truth and reconciliation commission, are not elucidated by the press. In fact, when the Western media uses prior ways of knowing and labeling history, in this instance, or in the label of the Islamic Revolution in Iran as "Islamic Spring," it selectively forgets and transfers knowledge—"forgotten substitutions," to apply Joseph Roach's performance terms, and a "dangerous fiction" of a "unified culture."[10]

So even as the news shifts from spring protests into winter, eliciting labels of miracles and nightmares, as academics decry the press for not being a better watchdog, and a few mainstream presses have offered halting apologies, I want to suggest an alternative lens. First, the case studies of blogs and performed protest in this book challenge the singular idea of a globalizing effect of mass media. Assumptions that the press failed are often premised on the notion that the public is one body, as if there could be a single response that receives, in shock and awe, the effects of the political spin, without diverse, global reactions. I argue that globalization—as in the circulation of 9/11 and protest icons—produces a multiplicity of national effects and diverse political springs, not a singular or hegemonic effect. And alternative media sources offer counternarratives of historical events. Resistance to mass media images, an important element in my paradigm of springtides, emerges as a Cape Muslim in South Africa performs a staged protest of the circulating images of 9/11 and its fallout of civilian deaths; thus, Nadia Davids redefines herself not just as "coloured"—as in the apartheid definition of certain communities of mixed Malay, Indian, and Black South Africans—but also in terms of a global, Islamic feminism.

Second, alternative media record distinct perspectives—in effect, counternarratives. As in a blog by a twenty-something, a computer programmer who codes her name as River or Riverbend; she recorded how al-Jazeera and al-Arabia were suspended from official press conferences by the Iraqi Governing Council for two weeks, but she reported that this is "no loss—they are becoming predictable. The real news is happening around us."[11] As a witness to events, River described "her 9/11," political disasters that have become sites of social memory, such as the chemical agents used in Fallujah. But the circulation of New York's 9/11 images made it difficult for Western readers to attend to her testimony.[12] And it becomes difficult to understand democratic desire, given Western uneasiness with hybrid religious and political identities, and blindness toward internal religious disputes. Indeed, the Western frame presented silent, tortured bodies—what Jasbir Puar decries as showcased subjects, caricatured as having repressed sexualities.[13] So River's claim to be a modern woman—a computer programmer—and a devout, Sunni Muslim—who wears blue jeans—is rarely understood, if the concept of "Islamic feminism" eludes Western media frames. But if we ignore River's voice, then we end our media blitz with images of tortured Iraqis, not listening to their stories, not attending to their ideas of democratic springs.

So while images of protesting bodies on television are an important witness, because they encourage other sites of global protest, these images can produce an icon of the crowd, blind to gender and religious pluralities, stripping away diverse histories. In contrast to mass media, charting out protest in creative sites provokes an appreciation for artistic form, pluralistic voices, and democratic desire. Let's not follow the "absent" body in flattened images that flow through television.[14] Instead, through global instances, starting with Iraq and Iran, then crossing into other protest spaces, regions, and history, let's pursue the bodies of the crowd! These performances locate—Diana Taylor argues—a new way of knowing through people's actions as they stage political claims based on traumatic events; in effect, a parade of a collective identity.[15]

But how do we track a crowd? Surely the reasons that people protest are located within their own experiences of loss, especially given the danger of participating in events whose borders are policed by military force. While there may be common experiences of political violence, what ties people through events—experiences of individuals, perspectives on politics, and priorities of a family or specific group—all suggest that every crowd is a body of individuals, each with different motives. The former political prisoner, tortured by a regime, has a different voice of protest than the young man unemployed five years after graduating from college. A mother in the crowd, protesting in the name of future generations, and a young woman, fired from her job, register a plethora of opinions. To find voices of diversity, we can look beyond mass media in order to find other archives of knowledge—other records of lived experience and street politics. Following witnesses onto innovative spaces, this book shows stages of controversy with histories of the guerrilla fighter, the female activist, the blog writer, the street poet, the performance artist—in effect, an alternative map of democratic springs.

And even as street protests are recorded in blogs, as part of a public debate about political choices and identities, it is not just televised sites and blogs that perform political identity, since other prolific forms of memory replicate and circulate—the blog published as a book, or the televised testimony incorporated into a sold-out theater performance. Interpreted as signs of democratic potential, such cultural transformations shift from silence to popular speech, and, at times, from frustration with global scenes to local protest. By simultaneously protesting global and local politics, these forums resist the Western frame, charting out complex, transnational sites. Performing loss and inscribing experience, these artistic occurrences are signs of hope for countries yearning not only for voting rights, but also for a voicing of the self.

But even as the protests record economic struggles and repression, these voices are political and personal, because after repressive regimes, public reactions, to use straight psychological lingo, divide into two camps: speaking or internalizing loss, as in wary silence, for instance, or even as expressions of altered identities after atrocity.[16] Narrating injury, as Nouri Ghana argues, has "political implications," since stories lament the injustices of the past.[17] In protest forms, such mourning of injustice can redirect the primary loss into idealism—what the postcolonial theorist Ranjana Khanna perceives as a common *nationalism*. But when loss is suffered—loss of a loved one or even a lost ideal—one's self-concept can shatter. When people internalize loss, a depressive form of self or social criticism emerges, what the forefather of Western psychoanalysis, Sigmund Freud, labeled as a "revolt" from painful conditions, the "crushed state of melancholy."[18] But given that Freud was a Jewish war exile, Khanna extends his idea into a political state of melancholy, wherein the painful past can convert into an uneasy "conscience," critiquing the "status quo," rejecting *state* and *global* domination.[19] Emerging in ever-shifting forms of nationalism and protest, tremors of the past, amidst economic and political crisis, and tendrils of worldwide images, continue to invade the postcolonial subject, and may, at times, be informing private scruples, public protests.

Yet psychoanalysis is a limited frame for recent protests. Throughout history, the Western world used racist psychology to hide violence.

As Mohja Kahf details, the West initially identified Muslim women in the Golden Age of Islam as powerful political players and queens—not depressed, silent women.[20] And African kingdoms, as powerful trading meccas, were later re-visioned, after colonization, as backward regions with melancholic natives. What is needed is a new mapping of social loss—a recuperative voicing, an enunciation of diversified histories and political voices. This refreshed lens is also critical since trauma theorists have dissimilar notions about how violence permeates societies and filters through expressions of culture.[21] In fact, psychoanalysis as a Western practice does not acknowledge the complex ways that local cultures work out trauma in alternative venues. *Performing Democracy* attends to alternate sites of creativity—emotional forums that simultaneously record violence and imagine community after atrocity. Public expressions often show dissent against the state; at the same time, these vocalizations, which often record street politics and embody voices in the crowd, enact various kinds of communal identity—a sentimental citizenship. Thus, public and private inscriptions of the past are not just psychological, for they illuminate political tributaries, resist state impediments, protest corruption and inequity, and, at times, attempt to imagine ever-flowing claims for human and democratic rights.

Unlike facile pronouncements of miracles or religious nightmares, at their core, the Arab and African Springs, as emotive ideas, must include a paradigm shift to chart not only unfinished mourning, executed as political protest, but also diverse identifications emerging as part of the politics of healing. Given how nation-states narrate (and sanction) their losses, grief is not to be dismissed as a simplistic, private, isolated action. Rather, loss links to the present political movement, argues Judith Butler, because reflecting on the dead is not solipsistic; rather, it ties the mourner to a "political community."[22] Many trauma theorists argue that violence reconfigures identity. This reconfiguration of identity suggests a model of continually shifting national affiliations, a stark contrast to stagnant concepts of violence, without historical nuance, such as orientalist ideas of ancient tribalism, unending sectarianism, continuous gender warfare. Violence alters subjectivity, as Veena Das and Arthur Kleinman insist, so survivors must not only reconstruct identity but are also in a sense "re-making a world," redefining their "political society," their concept of community.[23] This reconstruction of self is not limited to individuals, since neighborhoods are also distraught, displaced, reorganized—what Kai Erikson calls a form of social trauma.[24] Many of these permutations of trauma are passed to the second generation, even as youthful generations conceive their own protest narrations, their own forms of embodied and creative revolt.[25] Crowds hold divergent perspectives; yet public mourning of loss can also reconfigure communal bonds.

Extending this idea, these case studies show how creative forms attempt to imagine community after atrocity. One way that these losses are expressed is through emergent media, which offers new spaces for more voices. Self-expression resists the silencing alienation that often walks beside atrocity. In itself, this very limited movement moves toward healing, speaking of a self and a society that has not been buried in mass graves. Narrating the past is also essential for conflict resolution, contends John Paul Lederach, because it exposes how people cope with loss, conceive of a conflict, and imagine social change.[26] Even though staging loss is a critical enactment of subjectivity, cultural productions, as the performance theorist Peggy Phelan clarifies, are not an exact replica of the loss. Rather, it is a creative and subtle form of mimicry that can transfigure the "repetitive force of trauma," finding a "way to overcome it."[27] Artistic responses—unlike appalling expressions of violence played out in the streets—create nonviolent debates of political and economic power. This dialogue of subjects, in M. M. Bakhtin's philosophy, reflects distinct classes, an expressive and essential voicing of conflict.[28] These alternate maps of political power, economic experience, and personal emotion, while themselves not necessarily forces of revolution, are integral voices for imagining greater resolution, providing a needed level of civility, given the plurality of any democracy.

In short, a straight political analysis or a psychoanalytic framework does not fully allow for the intergenerational, gendered, hybrid, split, and virtual crossings between national boundaries, which this book analyzes in global sites of media and artistic expression. Given the *original* ways that people are coping with loss and creatively defining themselves in the midst of mass media, the chapters in this book offer a fresh paradigm for witnessing political events via creative venues.[29] But one final correction is needed in considering how popular expressions emerge in the media, for as a scholar of gender, I want to point out that "Arab Spring" is a *neutered term*.

Integral to each chapter is the way that masculinity and femininity are engendered in periods of violence and political transition. Furthermore, women's voices—a *forgotten spring*—emphasize their contributions to democratic expression, and amidst women there are multiple opinions about political needs. Not just social roles, but also gender roles, need to be considered in more concrete terms—part of political groups. In *Scheherazade Goes West*, Fatima Mernissi's approach suggests women's political identities need to be conceived in terms of a "minority" group, despite their population numbers, because they have been left out of key negotiations and have continually battled for political power.[30] Any study of gender requires a global vision of power, declares Chandra Talpade Mohanty, to see the experiences and actions of women from a more "cross-cultural lens." Because global and local not only interact but also "constitute each other," what is needed, urges Mohanty, is a *Feminism Without Borders*, not limited by physical territory.[31]

But how to chart out such gendered spaces? Women and men often gather together to make claims in public places, and in these forums, public articulations, despite being very personal expressions, map out political problems. These compelling stories transfigure political obstacles into a "public mood," claims Jonathan Flatley; in fact, these stories of loss, according to this critic, allow for altered perceptions.[32] Extending this theory, when women tell their stories, these narratives map out the political atmosphere. Such public and private venues—from open testimonies to covert blogs—register lively barometers of political aspirations, gendered views, global reflections, and social conditions.

These acts of protest, either on the street, or on the stage, or even at a state commission, navigate both gender and power. As forms of political performance, the possibility of change enacted by a group—the "field of action"—and the limits of populist conceptions—the web of "cultural production"—both need to be considered: concepts elaborated by Boal and Bourdieu.[33] While considering these two fields of action and production, I attend to alternative spaces of protest, following massive relocations after violence in order to challenge the way that we know democratic springs—a relocation of both time and place, an altered genealogy. Thus, what is needed is a road map of chapters, briefly sketched out, so readers can select from alternate sites and creative invocations of political identities—all integrating or responding to media.

The first chapter sets the context for this book by narrating my experience in a forgotten democracy, two decades past, in Kurdistan, Iraq, delineating case studies of televised and radio broadcasts of songs and stories of survival after ethnic cleansing. Chapter 2 considers how televised war impacts Shiite women, who have fled three waves of war-torn violence. Responding through poetry and experiential narration, these Shiite women protest the continual refugee crisis amidst political transitions and perform a resistant interpretation of religious and national identity, rejecting Western narratives. Not only do they tell their stories in venues to educate others and to create more political awareness, but they also enact divergent national placements, split intergenerational responses. Further analyzing women's voices, chapter 3 depicts a multivoiced protest, staged in the midst of the muezzin's call to prayer—the diverse calls for justice from nine women in *9 Parts of Desire*. While this political play suggests fluctuating locations of Arab identity, these transregional recollections, as part of the social memories of the play, also resist the media's determination to change conflict into a single avenue of ancient sectarian grudges, as multiple female perspectives add further context to emergent violence. Gendered sites of war are also discussed in chapter 4 through the self-positioning of youth culture in blogs, as a Sunni feminist computer programmer and a secular gay architect reframe national identifications.

Traversing national boundaries, chapter 5 follows an Iranian Spring marked by an ongoing political protest in Tehran and a generational divide. These intergenerational politics and emotional bonds are charted within *Persepolis* through sketched bodies of personal and public protest within multiple locations of urban space. While Western media suggests the Arab Spring is often shadowed by its dark nemesis—the Islamic Revolution—this chapter complicates this historical parallel by remembering a forgotten democracy. Continuing to study gender roles within political surges, chapter 6 considers a distinctly African Spring, since massive uprisings of popular testimonies are not limited to Arab populations. This chapter includes my work as a practitioner, facilitating performance workshops for former guerrilla fighters. Communal affiliations are further analyzed in chapter 7 when two female playwrights, from Muslim and Jewish communities, describe the gendered nationalism that they felt after watching images of 9/11 and an aftermath of wars. The final chapter challenges readers to rethink gender and cultural emergence in youth culture, in ritual performances of young democracies as bewitched states.

By using this critical paradigm of a forgotten spring, this book opens a budding space to revise outgrown modes of Western thought on gendered histories and appreciates the youthful bloom of politics within cultural forms. It is an invitation to listen to fresh voices: an arrangement of women's creative expressions, not yet picked by Western media. These public voices comment on transregional affairs, not just local events, and usher us all into a new stage of consideration about how we might reimagine one another, and how we might reimagine the politics of healing. Political responses are not just cognitive and artistic, they are also emotionally poignant arenas, in the language of affect theory—a "bloom space."[34] Not a singular or fixed body, cultures grow within tactile pollinations across state lines—a sentient xylem pulses across national affinities, a blossoming space of variegated identities. Therefore, public expressions by women are not just contesting state privilege, but they are also defining complex identities: not limited to one category of gender, class, minority, religion, or generation—hybrid blooms of democratic voices.

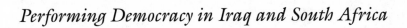

Performing Democracy in Iraq and South Africa

1 | Radio Songs, Kurdish Stories, Videos

Politics of Healing after Ethnic Cleansing

There was nobody guiding me to find my homeland
At the last moment, the flute started to speak.
　　　　　　　—Jamal Khambar, "No Body," 2007

Western media have not been consistent in their record of Kurdish protest, nor careful about the specific contexts and variegation of these diverse uprisings. This chapter remembers a forgotten democracy, voted in with nearly two hundred polling stations, in the spring of 1992, and records, during my year living in Kurdistan in 1993, its liberation songs, its Kurdish Spring. While in a taxi driving into Iraq, the driver explained the importance of a song on the radio about chemical weapons killing thousands of people in the urban town of Halabja. The lyrics also played in the mind of a guerilla fighter, reminding him of how he helped his brother flee Saddam's tanks. This song was played, performed, and televised during multiple moments of history. It began with the ethnic cleansing of Kurds—150,000 civilians murdered and 180,000 missing, almost all of the rural villages decimated in Iraq amidst chemical weapons, devastating, over a period of years, civilians and guerrilla fighters.[1] Long afterward, this song played during the Second Gulf War and on into the country's democratic elections of 2005. Even as televisions played videos of singing and dancing, groups reenacted these dances at gatherings. Both local expressions and creative media contextualized violence: offering hope, a creative arrangement of music to witness their

1

losses. However, unlike the private hearing of radio and television media, communal events embody local bonds of support. Kurds dance to these songs, shoulder-to-shoulder with neighbors and friends. This chapter considers how Kurdish cultural forms navigate various political, historical, and media spaces, to cope with their national trauma, to work toward democratic desires.

To introduce the context of this chapter, I want to position what Western media call the "Kurdish question" or the "Kurdish problem," since the press has not been consistent in spotlighting and then forgetting various Kurdish groups, despite their political roles in uprisings throughout Syria, Turkey, Iraq, and Iran at different historical points. For instance, the media of the Syrian uprising, such as Tim Arango's article in the *New York Times*, September 28, 2012, suggest that Kurds from Syria want an "independent nation," without quoting a Kurdish witness to this concept.[2] In fact, the quote by a Syrian Kurdish opposition figure, Mahmood Sabir, suggested that troops were training in Iraqi Kurdistan because after the regional collapse of the Bashar al-Assad regime there would be a "security vacuum" and we must "defend ourselves." But the article assumed that because Kurds were preparing for their local protection and hoping for Kurdish rights and the security of their families, that the Kurds were a spark of "volatility," part of an "all-out sectarian war that could drag in neighboring countries." Because these training units of Kurds were being helped by Masoud Barzani, this Iraqi Kurdish leader was labeled in the Western press as a "kingmaker." No mention of the importance of the Kurdish local militia in Iraq in keeping their people safe and creating a secure territory—unlike the upheaval of Baghdad after the American occupation—nor recognition of the current prosperity of Iraqi Kurdistan as an independent substate that has not broken from the Iraqi nation. No mention of the delicate state of Syria, given that over 95,000 Syrians have died in this uprising, and the number continues to rise from this U.N. Human Rights Commission estimate. Indeed, this article contains assumptions of ethnic groups with inflexible ancient memories, a suggestion, without specific quotes, of a bizarre history, a "cosmic retribution for Saladin's victories" over the Western world. The article does not state the more recent injury of 120,000 Syrian Kurds, which is pointed out in J. Michael Kennedy's coverage, Kurds who had their citizenship randomly and violently revoked in 1962.[3] Or, another tangible instance, a 180-mile landmass was stolen from the Syrian Kurds, given to Arabs, favored by the regime, in 1973.

From the very beginning of the 2011 Arab Spring, President Bashar al-Assad offered last-minute concessions to Kurds during the demonstrations, citizenship to those dispossessed in the sixties and their children, an approximate two hundred thousand Kurds living in a "stateless" existence.[4] While many articles suggested Kurdish caution in this conflict, a chronic situation where ten thousand people flee across the border each day, soon to add to about 4 million refugees from Syria, according to United Nations estimates, not counting the 4.2 million internally displaced, there have been many Kurds, such as twenty-somethings at the university in Damascus, fleeing to avoid conscription in the Syrian militia. And while Kurds have been selective in joining the warfare (state massacres) of other regions, they have been part of the protest. After the United Nations Security Council offered a weak resolution with possible sanctions, one that Russia and China quickly voted down, the Syrian government was believed to have assassinated the Kurdish leader Mashaal Tammo, who had previously served a three-year prison sentence for his activism against the regime. Afterward, a crowd of almost fifty thousand people, indignant Kurds, protested the government, and at the funeral of Tammo, security forces shot two mourning citizens. Not only are some Western presses, evident in Arango's article, labeling conflict in terms of sectarian warfare without considering the challenges inevitable to any new democracy, deciding state lines and economic or political power, but also the orientalist leap, a bit outside of contemporary history, is disturbing.

On top of this, Western media often detail a schizophrenic view of "friendly Kurds" in Iraq (who are American allies), or Syrian Kurds (unreliable sovereignty seekers), and "bad Kurds" in Turkey (who fight against our Turkish ally). There has rarely been any coverage of the human rights violation of torture and disappearances, nor the removal of elected Kurdish officials from parliament, nor the land grabs and military occupation that are the fate of Turkish Kurds; only the desperate acts of violence in

Istanbul by the Kurdistan Workers Party, the PKK, and their recent desperate hunger strikes in prison make the press. Each Kurdish group needs specific contextualization within its nation-state and some attention to internal tensions, not media labels or overarching generalizations. There are 4 million Kurds in Iraq, 23 percent of the population, in contrast to the 2 million in Syria, roughly 11 percent of the population, as well as nearly 6 million in Iran and 13 million in Turkey, according to a study of displacement and dispossession by Dawn Chatty.[5] The nation-state lines (formed in Paris in 1919) have left the Kurds a minority in each of the four countries. So even as the war-weary feet of ten thousand people in flight cross daily as refugees from Syria—reported by the United High Commissioner for Refugees—including former Iraqi exiles and Syrian Kurds, and as Turkey has voiced political anxiety, given its own crackdown on Kurdish regions, Western media slippage and schizophrenia in discussing "Kurdish" regions suggests a need to contextualize an earlier history. Returning to a forgotten spring in Kurdish Iraq, I want to remember a democracy established in 1992.

The mass media have been inconsistent in their favoritism and rejection of Kurdish groups, and video media have altered meanings over time, as in a single video, for instance, interpreted differently by various groups. When a police video, a recording of a mass execution of Kurds, was handed to me shortly after I moved to the large town of Shaqlawa in northern Iraq, it had multiple meanings. The video was created by Ba'athist military, proving to Saddam Hussein that they were controlling the "Kurdish problem." During the First Gulf War, the video, however, was captured by Kurdish guerilla fighters at a police station and changed meaning. When my friend gave me this recording, the video was valued as evidence, proving the slaughter of his people. After watching the video, I mentioned the filmed massacre to my Iraqi neighbor, and she told me the story of a young boy who pretended to be shot and hid under bodies, crawling away at night. The media can both portray tragedy and trigger an array of traumatic histories. When I told stories of Kurdish persecution, liberals listened during the Clinton administration, and during the Bush administration conservatives wanted to hear these same stories. Changing responses, such as mass media directions in the news, demonstrate how these local stories have been given altered meanings. All of these distinct forms—from public media to oral and communal performances—do not replace one another; rather, each can be a way to embody loss or political identities. Technology dressed these stories in contradictory fashions over time, and Western media have ignored local contexts.

While media often position Kurds as a tribal identity, when the western no-fly zone relieved political pressure on the Iraqi Kurds, the Kurds established a democracy, agreed upon by its two central political parties (the Kurdistan Democratic Party—the KDP, and the Patriotic Union of Kurdistan—the PUK). Redefining Kurdish identity in an insightful political analysis, Denise Natali denotes that there is "nothing natural about Kurdish national identity, Kurdish political behavior," nor any set pattern between Kurds and the governing power. Furthermore, this political scientist rejects that there is any "natural hatred" between Shia and Sunni, or Christian and Alevi, and Kurdish groups; in fact, there have been time periods when Kurds have not "differentiated themselves from Arabs, Turks, or Persians." Indeed, Natali claims, "Kurdish nationalists are not inherently defiant toward the state."[6]

Positioning an essential hatred (or claiming that individualistic Kurds are tribalists who despise state authority) disregards the complex "political spaces" and uneven power dynamics of nation building, which Natali critiques.[7] The complex identifications are mapped in a memoir by the well-known Iraqi Kurdish writer and filmmaker Hiner Saleem, who lists his given name of Azad Shero Salim in his memoir *My Father's Rifle*, and charts out his genealogy in a single passage.[8] He described how his grandfather was "born a Kurd, in a free country."[9] But when the Ottomans arrived, they said: "You're Ottoman." In response, he "became Ottoman. At the fall of the Ottoman Empire, he became Turkish. The Turks left and he became a Kurd again in the kingdom of Sheikh Mahmoud, king of the Kurds." When the British fought against the Ottoman Empire, they changed the region to a nation-state. Saleem's grandfather, who learned some English after the British came, became "Iraqi" when the British "invented Iraq." Not only has self-positioning fluctuated, but different languages and politics also divide Kurdish groups, who affiliate with certain communities and live in distinct nations.

Yet within Kurdish songs, there is a Kurdistan—a place of refuge. Kurdish ethnicity is not just a blood line; it is an imaginative response by Kurdish groups to state powers—what Christopher Houston calls a "relational and creative act."[10] Charting the history of this "imagined community," David McDowall traces how Kurds have been increasingly "drawn into the national fabric," and in the diasporic history of Chatty, she explains these state bonds as "practical requirements of economic survival."[11] Then, too, political self-determination now gives control to the Kurdistan Regional Government in Iraq, creating a safe and economically viable space that is quite different from the ethnic cleansing of the Ba'athist regime and of World War I.[12] For WWI, Chatty researches how the Kurds were caught in the middle of three armies—the British, Russians, and Ottomans—and in the city of Bayazid this resulted in an "ethnic cleansing" in which "very few, if any" of the Kurdish Muslim population survived.[13] Given these tangled early and modern political identifications—two periods of ethnic cleansing, innumerable pacts between Iraqi Kurds and the changing guard of governing forces, political experiences of self-determination, but not separatism, and now a Kurdish state within federal Iraq—I want to reconsider national sentiment. It is not just envisioned as sovereignty or even as the more politically apt self-determination, but also as an imaginative force to personally cope and socially reconstruct community after the ravages of atrocity. What I hope to show in this chapter is how Kurdish sentiment flows through sung media, operating not just as a political ideal, but also as a force of collective healing and a map of changing affinities.

Given controversy around the "Kurdish question," I want to begin with my perspective, which has been influenced by living in Iraq during the sanctions and during the Kurdish civil war. In 1993–1994, I became close friends with the Gozeh family, a Kurdish family in Shaqlawa, who adopted me and have remained friends for over twenty years, as they relocated in the United States. I taught English courses to former guerrilla fighters, as the no-fly zone established a cessation of violence for a period. Even during my first trip into the country, I was struck by the fact that I was entering a nation that existed in the minds of its inhabitants, but was politically denied and economically crippled by Baghdad,

Istanbul, and Washington, DC. After the Turkish security stamped me out of their country, I did not receive an official stamp in my passport, since other governments did not recognize this democracy, and the Iraqi state was divided by no-fly zones. There was a year-long gap in my passport. Crossing over the border, the usual security check was replaced by a friendly Kurdish greeting, and an enormous sign: "WELCOME TO KURDISTAN." Trying to register with various official agencies, such as the United Nations station in Shaqlawa, I was placed on a notification list, in case Saddam Hussein's military invaded the no-fly zone. Although the taxi ride was full of music and conversation, I noticed paucity in the general landscape—very few people outside the cities. Only a year later did I realize that the emptiness was the result of an ethnic cleansing that had destroyed all the villages and had shipped their inhabitants to concentration camps. Or killed them. I began wondering how ethnic minorities survived under such conditions.

One of my students described how his house had been destroyed by Saddam Hussein's military, after which he came to the city of Shaqlawa to join the resistance. When he was not training or in class studying English, he sat in a closet-sized shop, selling rice and beans to support himself and his mother, on the outskirts of Shaqlawa, next to the highway. Speaking of his destroyed home and decimated village, now void of people, he dreamed of rebuilding his childhood home. What hopeful resilience he modeled, after losing everything! In Shaqlawa, the stories of collective loss and hopeful dreams were accompanied by another medium: song. The music swelled from the crackly speakers of radios, emitting Kurdish music from precariously perched stands on outdoor tomato and cucumber stands, and in restaurants, televisions, securely shelved next to the plates, boomed forth the sounds and visuals of Kurdish musicians. Since I had limited cooking tools and even fewer culinary skills, I went several times a week to my favorite lamb kebab joint. Tucked in a corner, my husband and I talked with the restaurant owner or watched groups dancing to the tune of Kurdish songs. So it came as no surprise that when we were invited to the Gozeh house, they would draw our attention to their television as well. "This is a Kurdish song," Asad would say, translating part of it. "This is our Kurdish dance." The TV was always on.

There are lots of Kurdish songs: songs of war, songs of love, songs for children, songs for dancing. Small children learn to dance as they are tenderly held on the laps of their parents, gently moved to the rhythm of their songs. In her travel journal, Christiane Bird noticed a range of songs from religious songs and lullabies to expansive histories and "epics that tell heroic legends."[14] Songs and dances were part of all major celebrations, especially the weddings that I attended in 1993. Even a fishing trip, during which one of my friends threw a hand grenade into the water to stun the fish, ended with a picnic with songs and dancing. Always invited to join in, I learned the line dancing that bonded the community together, even in hard times.

Despite a major historical fluctuation, Iraq's political transition out of a terror-based regime has not guaranteed that individuals will automatically shift out of their traumatized states. Yet cultural forms have recorded historical events and created communal forums that work toward reconstructing identity after the silencing effect of torture, terror, and ethnic cleansing. In stark contrast to the helplessness of the experience of torture or severe oppression, public commemorations can break through the individual's traumatized alienation; furthermore, a story or song—especially through the acting agent's choice of movement, pace, length, and participation within a community—offers a measure of reassuring control. This degree of artistic control and this group setting for performed memories of the past offer psychological closure and a public, embodied sign that a *shift in context*—from former terrorized state to a transitional state—has occurred.

Talking with Kurdish fighters about whether songs ever brought consolation, I was moved by Asad's account of how a popular song provided comfort after the chemical bombings during 1987–1988. While the most well-known chemical bombing is of the town of Halabja, Iraq, where an estimated eight thousand civilians died, many lesser-known incidents occurred, as in the village of Sheikh Wasan. Asad spoke of how an "eerie silence enveloped" him as he walked through the village.[15] The previous day the village had been full of people, since several hundred people lived there. But as he walked through the town, a day later, the corpses of goats and cattle were strewn about the village. Dead chickens were lying next to the houses. Then he saw men, women, and children, too, some dead, some alive, "blind and crying for each other." Haunted by memory, he remembers these two images: the village alive with people, the "ghost village" filled with the dead and the blind. The state government policy was to eradicate all the villages: four thousand small towns were destroyed, the people imprisoned in concentration camps, murdered in mass graves, or chemically annihilated. Despite the fact that the majority of Kurds followed the Sunni religion, the government termed this ethnic cleansing *Anfal*, Arabic for the "spoils of war," positioning the Kurds as infidels.

These systematic killings, this genocide, continued, for the helicopters returned, Asad said, over thirty of them, to bomb the village again. Reverberating sounds of the chopping propellers descended on the survivors and guerrilla fighters. An attempt to "kill all survivors," Asad thought. A second round for extermination. Warning the civilians that tanks would come after these helicopters, the guerrillas had begun to escort people toward the mountains. Everyone "tried to escape." But with the thudding of the propellers and the grinding sounds of oncoming tanks, "panic deepened"; some civilians hid in their houses, not following the fighters. In this second attack, Asad smelled mustard gas, a carcinogenic that was sprayed on the village. While the mutagenic chemical caused intense skin inflammations, similar to first- or second-degree burns, this vesicant with its blistering effect rarely appeared at the onset. An incubation period—up to twenty-four hours—transpired before the skin blistered and eyes were inflamed, affecting the pupils and swelling the eyelids, leaving its victim temporarily blinded. There could be bleeding and blistering within the respiratory system. Disfiguring third-degree burns resulted for some, and if more than 50 percent of the person's skin was affected, they died.

As the guerrilla fighters were leading the villagers to safer terrain in the mountains, the incubation period of the chemical weapons terminated. "The real horror was just beginning," Asad recalled, as the fighters felt the raw burning of their skin and the hazy, nebulous vision that turned toward darkening blindness. Stumbling further up the craggy mountains, the resistance fighters and civilians painstakingly scaled up the hills, but the helicopters charged ahead to gas bomb the surrounding mountain passages; they became entrapped in landlocked poison. A few people were able to find their way, even though blinded, to the houses of relatives in nearby villages. Some found doctors to treat them for the chemical effects, salving their excruciating burns. But for many, the "secret police rounded them up the next day and murdered them all." A few mass graves were discovered after the First Gulf War. Yet given that 150,000 died, and 180,000 disappeared, more and more mass graves were being located after the Second Gulf War, and people still searched for the bones of their dead.

This annihilation occurred almost two years before Saddam Hussein had bombed Halabja, suggesting years of chemical attacks. So when a popular song, created by Shivan Perwer, mourned the thousands of deaths in Halabja, the song would remind Asad of how he had saved his brother during this chemical gassing, bringing tears to his eyes. Perwer's song recalls the rumbling sounds of planes followed by the fiery onslaught of the land. "From the land comes" a chilling sound, penetrating all the dust, the "sound of crying children." The refrain was a penetrating cry of "Halabja, Halabja." For years after, hearing this song reminded Asad of how their small group of fourteen survivors had escaped out of the chemical bombings. As a public form of mourning, this song remembered the long-term suffering and resilience of the Kurds, and their perseverance as they continued on, despite the despairing sights they had seen. In effect, the song reminded him of the group courage and solidarity in their search to escape the chemical weapons.

Cognitive processes usually break down in the face of such traumatic sights. Popular songs—as embodied memories—offer an alternative to cognition, an important coping mechanism amidst trauma. In *How Societies Remember*, Paul Connerton distinguishes habitual recollection from personal or cognitive memories.[16] Through habitual practices like songs and dances, another form of recollection is accessed. Even though songs can trigger traumatic memory, they expand the moment of horror into a larger context: in this instance, a group presence that refused to capitulate, an intonation of community action and determined survival. Thus, the physical process of remembrance through music—unlike cognition, or more accurately, unlike the inability to process traumatic memories in

1. Asad Gozeh (Iraqi Kurdistan). Courtesy of William Segall.

the case of shock and stress disorders—adds a healing dimension. With their well-known patterns, songs may interrupt, replace, or impede the traumatic images that repetitively drown out other incoming senses. The habitual rhythm, for Asad, was also a lyrical history, a working model of courage and collective bonds.

At first glance, it may seem that such songs only exacerbate the old wounds, preventing rather than permitting healing. General Western perceptions of the Middle East associate these areas with cycles of violence, without any subtleties about the changing development of history;

thus, any public recollection of tragedy is conceived of as a preface to vengeance. In considering these cultural forms, I am not suggesting that there is instant closure in songs, but rather that it is one of many building units in recovering a sense of community after the alienation of trauma. Often, trauma crescendos toward a crisis of meaning, and in this context, musical associations become complex players—both communal cantors and incantations of the traumatic past. Music can be deeply linked to "our emotional lives," states William Forde Thompson in his cutting-edge text of music and psychology.[17] Research suggests that music, with its affective tones, facial expressions, and body language, composes community, orchestrating social interactions with others.[18] Unlike the trauma scene, music structures communal bonds.

With raw trauma, it is difficult to compose an ending to stories of the past. Pain and humiliation—for instance, the inability to protect one's own children from harm—does not mesh with one's sense of an able self or a competent parent. To fully consider how cultural forms penetrate trauma, as a healing step from silence to a relocated sense of self, one must first confront Western bias. Generalizations fail to consider how years of ethno-genocidal attacks must find a release valve. Cultural forms are not only about vengeance; they also incorporate and contextualize complex emotions—alienation, anger, revenge, repressed silence, shame, regret, relief, recovery, conciliation, community, and even anxiety over horrific, invasive memories—into a larger narrative, an artistically bound and controlled form. After war's destruction of the social fabric, it is an expressive reconstruction of both social and communal identity.

Examples of how rural women responded to ethnic cleansing can be found in a young Kurdish researcher's study. Choman Hardi details the lives of widows, such as Nazdar and Nasreen. Passing by so many corpses after the napalm bombing of her village, Nazdar felt that the "dead were following me."[19] When the grave of her husband was uncovered, years later in 1992, Nasreen became so ill that she had to be hospitalized (165). Slamming doors triggered the feeling of prison gates for many survivors: common flashbacks, emanating long after the village was destroyed. For these survivors of ethnic cleansing, the Western response to trauma is inadequate, predicates Hardi. Even as economic care must follow this massive displacement, these survivors also need more than an "individualistic approach"—foreign to the "communal identities and communal ways of coping used by survivors" (165).

Delivering humanitarian aid through a Swiss relief agency while living in Iraq, I met many of these widows. During sanctions, the markets were bare of produce, especially compared to the markets of Istanbul, where we had lived earlier while teaching Iraqi, Iranian, and Sudanese refugee children. During the sanctions, the orange lentils were full of pebbles and rock chips, and it was labor intensive to sort out the beans before cooking them on my canister of propane—topped with a burner and pan. At a humanitarian center, I selected clothes from piles, donated from Switzerland, to give to widows. Asad gave us a list of children and their ages, and we brought the warm clothes for these war-afflicted families. The cold winter nights were coming. Carrying large sacks of rice, a can of propane for cooking, and clothes, we went to various parts of the city to bring aid. I remember one family, who lived in a cave, the three children and their mother emaciated, the walls of the cave blackened by the smoke of their fire. Nearby we saw the rubble of their house and a neighbor's cow. The mother wanted to tell her story, to protest Saddam's wreckage, since his tank had destroyed their home and then her husband had died. It was a selective urban destruction; family houses were torn down if male or female family members were fighting as *peshmergas* in the mountains.

Traveling to various locations in Shaqlawa, some women spoke of living in tents with no water supply nearby. Some widows from the Iran-Iraq War still had houses, but had no income. Although I studied Sorani with a language teacher four mornings a week, I appreciated that my friend Loqman accompanied us, translating the words of these women. In contrast to this work with the widows, I also taught courses to the sheik's son, who wanted to improve his English, and to twenty-year-old guerrilla fighters and older political leaders in the community. After six months, I wanted to work with women and opened an English course just for English teachers, who were mostly female. Some of my students were hopeful that the West would recognize the democracy that the Kurds had established, and then lift the devastating sanctions; others

2. House destroyed after uprising (Shaqlawa, Iraq). Photograph by author.

talked about leaving because of the difficult inflation and limited job market and pay.

The importance of women narrating their lives struck me again while living in a section of a house, owned by Kaka Muhamad and his two wives. Initially, when the Gozehs arranged for us to live alongside this family, I was overwhelmed, but I found my preconceptions tested as the eldest wife, Khadija, asked me probing questions about my life. Since her son was learning English in school, we had a good time talking about cooking and family dynamics. She had selected the second wife, and she wanted me to know that, because it was an upper-class sign of her power and prestige. When she could not have children after ten years of marriage, her husband did not choose to remarry and was content with her. But she returned to her home village and selected her favorite younger cousin as the second wife. The two women were content together and shared the domestic labor and childcare of their five children. In other ways, too, these women had considerable authority; during the sanctions and the loss of jobs and economic opportunities, wives selectively sold their gold and family furniture to provide for the family.

Given the hardships of war and sanctions, the Kurds commiserated at funerals with public lament and celebrated group dancing with cherished songs, creating a space for community, both mournful and heroic. A "public space of trauma," as Laurence Kirmayer relates in his cogent analysis of culture, offers a "consensual" framework for collective memories, a lens to assemble "fragments of personal memory," a memory reconstruction that has a "tacit assumption of validity."[20] Where memories of injustice are recognized, memory bonds and attachments occur in this shared space. However, in contrast to the widows, who were living as refugees after being released from concentration camps, the resistance fighters stated that they did not have time to mourn as they fled in the mountains and engaged in guerrilla tactics. When one of their companions died, they had to quickly bury him. Then they moved on to the next attack or hideaway. Little time was allotted to grieve.

When I asked these former guerrilla fighters about public forms of mourning, they remembered various rituals, common in times of peace. For instance, when one militia soldier died, a kinswoman composed poetic laments about the dead person. It was often the role of women to publicly lament the dead and to engage the community, ululating their personal and shared grief. Laments remember heroic acts, personal attributes, and family connections of the lost loved ones. Not political protests, these ululations recollect positive attributes of the beloved. In discussing postwar Iraq with the Kurds, I asked if it would relieve some of the frustration and anger of the past to have commemorative ceremonies for the dead, and this option was commonly embraced. Still other research has shown that Kurdish widows of war often attend public funerals as a way to publically mourn their own losses and to feel part of a community.[21]

One funeral that we attended was conducted years after the person had died. Mustafa Barzani—a leader who negotiated throughout his life (British, Qasim, Ba'athist) for Kurdish self-determination in Iraq—was being buried in Iraq, after interment in Iran. Invited to this jubilant funeral procession, we were summoned by our politically passionate neighbor Khadija when it was time to depart. Khadija insisted that we attend the funeral procession, since the motorcade with the corpse of the political founder of the KDP went through Shaqlawa. Dressed in my ankle-reaching green dress, I attempted to blend in by wearing this recognizable Kurdish fabric, one of two outfits that I owned, which Khadija had complimented me on. Grabbing the edge of this verdant-colored skirt, Khadija shook her head in disapproval; her teenage son sheepishly translated that it was the wrong color. Green was the color of the other political party. Finally there was a nod of approval before we set off for the communal gathering. Although the azure dress was not the flaxen color of the party, at least it was better. As the car carrying the casket came by, shouts and celebratory gunshots filled the air. After years of exile, the bones of their hero, the father of their current leader, had come home. The no-fly zone created a measure of security, even the dead could return.

Recognition of past sorrow can also be combined with joyful celebrations of bravery, as in dance songs or "Shayee." As one common song states: "if you are not sharing my sad as well as my happy days, then I will not be there to share your sad or happy days." The idea is that individuals and families help one another; for instance, during the three days of the funeral, community members visited and brought food to console the family. The bonding of the community was also present in the line dancing, where men and women responded to the songs and formed a line to do a series of steps with linked hands in a circle. The same song may be used, as Dieter Christensen enjoins, in a wedding celebration or as a spontaneous song and dance when a feud was resolved.[22] Through singing and dancing, isolated obsessions with traumatic images and personal violation were now acted out with more expressive, physical interactions. In Thompson's research in music, he argues that both emotion and melody share similar "patterns of tension and relaxation."[23]

Haunting local songs attest to the fate of the many disappeared—those arrested and never heard from again. In one Kurdish village, the people were persecuted because they were from the Barzan clan. The military had placed people in collective camps at three different locations, and they arrested all the men from ages thirteen to seventy. These

3. Decimated village (Barzan valley, Iraq). Courtesy of William Segall.

men were never heard from again. Even when the remaining residents were relocated to a northern location, they could not find the living or their remains. Some have surmised that these grandfathers, fathers, and sons were taken to the south where they were killed or buried alive, especially given the reported speech of Saddam Hussein that "they were sent to hell."[24] But in her analysis of the surviving women and their songs, Christine Allison studied how their laments warbled between recalling the dead and hopeful desire to find the men alive in prisons. In their communal lament, "a single voice would sing, usually in stanzas of three lines, pausing to weep between them. Other women would take up the song, or interject when they felt moved."[25] The songs expressed both grief and hope in a community forum. Women supported one another in a song. Carefully skirting details of death that would retraumatize, the songs embraced a communal history that solidified female bonds. After the murder of all male kin, the lament was just one piece of this supportive community: women worked together to survive, collectively providing for their children.

Second-generation children of resistance fighters—also affected by state oppression—identified with these Kurdish songs; for instance, patterns of musical enculturation are suggested in the short memoir of Saleem. As a child, he remembered when his father was arrested and relocated to southern Iraq. Under house arrest, the family was beleaguered in a shoddy hut, which could not keep out the assault of the simplest rain. Besieged by watching guards, Saleem's father listened all day to an old Soviet radio. Meanwhile the boy went to school, where he learned the Kurdish national anthem. At several points in his narrative, he remembered this anthem: "be assured the Kurdish people are alive and nothing can bring down the flag" (10). Even as singing provides evidence of surviving voices, songs cantor the national imagination, assuring its besieged bearers of a greater communal bond. Back at home, Saleem's father translated Radio Baghdad from Arabic into Kurdish. After the election of a pan-Arab party, the politicians were celebrating by hanging "enemies" like Iraqi Jews from the gallows. With growing consternation, the family thought of Saleem's Jewish grandmother. Then, Radio Baghdad accused Kurds in 1968 of being "Zionist agents and enemies of the Baath Party" (16). Even as Voice of America named the Kurds "rebels and bandits," Radio Moscow presented General Barzani as the Kurdish liberator, condemning the new Iraqi leaders. Unlike the anxious discord of radio media, Kurdish songs reassured people; despite all the political upheaval, the "magic violin" of Saleem's music teacher played on (10). The music planted seeds of healing, the possibility of survival and hope.

Songs interspersed news again, when Saleem heard that the Kurds and Saddam Hussein had made a deal for Kurds and Arabs "to share everything like brothers!" (22). After the reconciliation, not only could the young boy buy two cokes for the price of one, but there was even dancing in the streets with flutes and drums. Given this brokered peace, the family was released from house arrest, they could return to their city. Packing their meager belongings, they discovered that in their absence, their house had been burnt to the ground. Despite this accord, they rebuilt their house like a fortress: few windows looked out at the hostile world, which had consumed their first home. In this interim, the local school was renamed the Peace School, and all students were required to take courses in Arabic. Although Saleem returned to school, he failed and had to repeat a grade because he had not learned Arabic. While learning

Arabic, he simultaneously discovered a subversive study: Kurdish poems, "little songs without music" (29). In contrast to Arabic, the language of the oppressor, Kurdish songs and poems were part of his identification with his culture.

When the peace eroded, he recorded songs with other students for the radio station Voice of Kurdistan. Consistently, the students were told that "our country couldn't be liberated just with guns," but also needed "violins and drums" (47). While the Kurdish songs were hopeful, there were times when poetry and politics were striking dissonance. As a poem described the beauty of Kurdistan on the Kurdish radio, Saleem imagined the harsh mountains and sky, full of chemically loaded bombs. In 1975, their fragile Kurdish state further eroded. After Saddam Hussein signed a peace treaty with the Shah of Iran, Mohammad Reza Pahlavi, the Kurds were bereft of allies, forced to flee to Iran. While this Algiers Accord broke down in less than six years with the Iran-Iraq War (1976-1980), the political treaty devastated the Kurdish front, causing a mass exodus of Kurds. During this diaspora, Saleem witnessed the weeping of Kurds, the packing of belongings onto trucks, and whispers by family members of Kurdish fighters committing suicide in despair. After arriving at the U.N. refugee tents, Saleem heard someone singing: "The more time goes by, the more my heart beats slowly, my beloved" (51). The mournful love song was also a song of lament for Kurdistan.

Debating between immigrating to Europe and returning to Iraq, Saleem and his family accepted the offer of the state to return, and received identity papers with the stamp of *aidoun*—the ones who are now back in line. But upon their return, their house was occupied by other refugee Kurds, who initially refused to leave. His school was now the Ba'ath School, and to avoid the scrutiny of the secret police, people were pressured to join the state party—a precondition for state jobs or attending state universities. Running away from school, Saleem joined the Kurdish resistance army in the mountains, and one of the soldiers told him the story of a bird. During the time of Soloman, there were two sisters who could not find each other. As they searched, they transformed into birds, flying all over the mountains. Each was seeking the other and grieving. While the story personifies the Kurdish flight and lament, for Saleem it was a turning point, and he decided that he did not agree with their guerrilla strategies and political melancholy.

Returning to school, he learned that during music class his cousin Zilan had sung a patriotic Kurdish song instead of the national Ba'ath party song. The little girl was dragged to the principal's office and interrogated about her family's political views. Nervous about this public scrutiny, the family warned her, "you could endanger your father's life if you sing that kind of song" (85). Afterward, Zilan became sick, and even after weeks had passed did not seem to get better. Saleem's father comforted his niece, telling her that the Iraqis couldn't hurt her father, who was safe in the mountains. As the niece grew deathly ill, Saleem took her to the hospital. Paid by the secret police, the doctor refused to treat her. Pounding on the doctor's office door, Saleem begged him to come, stating, "she's stopped breathing!" (86). Finally opening his door, the doctor answered him: "She's the terrorist's daughter" (86). In desperate response, Saleem cried out, pleading that she was only a child. Reluctantly the doctor gave Saleem an oxygen bottle. Running back to his small cousin, Saleem noticed the bottle was very light. Trying to figure out how to connect the oxygen, Saleem was finally joined by a nurse, who placed the mask on the little girl's mouth. But the bottle was empty, and she died.

Devastated by her death, Saleem started planning his escape to Europe. Not wanting to raise his parents' suspicion, he kissed each of them before sneaking across the border. In Europe, Saleem became a Kurdish filmmaker, whose work floods the screen with images and lyrics of his people—songs from a country he fled. So it is that such songs become an influential and emotive connection even for the second-generation child of a resistance fighter. The son of a *peshmerga*, one who fights death.

Much later, songs were also a force during the 2003 Gulf War. Played every hour during the war, one political song remained on the television and on radio stations to urge resistance to Saddam Hussein. This song reminded the Kurds of how other dictators had historically been defeated in Iraq: "But Saddam Hussein, go and build your castles, but you will not stay there! / You have tried to build castles where Alexander the Great failed!" In this song, the televised images focused less on the singer than on images of Kurdish fighters advancing toward Baghdad. The song of protest encouraged people to identify with a common history and motivated political resistance. The songs, like the poetic laments, suggest a certain poetic potential for group identification through cultural forms.

And also during the Second Gulf War, the Halabja lament played again and again, recalling past oppression and continual desire for liberation; however, the actual town, where almost everyone lost a relative and where whole families are buried together in the cemetery, was still in mourning. Long after television footage showed the statue of Saddam Hussein fall from its perch in Baghdad, a *Washington Post* journalist, Pamela Constable, reported that there was little celebration in Halabja, the town devastated by a chemical attack. The town's largest landmark was a "stark white monument to the dead"; it was "a plaster tableau of lifelike victims frozen as they fell, covered with chemical ash and cradling their children for protection."[26] It was a monument to the dead, not counting the thousands that died from contamination years later. In 2003, the U.S. secretary of state, Colin Powell, attended the opening ceremony, followed by numerous foreign, state, and local Kurdish leaders. Touring the central rotunda, they saw a stone carved with the names of over five thousand identified victims.

However, while many leaders pledged economic restitution to this city, the promises were not kept, so the site of commemoration shifted toward a site of protest. The chairman of Halabja's council, Khadar Karim Mohammed, reported to a journalist in *The Guardian*: "We got lots of empty promises from visitors. The only money we got was to build two schools."[27] At the memorial, high school students protested the lack of development, including the absence of running water, power, or sewage in Halabja. "Why don't they build power stations here, so we don't have constant cuts?" asked one student. After accusations against the older generation and current Kurdish political leaders of internal favoritism and lack of economic support, fighting erupted between the youth and the guards of the monument—Halabja's Spring. As a site of memory, Halabja has changing associations. During the democratic elections, documentaries about the genocide were played on Kurdish television, and the

Halabja song was broadcast—an implicit reminder for people to mobilize and vote for Kurdish leaders.

The memory of Halabja has manifold meanings: it does not have the same intonation for city dwellers as for the survivors of the genocide, refugees from ravaged country villages. For instance, in her survey of Anfal survivors, Hardi describes Srwa, who was fourteen years old when the soldiers came to load the trucks that were headed to the mass execution sites where families were shot down or buried alive (161). At this time, her parents were away from the village, and further complicating the situation, a Kurdish man—working for the state as part of the *jash* forces—felt pity and offered to save two of the five children, while the rest had to die. At first, Srwa and her little brother hid in the collaborator's house. But as the other three children were loaded into the collaborator's truck, her little brother could not bear to be apart from them. Before Srwa could stop him, he ran out to join them, and the truck drove off, leaving Srwa alone in the collaborator's house. Eventually Srwa found her parents. But she suffers from depression and survivor's guilt, since her four siblings were killed.

One of the ways that Srwa sought to mitigate the horror of the past was to write poetry. However, one day when she was struggling with the memories of the past, she burned all her poems, stating that poetry "could not solve her problem" (169). And yet, even as her words did not solve the problem, words offered an altered form of memory, and they became part of a larger process: unlike the past when her village and siblings were extinguished, this time, it is she who gets to light the fire. Working in a government office in 1996, Srwa found another form of healing, sharing her story with colleagues who also lost loved ones in the Anfal. But this recovery was disrupted, as Hardi charts out, by the civil war (172). When the opposing political group took over the office, Srwa was displaced from her job. Group support and poetic mediation can be healing, even for the most shell-shocked survivor of genocide; however, violent instability creates regressive tremors.

When the civil war began, frustrations over sanctions were running high. Agreeing to share power, the two central political parties established a democracy. Yet it was hard to run a democracy, or any form of government, without money. Even the *peshmerga* military and civil servants were not getting paid and many within the general population were desperately poor. The only lucrative business was illegal oil smuggling, across the borders of Turkey and Iran. Territorial disputes over these borders erupted into a larger skirmish, spilling into a turf war between the PUK and KDP for northern "Kurdistan." Many were upset over the outbreak of violence. Invited to the Gozeh's house for dinner, Asad's mother was distraught, stating that it was a sin to have this war, crying out, "*Haram! Haram!*" She repeated this single word, then a single sentence, which Asad translated for me: what a shame, after being attacked by Saddam, we are attacking each other! In some ways, this civil war was a traumatic residue of the Anfal, as survivors, with few economic options, had turned frustrations on one another. At night, the power flipped on and off, lighting up for the firefights in the nearby hills. When half of my students from the English language class were missing the next day, classes were cancelled, and Asad announced that, tragically, this skirmish had become a prolonged battle. The Gozeh family disapproved of this civil war, and when the opportunity arrived, they decided to leave Kurdistan, the country they had fought for all their life, and resettle in the United States.

Perhaps, a decade later, this civil unrest further situated hopes in Iraqi nationalism, suggested initially by the multicultural nationalism first proposed by the forefathers Mustafa Barzani and the first Iraqi president, Abd al-Karim Qasim, in 1958.[28] Today's democratic Iraq has a Kurdish state governed by Barzani (KDP), and on a federal level, a Kurdish president, Talabani (PUK), keeping these two power groups separate. Most Kurds want to forget these brief years of conflict, especially when situated in the larger tragedy of Saddam's genocide. From the early years of the Ba'athist regime in its ethnic cleansing, tension remain in the mapping of Iraqi land. As in Saleem's memoir, when his family had been placed by the regime under house arrest, they returned only to find their house burned down. After fleeing across the border, the family found that another Kurdish family had taken over their house, and they had to negotiate to return to their house. Moreover, imagine the dispossession of the Barzan clan, where entire villages had been bulldozed.

When the women and small children were finally allowed to leave the concentration camps, they had to find new residences, especially since the regime had destroyed their orchards, filled in their water wells, bulldozed every house.

And these disappearances were simultaneously occurring in the southern regions. Moreover, the regime drained the natural wetlands, depriving families of the fish and resources of this region. This attack on land and bodies was evident in the case of eleven men from the al-Musawi family who went missing; their loved ones did not know if they were dead or alive. Eventually they located one son at a prison. The guards had tied "Husayn's hands behind his back and hung him from them, dislocated his shoulders and tortured him with electricity. They beat him with cables and metal rods until he was drenched in his own blood," Rosen reported in his article, "Uncovering the Dead."[29] These Shiite families were often forced out of their communities and displaced to other regions. In a cunning machination, the regime placed Shiite families into homes in Kirkuk that had been emptied of Kurdish families. Given that Kirkuk is a city in an oil-rich region, current disputes continue as Kurdish families, still holding their house keys, knock on the doors of their old homes and are answered by Shiite men, women, and children who have previously lost everything familiar from their hometowns. The importance of forgetting, the need for reconciliation, the difficulty of establishing justice in circumstances of nefarious loss and jarring dislocation continue.

Considering such unbearable memories, I asked Asad what public forms of justice or reconciliation he could imagine for the Kurds in Iraq. But in 2003, Asad did not speak of Kurdistan, but rather positioned himself as an Iraqi. He answered that there needed to be forgiveness. While some of the most severe offenders of the secret police or the torturers who specialized in rape needed to be brought to justice, Asad envisioned amnesty for the thousands of militia, the conscripted foot soldiers, since Iraqis were forced to serve and all Iraqis have suffered. While top leaders, like Chemical Ali, who advocated for the chemical bombing of civilian villages, needed to be punished, Asad emphasized that the society needs to recover, to move on after these trials. "We need to forget about the crimes of the past," concluded Asad. Advocating a forgiving and forgetting to propel Iraq into a secure and prosperous recovery, Asad showed a generous disposition. How can anyone forget genocide, followed by massive land relocations, which have created tensions among multiple groups that have all been persecuted? It is not a "simple forgetting," but rather a selective memory—what Paul Antze and Michael Lambek define as a "preoccupation with a particular fragment of the past."[30] One form of selection is commemoration, wherein certain narrative pieces gain prominence. Thus traumatic moments do not end the story; rather, another ending adds closure in a personal history. Not just focusing on the history of genocide, he also recalled the number of people conscripted, the number of people who have suffered—a sympathy across neighborhoods, across regions, embracing all of Iraq. With beautiful simplicity and heartfelt hope for all of Iraq, Asad stated, "we have all suffered."

Asad cited the story of Salahadin as an exemplary model for the nation. This ancient Kurdish leader is important as a historical and mythical figure passed down in collective memory to the young Kurds, and as a heroic lineage, since Salahadin is a popular Kurdish name. Being Kurdish is not just about bloodlines, but also about important ancestral and mythical associations, like Salahadin, to return to Chatty's diasporic research.[31] This famous warrior, Asad recounted, Salahadin al-Ayoubi, arrested King Richard (the Lionhearted) of England during the crusades. Then, Salahadin decided to free him—an act of generosity in frank contrast to a historic period when people often killed all prisoners. For instance, when the European crusaders conquered Jerusalem, they killed Christians, Jews, and Muslims alike. In contrast, Salahadin is an important myth of origin for the Kurds, encouraging conciliatory trends. Indeed, whether it is history or myth that when Saladin conquered Jerusalem he picked up a cross that was on the floor, kissed it, and set it in its place, for Asad, relating the story, it is a fact of reconciliation.[32] Founding figures are crucial to any national conception. If research on nationalism and traumatic memory is accurate, then in order to "constitute themselves, nations need to discover (or construct) a past, a collective memory."[33] Why not follow this Kurdish model of Salahadin as a national icon of reconciliation for Iraq?

What both songs and stories can emphasize is conciliatory patterns in commemorative memory. Like the sung histories from Homeric times, creative oratory extends beyond the power of text-bound Western imagination. It is a type of memory that (paradoxically and partially) forgets the toxicity of trauma, by placing this mnemonic corpse inside a respected monument: the nation. Recollection, for instance in a poem about Halabja, written in 2000, reminded Kurds to reconcile with each other; after the chemical attacks against the Kurds, followed by the devastation of civil war, "were they able to reconcile / Have they learned a lesson meanwhile?"[34] This poem by Shahin Sorekli uses the traumatic memory of Halabja to encourage contemporary reconciliation between Kurds.

The past, also encapsulated in Kurdish mythology and ceremonies, suggests a state of political resistance, and in many ways might even promote conciliation. In the New Year celebration of New Roz on March 21, burning fires are lit, symbolizing desires for freedom. This holiday is associated with legends, recalling uprisings, resistance, and the strength and cunning of Kawa—a brave Kurdish blacksmith who lost six sons to the depraved king Zahak and decided to kill this nefarious ruler and then light fires to signal liberation. In recent times, fire was also lit to signal quickly between locations that the time for an uprising—an Iraqi Spring—was at hand. The Iraqi Kurdish city of Sulaymaniyah has a statue of Zakia Alkan, who lit herself on fire, during the fiery spring of New Roz to protest the lack of human rights and cultural respect in Turkey. This statue of protest would be torn down if resurrected on Turkish soil. The spring festival has seasonal roots, celebrating the survival of the Kurds throughout the winter and the possibility of growth in the spring. And the week following New Roz, according to Mehrdad Izady, is also a time when old feuds are settled within communities.[35] Ritual celebrations of New Roz not only recognize the culture's uprising against external oppression, but it also is a time when internal divisions should be reconciled.

So why are these public performances important? Since traumatic memories remember what one most desires to forget, performing them is a painful process that is worked out in communities as well as in state institutions. These songs, dances, and stories are not mere reflections of culture, but as Victor Turner argues; rather, they may "themselves be active agencies of change."[36] While we recognize that countries need ceremonies after political transitions, we often forget that community groups have ceremonies and cultural traditions that can also assist individuals in transitioning out of terror. Not just forms of lament, jubilant songs celebrate periods of amnesty, times of self-determination; and today's autonomous Kurdish Iraqi state, flying its Kurdish flag high over public buildings, enjoys more security and prosperity than its two southern sibling states.

Much later, I visited the Gozeh family in Colorado Springs, since they had received papers to the United States in 1997, after three months in an American refugee camp in Guam. They had separate apartments that were all part of the same complex. An adorable little girl with black ringlets and a spunky Mickey Mouse shirt clambered into the lap of her grandmother. It seemed ages ago that this mother, with her harsh cries, had signified how the Kurds must not be divided, during a time period still reeling from genocide in an unrecognized, young democracy. Unlike her grandchildren and her grown children, who were decked out in T-shirts and blue jeans, this regal matriarch still wore her Kurdish fabrics, gold threaded, passionately colored, along with a seraphic smile. And, years later, when I talked with Asad again in 2005, his concern over the state of the nation, especially the safety of civilians, was no longer limited to Kurdistan, for he referred to all situations in Iraq—an identification of himself not just as Kurdish, but also Iraqi. Indeed, the Gozehs, loyal to the vision of Iraqi independence and American intervention, were also contentedly settled in the states. As Asad reported to a local newspaper journalist, he did not like the terminology of a mixed identity; rather, he felt grateful, after surviving seven chemical attacks and fighting for ten years in the mountains, that he could be in a country where human rights are freely given and daily living is not such a challenge. He declared a distinct identity. "We are American Kurds," and this is "our home."[37]

While Asad still tells stories of his Iraqi past—walking through the mountains with 210 bullets ready to load in his rifle and 2 hand grenades by his side—he mentioned to the Colorado Springs journalist that he has not told his nieces and nephews these stories. "Why should they know?"

Asad asked, putting the floral-colored album with his peshmerga photos back on a shelf. "Why make them sad?"[38] But at the same time, the children are taught the dances and songs of their heritage; and young Layhat recalled visiting her father when he was imprisoned, while young Halat saw a book about Saddam at a garage sale, and said, "this is a good book for uncle Asad."[39] The journalist noted that the children quickly returned to their game, "Go Fish." But even so—there are still strong, collective bonds of family, of place, of time, recalling a genealogy of resistance against genocide and a hope for democracy—all placed within the space of a family's courage.

Hanging on the wall of the living room of the Gozeh apartment is a massive photograph, framed in clear glass: perhaps twenty or more people in a wedding celebration—a family portrait of Iraq. The vibrant green, yellow, red, white, and blue dresses of the Kurdish women seem incandescent in contrast to the plaster wall. Before leaving, the Colorado journalist had one more question; for her interview was just one year after the Twin Towers had fallen. Asad said that he was shocked by 9/11, but that he did not feel unsafe in the states, and if he left the states, then where would he relocate? He would have no place to live. Over the past thirty years, Asad has "lost everything"; he has had to start over nine times, just to obtain the "simplest rights." He felt safe in his new national home. In spring, the Kurdish flag fluttered outside his door to remember the New Year on the twenty-first of March. In summer, Asad's American flag waved from its post to recall independence on the fourth of July. As a survivor of genocide, Asad celebrates democracy and these new years—springtime for his family and springtides, he hopes, for his first homeland, for the emergent democracy, Iraq.

And in another situation, after the statue of Saddam Hussein came crashing down, Saleem finally returned to his childhood home. Reflecting on his memoir of his youth in Aqrah, he stated, "we Kurds didn't have a childhood."[40] He recalled how Kurdish towns used to have "mosques, synagogues and churches"; there were tolerant and peaceful neighborhoods for Jews, Christians, Sunnis, Shiites, and all others. When reflecting on the estranged history of Arabs and Kurds in Iraq, Saleem stated, "we are all human, but we take different directions in life." He suggested the possibility—in the simplest terms—that we could all "get along." But there was also sadness because when he returned to visit friends, "so many had been killed." At the reunion, the "emotion was intense, we went from euphoria to tears." While the war was widely unpopular with so many in his hometown of Paris, he recalled how "Saddam destroyed a country, provoked the death of millions"; in fact, "he wanted us wiped off the map."

In a completely distinct region, a very different Kurdish group brought another statue crashing down. In this crash—without the occupation and its urban disruption in Baghdad, and without the contestation over land, as in Kirkuk—Syrian Kurds had their own unique struggles, history, politics, and specific dialect of Kurmanji (not Sorani) Kurdish. Hoda Abdel Hamid reported on al-Jazeera that Syrian government forces began pulling out of Kurdish regions starting on July 19, 2012; as Kurds filled the security vacuum to protect civilians, people in the city of Qamishli held elections, and a women's group, which used to meet only in private, now held public workshops on the role of Kurdish female leaders in a self-ruled region.[41] In the town of Derik, celebrations began as al-Assad's soldiers pulled out of this largely Kurdish city; the town square was filled with dancing as Kurdish music was "blasted" from speakers of a truck.[42] Climbing onto their vehicles, people "delivered speeches," according to a report on al-Jazeera, in a language long forbidden. Just as they have shattered the dictatorial face of Bashir Assad in this region, perhaps they can also find, as the Iraqi Kurds have done within national boundaries, economic prosperity after their endless trauma. One can only wish those seeking rights, voices, votes, opportunities, a chance at recovery from their current struggles and their own unique and challenging past.

2 | Televised War, Poetry, and Shiite Women

A Case Study of Generation Gaps

The dead
come in shifts.
                    —Dunya Mikhail, *The War Works Hard*, 2005

I f Western media have created certain boundaries of the imagination, restrictions of our global lens and ethical borders, attuning to Iraqi voices allows us to enter the jails of perception, rejecting blindness toward emergent political springs. Given that the first case studies focus on Iraq, before trekking to other global locations, it is important to understand more of the context of Iraq's Spring, not only the strife but also its small acts of reconciliation, such as the 2013 meeting of Kurdish state president Barzani and prime minister Maliki, and its mass protests that persuaded the prime minister to resign at the end of his second term instead of changing constitutional limits. Tens of thousands of protestors have held demonstrations across Iraq, according to a single 2011 press report, which is otherwise disregarded in Western media.[1] Maliki has responded to these men and women by cutting his $350,000 salary in half. He has also cancelled the planned purchase of eighteen U.S. fighter planes, in order to allocate more funds for food rations for the poor.[2] But such cultural protest did not begin in 2011. The first section of this book begins by tracing the way that voices of Arab women have mixed with politics, artistic forms, and media like television, radio songs, and blogs, all wellsprings of protest. In this gendered context, this chapter maps out the particular protest of two Shiite women, who cross boundaries. Their dissent is marked not only by revolts within changing historical contexts and their concern over political upheaval, but also by their resistance to the media's depiction of sectarianism and their own demands to be recognized for their intergenerational differences.

Why begin with the staged protests of these two Shiite women? While Western media refused to show civilian deaths, alternative media debated Iraq and lamented its hundred thousand dead; in fact, as some scholars have claimed, these dead bodies, forgotten within the Western world, were one of several sites of resentment and resistance, further fueling the Arab Spring of 2011. Indeed, "Iraq became central to Arab identity" because of "arguments in the new Arab media," claims Marc Lynch, especially in debates on al-Jazeera about dictatorships and their failure to speak out in Iraq: not just with the Western invasion and civilian casualties, but also previously with the mass graves of the Ba'athist regime and the suffering under sanctions.[3] In fact, what started out as a protest of American violence in Iraq turned into a street uprising against Mubarak's desire for another re-election, as Lynch points out, an "unprecedented anti-Mubarak demonstration"; so that these Kefaya protests in Egypt, March 2003, along with other widespread protests, such as bread riots, form critical precursors, according to Lin Noueihed and Alex Warren, to recent uprisings of the Arab Spring.[4] Even as protests mutate, when global lament turned to local fury, this regional anger at civilian casualties did not deter widespread attention to Iraqi elections on al-Jazeera.[5] So while these images of Arab suffering and political debate must be situated in historically specific protests against local politics and economic hardships, these (inter)national identifications, as Lynch claims, may indeed be one of the most "pivotal questions shaping the Arab future."[6] But this legacy of border-crossing protests and sympathetic identifications is far from over, as lament over the dead and public debate over political policies of dictators and Western players continues, as the Arab public watches civilian deaths, for instance, in the bombing of Gaza and massacres in Syria. Given this trend of lament and debate that developed with press coverage on Iraq, what happened during this time period needs to be revisited, especially in light of polarized perceptions and ways that Western media of war zones have also crossed global turf, as people watched multiple news sources. Considering the entanglement of press and oral histories, as in this case study of women's stories, complicates misperceptions of gendered and generational views, and further challenges our ways of knowing both media lenses of the past decade as well as ongoing protests.

To address these protests, a bit of history is in order. Much has been forgotten about Iraq. Two Arab Springs—uprisings against the British and Shiite resistance to the Iraqi regime, after the First Gulf War—received minimal press. Even less is known on the slaughter of Iraqi Shiites, especially after the promised air support of the U.S. military never arrived in 1991. Since, overall, Iraq as a state was established in 1920, controlled first by the British and then by Iraqi governments, the state made "new demands" on the people, and, in response, residents began adapting, resisting, reconceiving their political identifications, as Charles Tripp argues in *A History of Iraq*.[7] Thus, altered narratives of identity and history were constructed to "justify their political engagement," to match their "self-image."[8] But how are political protests and national identities currently changing in response to urban violence, political upheaval, widespread exile and internal displacement, and continued desires for an Iraqi Spring? In what ways have these violent relocations of place influenced gendered and generational narratives of identity? How are creative spaces of witnessing speaking back against Western media depictions that selectively remember (and are now silent) about Iraq? How does this political performance by two Shiite women enact both communal loss and collective desire for an Arab Spring?

What has been forgotten in specific mixed media testimonies, such as Khawla Hadi and Marwa al-Mtowaq's public protest, are grave oversights. Their public dissent, organized around poetry and autobiographical protest in a collaborative workshop, showed how both women remonstrated the lack of support to refugees and spoke of mass media as a form of loss; yet by the end of the workshop, they also narrated mother-daughter bonds within heroic female histories, divergent views of sectarianism, relocations of identity while crossing national boundaries, and variances in national perceptions. This particular protest extended across national boundaries. Indeed, few guessed that three women at a table

4. Workshop with Khawla Hadi, Kimberly Segall, and Marwa al-Mtowaq. Photograph by Luke Rutan. Courtesy of Seattle Pacific University/Luke Rutan. Reproduced with permission.

in Starbucks were reflecting on injustices. We had gathered over coffee, crammed around a wooden table, near a bustling parking lot, just outside of Seattle. Not that there was no interest in our group. While talking with my two friends, who were both fully veiled, I realized that some of the other coffee patrons were staring at us. Perhaps they wondered why the tall woman—blond hair neatly pinned in back—was so engaged with these two Shiite women. Many in America see the scarf, but not the people. With her piercing eyes and compassionate voice, Khawla, who wore a purple spotted-leopard scarf, is a striking woman. Marwa—with her youthful political passion—studies fashion design; she sported a tasteful black silk headscarf that set off her rose-colored jacket. When I tried to buy the coffees, Khawla pressed forward to the cashier and gently pulled me back. "You can't win against an Iraqi. It is our tradition of hospitality." Forgetting all about my coffee, I began listening to their stories. Both of these women claimed a family heritage of struggle against dictatorship, and this chapter records their stories of revolt.

Also, our conversation, launched in the middle of the media press of the Arab Spring in 2012, was not just about political transition, but also about the refugee crisis in the midst of this vast spring tide. Many families are fleeing out of Syria and into Turkey, after having left because of death threats out of Iraq. Over a million fled into Syria, a million into Jordan. These journeys—unbearable sojourn and painful diaspora—have consumed all their life savings, so that they arrived with no money and few job options in the pricey urban zone of Seattle. One family, living in a car, was attempting to survive on the meager state support for refugees, Khawla lamented. Then she spoke of the inflow of refugees to the trauma center, where she works as the translator for Arabic speakers suffering from stress disorders. The Arab Spring—often discussed in distant terms—flows past our urban cities, entangles with media images, crosses in transnational treks. For both Khawla and Marwa, their families were part of heroic traditions of fighting for survival and revolt—the spirit of Arab Spring—and they spoke of the current protest, identifying feminine histories of resistance and concerns for Arab refugees. Their public protest emerged through workshops on poetry and testimony and then public performances on academic campuses. It began with a series of workshops from 2008 to 2009, where these two women first told their provocative histories, responding to poems written by Iraqis. Having started this workshop as a response, since it was not enough to research the flood of refugees out of Iraq, I wanted to inform others about the crisis. The project was not only a testimonial play created through a workshop, but it also began earlier through interviews and contacts with directors of refugee centers. I invited these directors to speak on campus, to inform students how they could assist Iraqi refugees in Seattle. As over two million people fled from Iraq across Middle Eastern borders, largely to Syria, some in Jordan, the United States, after a period of extremely limited admission, is finally admitting more Iraqi refugees. Thousands are rejected. Moreover, further displacement has erupted as the political movement of the Arab Spring has emptied Syria of its Iraqi refugees. In Iraq's neighboring countries, the majority of refugee children have fallen behind in school, and their parents are legally prohibited from working.[9] *Iraqi Voices* is a poetic rebuke of the United States' minimalistic, locked-door policy. Raising awareness of the refugee crisis, these witnessing performances generated income for the women and publicity for the refugee centers. In this process, these Seattle venues clarified profound disjuncture in Western media and the experiential narratives of our Shiite neighbors.

Within their public protests, both women described the impact of the mass media. To live in a foreign country is a dislocation, but to peer at a televised version of violence against your home country is another level of displacement. For these two women, technology became part of an emotional landscape: traumatic, precarious, and precious. Televised images hint at deaths that are not shown—a live wire, an imagined pulse between exiles and their family members in Iraq. As a result, these two accounts configured both the television and the telephone as paradoxical agents: mechanizations of hope and of unreliable despair. Globalization—characterized as a journey of peoples and information—is also a gripping entanglement for these two women; it is part of a personal struggle for healing that led to shared protest about displacement and dictatorship alongside divided ideas about national identity—a generation gap.

To engage the protests of Khawla and Marwa, we must trace the journey of two different families. In terms of generations, Khawla is a forty-year-old woman; the younger woman, Marwa, is just entering her twenties. These stories have distinct chronologies, since Marwa al-Mtowaq's father protested against the regime with its Ba'athist dictator. Then, after being tortured by the police, his house was destroyed by an American bomb. Forced into exile, Marwa's family—part of a massive exodus of Iraqis between these two Gulf Wars—is part of a transnational body that has watched the mass media depict its fate. The story of Khawla begins earlier, during the Iran-Iraq War. When Iraq invaded Iran, claiming an unfinished territory dispute, Khawla's husband was in the military, and this deleterious clash became a killing field: a million Iraqis, a million Iranians dead. Shortly after this war, Saddam Hussein entered Kuwait, claiming a historic territory from Ottoman times, with aspirations of attaining oil-flushed lands. The United States declared war after the invasion. Deploring another cataclysmic, blood-drenched battlefield, Khawla's husband crossed into Jordan beyond national lines, where he was held as an American prisoner of war for nearly two years. Throughout these two years, Khawla did not know if her husband was alive or dead, and even fourteen years after the event, his state of unresolved loss, when described by this mother of four, still brought tears to her eyes.

Further aggravating this loss, the family became a target for the Ba'athist party after her husband left the military. One method the regime had of locating deserters and dissenters was to find their families and place them in prison, a suppression strategy that held them hostage. When the dissenter learned that his family was in prison, he surrendered to release his family from incarceration. Since racking maltreatment and rape were prolific acts in these Abu Ghraibesque prisons, jailing a dissenter's family became an efficacious but grisly shackle of control. So Khawla retreated far from her house with her four little kids. Every week she relocated—dusty back rooms, barren garages, mingy hideaways—the covert spaces of relatives. Navigating her family's survival while hiding underground, this sole provider kept her young brood far from the regime's panoptic clutches.

With a letter and a phone call, her circumstances shifted. When an unknown man handed her a letter, she knew that it was not delivered by the state. Opening the letter with trembling hands, Khawla read through the coded letter that her husband was alive. She waited in suspended yearning for several weeks, expecting the return of this messenger. When she finally received a phone call, someone informed her that her husband was alive and had been granted refugee status in the United States. Advised to cross the border to Jordan, Khawla had to take on another intrepid role: crossing the border with four small children into another country, she sedulously deceived the policing eyes of the state, who would have imprisoned her.

In search of a secure locale for her children, Khawla had to leave Iraq—a taut journey into Jordan before crossing to the United States. Usually women are not allowed to take children out of the country: as the wife of a dissident (her husband deserting the Iraqi army) she would have been arrested. So she had to say that she had a health condition and needed a Jordanian hospital, and that her husband was dead. Mendacity was needed in another contrivance: to tell the children that their father was dead, because the children would be questioned too. Irrevocably devastated, the children, especially the oldest daughter, grieved their father. After her cousin drove the young mother of four to the border, Khawla answered hundreds of prying questions, elaborating on her constructed story about needing health care. Initially, the authorities did not believe she was sick. After finally convincing the border guards, Khawla and her family crossed the border into Jordan by taxi. Then she started to laugh—a sound of relief, just shy of tears. Accounting for the emotional dissolution of her mother, the oldest daughter responded with rancor: "Are you so happy that my father is dead!" At last, Khawla was able to tell them that their father was alive and that the family would see him soon in the United States. The eldest daughter, shifted around several houses and in hiding in Iraq, taken out of school, traumatized by the "death" of her father and childhood security, suffered from depression when they first relocated to Seattle. Khawla still harbors the pain of this mother-daughter crisis—a key juncture in her diasporic journey. As a mother she succeeded in crossing borders and protecting the bodies of her children, but the pain of her daughter was a costly reckoning.

When in Jordan, she met with a friend, who gave her tickets to the United States and informed her that her husband would meet her at the airport in Seattle. Warned that people steal children in America, she left for the airport with her children; alarmingly, when she arrived in Seattle her husband was not at the gate to meet her. After waiting for some time, she began to walk around the airport, clutching her small children. Since she did not speak more than a few words of English, her attempts to ask where she could find her husband were proving futile. Finally, while she was walking around the Seattle airport, an airport security guard said, "Salaam Alakuum." Responding in Arabic, she asked him to help locate her husband. Another man approached; in terse Arabic he questioned if she was Khawla Hadi. After she affirmed her identity, the man replied, "We have all been looking for you and couldn't find you." Indignantly, Khawla rejoined, "How many other covered women with four kids do you see in this airport?" Recounting this story to college students, Khawla told her story of harrowing displacement with vulnerability, resilience, and at the end, humor.

Finally rejoined with her husband, after trumping the Iraqi authorities, she spoke of her next aspiration. She had come to a new country, whose language she could not speak, and after her harrowing voyage across borders she resolved to learn English. With a winsome smile playing on her lips, she jokes, "I vowed to learn English before my children, so that they would not say things in English that I wouldn't understand." Not only did she learn English, but she also tutored her children in English when they went through grade school. Advancing on, she became a translator at the trauma center for Iraqi refugees, working full time while her older kids attended university classes. When asked by her husband if she would like to return to Iraq, she told him, "I'm not going back to Iraq. I like it here in Seattle. I almost lost you once in Iraq, and I don't want to go through that again. If you want to return, you will have to go without me." Detailing her past and claiming her new location, Khawla expressed how she feels changed—a transnational metamorphosis. When she returned to Babylon, she realized how different she was from her sister, who stayed in this small southern town in Iraq. As a translator, engaged with newly arrived refugees, she provides a bridge between two regions.

Khawla's response contrasted with Marwa's first reaction. When Marwa first told her story in 2008, she did not feel acceptance as an American citizen. She wanted to return to Najaf, to her homeland of Iraq—a country that her mother fled when she was two years old. Her account, a narrative of exile, also had strong mother-daughter collusions. The al-Mtowaq family had to escape Iraq after Marwa's father protested against Saddam Hussein. He was arrested and tortured for several days, and he still bears the fulsome scars on his leg. Released by the police, he apprehended that he was on a second hit list, pinpointed for refusing conscription into the military. On a wanted list by the regime, he went into hiding in the city. After his concealed relocation, his house was bombed—the opening round of American bombing, during the First Gulf War. Splintering glass from the windows cascaded around Marwa's mother, who was alone with her small children. Part of the house caved inward, collapsed, but no one was hurt. After this double attack, the family secured a few items and vacated. They could not travel together to the border because the father had to cross illegally and he did not want to endanger the family. So Marwa's mother, pregnant with her youngest son, her infant and toddler children in tow, headed out on foot across the border to Saudi Arabia. This diasporic narrative—the mother's narration and the daughter's impressionistic memories of the journey and their years in a refugee camp—were central to Marwa's national identity, even though she has grown up in the United States.

At the Saudi border, Marwa's father and mother were reunited, and they applied for refugee status while living in a border encampment for war refugees. Highlighting the difficulties of living for several years in a refugee camp, Marwa's impressions of trauma were vivid, but many of the details were not clear. When I asked specific questions about why they left and what happened at the camp, Marwa did not know the answers. The mother's traumatic memories were impressed on the child, but there was no detailed sense of the mother's experience. Fulminations of "rape, kidnappings, and sand storms" were saturated with ethical furor, but there were few traces of contextual specificity. Marwa did not have any clear idea about the identity of the aggressors in the camp. This second-generation trauma, passed from mother to daughter, created gender-based nationalism, but not a detailed sense of history. Since Marwa exited the refugee camp at the age of four, her memories were of changing winds, blustering sand. She recalls how the sand storm beat against her skin, seeping through the thin blankets, covering her face and arms. This diasporic narrative deeply attached Marwa to a maternal story. This mother-daughter bond also binds Marwa to an emotional identification as a Shiite Iraqi.

Many of the details about the refugee camp were filled in by Khawla, who had heard the story from Marwa's mother. Khawla recorded it in her memory in a very different way, with attention not just to the family trauma, but to the political details as well. The refugee camp was in Saudi Arabia, where the Sunni government was predisposed toward the regime of Saddam Hussein, because it was a largely secular dictatorship with a Sunni president. But the majority of the refugees in the camp were dissident Shiites. Some Ba'athist informers were planted in the camp, and in conjunction with these informers and a few corrupt Saudis working at the camp, a number of young women were stolen away from their families, and sold into slavery to Saudi families. Diasporic identity for the al-Mtowaq family included these stolen lives—part of a larger historic record of loss and a gendered narrative of origin.

The collective bond of mother and daughter was also a form of gendered loyalty. This cultural bond fueled Marwa's resentment toward the West: first, for assisting the Ba'athist rise to power, and second, for bombing urban cities in two Gulf wars. In the First Gulf War, American bombs destroyed her childhood home. During the Second Gulf War, Marwa and her family watched their country explode on the news. One night, Marwa's mother thought that she saw her own mother on the television screen, a figure in a bomb explosion. She thought she had actually witnessed death, watched her mother die on the news footage. Since the phones were out, there was no way to contact any family members in Iraq. Completely distraught, Marwa's mother became increasingly unstable at home: eventually she became mentally ill and had to be hospitalized. Not only had Marwa watched her homeland be destroyed by bombs, but she had also witnessed how the war nearly destroyed her mother's mental health. Every day Marwa would attend her public high school, where relatively contented teenagers continued with their text messaging, chatter, and studies. Even as Marwa carried the war and her worries about her mother to school, like suitcases tied with fragile ribbons, decorated with identity tags from dual nations, such second-generation children of refugees carry the memories and emotions of their parents.

When the phone lines were restored, Marwa's family found out that her grandmother had not been killed. She was still alive. While the war led to thousands upon thousands of Iraqi deaths, this story nonetheless exemplifies a technological death. In between global forces—a Western-narrated violence alongside distant televised images—was an imagined space of loss. The envisioned death of Marwa's grandmother led to a second type of mental death: the temporary death of motherhood. Marwa lost her mother for a while; she was removed from her home and her children because she had lost her mind in grief. Transnational loss and media entangled three generations, bound with tight strings of mother-daughter-grand-daughter bonds. Even domestic spaces became wrapped in a war psyche.

Speaking of her grandmother, Marwa recounted an oft-told childhood story. When Marwa and her mother trekked on foot across the border into exile, her grandmother walked several miles to the one public phone, hoping to receive a call that her daughter and her family were still alive. Every day she treaded this path, waiting by the telephone for a year. After two years of uncertainty, her grandmother began to mourn for the deaths of her daughter and her family. These unresolved losses permeate Marwa's sense of Iraqi nationalism; these gendered stories of courageous perseverance inform her sense of Shiite feminism.

Several weeks into our workshop, Marwa spoke about her return visit to her hometown of Najaf in 2008. It was a homecoming to a place that she couldn't remember. After her visit with her extended family in Iraq, she returned to school in Seattle and faced a long battle with depression. In one of the poems that Marwa wrote, she compared the laughter and noise of an extended family to the silence of her own room, in suburban Seattle. Second-generation trauma is entangled with current devastating conditions in Iraq. Marwa simultaneously witnessed war's devastation: through the trauma of her mother, the economic lack of opportunity for her father, war survivors who were family, and then an urban American population, for whom the violence of war was a kind of media-fenced video game.

Responding to Marwa's story, Khawla reflected on the transnational location of Seattle: "I know your mother," she said, and in her house, "she made sure you learned the traditions of Iraq and always spoke Arabic." Despite the intensity of a mother who wanted to re-create Iraqi culture for her children, and the economic disappointment of an exiled father who lost his business, Marwa expressed attitudes about national identity quite different from that of her parents. Marwa tells me that her parents are confused by her ardent patriotism toward Iraq. "You haven't even lived in Iraq, and yet you love the country more than we do." The two generations of Iraqis do not have the same reactions.

Unlike Khawla's resilience, Marwa, as a second-generation Iraqi who has grown up in America for the past nineteen years, seethed with anger after the Second Gulf War. She writes poems about the treasures of Iraq and her fury at their destruction. Her understandable anger at the devastation, alongside her secondary trauma in connection with her mother, created a militant nationalism. She brandished statements like, "I wish I could live in Iraq. Even if it is dangerous, I consider it a privilege to die, just like my fellow Iraqis risk death every day." Half jesting, she held up her U.S. passport and proclaimed, "Who wants this American passport? All I want is my Iraqi passport, my Iraqi home." Her two best friends, who accompanied her to the workshop, chided her. They called her actions shameful—*haram*—for "people are dying because they can't get a passport out of Iraq." And one of her friends explained to me that her own return to Iraq was a romantic dream, just like Marwa's initial return. After returning to Iraq for six months, however, her friend said that her attitude toward her homeland had shifted again, since it was difficult—the lack of electricity, of employment, of resources. Her friend claimed that Marwa would change her mind about returning to Iraq too, if she had spent more time there.

In this intergenerational distinction, there is a shifting romanticism by an Iraqi American to her first country. Marwa's return to Iraq in 2008 was very different from the experience of her parents. When Marwa walked down the streets of Najaf, she received a great deal of attention because everyone knew she was a foreign Muslim. Young men would yell out their names and phone numbers, hoping that she would take notice of them. But she and her brother were not allowed to say that they were from America because her parents were afraid that they would be attacked. Wanting to return to Iraq, Marwa felt nostalgia, a longing for extended family and Iraqi society, and she felt alone at her local community college, where there are few Iraqis.

Since these stories are also painful journeys, perhaps I should explain how I planned out this workshop, selecting poetry as the most therapeutic mode to engage traumatic narratives. Poetic images are important ways to cross into protest and into cultural sites of conflict. Not just a creative form of entertainment, poetry is an intimate, fresh voice of the workshop. Poetry gives voice to a global network of Iraqis within the country and in exile. In contrast to the novel, which is often upheld as the form that narrated nationalism in the West, as in Benedict Anderson's work, it is poetry in the Middle East that promotes the "cause of nation," according to Yasir Suleiman.[10] The form changes suffering into a pathos-laden image, a question, or a challenging idea. Images of the nation, envisioned by Iraqi poets, show both conflict and hope, diversity and nationalism. These images are full of emotional resonance—sublimated with what Sara Ahmed terms the circulating emotion that suggests sites of "social tension."[11] Even as images of the nation imbibe traumatic emotion and transfer sentiments onto group relationships, poetry also crafts passionate personifications and political metaphors, re-visioning transitional violence. As conflict bleeds not on the street, but in written bodies, these descriptions—the compact bandages of metaphor, with their comparisons between historical events and objects—can tie in a measure of detachment from the violence through a counseling metaphor, a powerful symbol, a protest apparatus, or an imagined community of readers.

While all the poems used in this workshop were written by Iraqis, the poetic images of Iraq—as a woman, a needle, or a shackled lover—exposed diverse national sentiments. This multiplicity was helpful, since Khawla and Marwa had extremely different perspectives, and they could speak to each other about their views. Interacting with a few thin lines on paper offers a safe space, which indirectly positions the history of Iraq into images. These national icons helped Marwa articulate her personal story of a gendered legacy, which was initially separated from her ardent militancy. Literary forms record the suffering that results from political policies—what Flatley describes as an "affective mapping."[12] After responding to the poems, Marwa's personal experience, family memories, and transnational affinity became more integrated into her public narrative. She was able to mourn her own losses, which were not included in her first session with her jingoistic poetry. Perhaps her personal losses had previously seemed unspeakable, especially compared to her mother's breakdown and the destruction of her birth country. When she selected or rejected images of Iraq within poems, Marwa experienced a form of control over how Iraq was being globally mediated.

Marwa also felt empowered in her protest because of her role as an educator. Appreciative of the interest and questions of the American students, Marwa's mediating role was a stark contrast to her initial helpless fury at how uneducated and uncaring the urban population in Seattle had been. Unlike her declaration at the first workshop, Marwa's self-stance was no longer only connected as an Iraqi, despite spending her life in America. At later workshops and public performances, she had begun to position herself as an Iraqi in America. This stance was still distinct from Khawla's fluid self-positioning: an Iraqi American in Seattle, and a dual identity as an American and an Iraqi when returning to her birthplace of Babylon. Built on collaboration, the workshop was a welcome alternative to the passive horror of watching Western media narrate the destruction of one's country in detached terms. For Marwa, the workshop integrated experience and national sentiment, and as an exterior sign of this integration, she posted the recorded video of *Iraqi Voices* on Facebook. There were three central features of her visual site: her nationalistic poems, her photo of her return visit to Najaf, where she holds the Iraqi flag, and the video of her narrated history. This self-portraiture circulated to her Iraqi friends and relatives in Iraq.

The other reason that I selected a poetic entrance into protest was because of the prevalence of this cultural form in contemporary Iraq. Splits in identity after the war are often expressed in poetry. In Baghdad, poets gathered together in an event called "Freedom Space." They gathered to hear one another's poems, and their central goal was to bring Shiites and Sunnis (mainly from Sadr City and Madaan) together. The event was sponsored by a local women's group, *Women's Freedom in Iraq*, and was organized by the Kurdish female activist Yanar Muhammad. On October 19, 2006, taking his turn, Sadiq Hattab read his poem: "You harbor grudges against me and I against you / Forgetting that we shared lovely times together."[13] The poem suggests the shifting location of identity, situated as a historical change after U.S. violence.

As a form of culture that discusses loss, poetry can also form a bridge of reconciliation. Arguing for the common use of poetry within Iraq, Harith Ismail Turki, an Iraqi professor of English literature, confided, "people sometimes resort to poetry, not as a way to escape, but as a way to mitigate the agony inside themselves."[14] Poetry is also a changing form; for instance, oral poetry called *darmee*, once a formal genre written by men or women to complain about the absence of a beloved, is now a pop form with Shiite slang, a type of Iraqi rap. A political voicing, poetry also extracts an emotional signature—a needed sentiment for modern democracies.

Using poems to start a conversation is not a neutral act; indeed, poetry has a long history of resistance in Iraq. During Saddam Hussein's reign, one of the longest terms of political power by an Arab leader, poetry was a popular form of resistance to the state. The Ba'athist state implemented policies of force and posited a collective history that glorified pan-Arab ties, but the intelligentsia resisted with poetic countermemories, producing what Eric Davis calls a "domain of struggle."[15] Many poets, who recorded their views of history and society, were targeted and imprisoned by the regime.[16] The Iraqi poems used in this workshop, challenged violence, reworked national identities and sublimated victimization into powerful images of self and society.

Many of the poems were from a translated collection called *Flowers of Flame*.[17] Collating these poems in Baghdad in 2005, Soheil Najm and Sadek Mohammed, bereft of electricity and surrounded by road bombs and death squads, met with poets to select poems that were an outcry against the invasion and the deprivation of human rights in Iraq.[18] While the initial intent of authors would be clearer in the original Sorani or Kurmanji or Arabic, I was interested in this altered product of translation, intended to cross to a Western audience. I was challenged by Saadi Simawe, who argues that Western perceptions of translation are another marginalizing tactic used by the West. The Anglo world has the luxury of writing in English, which is an easily commodified global form. Translation should be viewed as "creative, not inferior literature at the margins of the imperial culture."[19] It is a hybrid meeting point, says Simawe, since many poets work with their translators, and it is its own unique product, inscribed in English to engage the West. Published after the American invasion, *Flowers of Flame*, as a traveling product, was a historical confrontation.

Bringing several poems to the workshop, I asked Khawla and Marwa to select poems for our educational venue. We began by reading poems that imagined Iraq as female. For instance, in the poem "Bombardment," Baghdad is imagined as a mother who cannot hold onto her children.

"The city cannot gather in her children," Haider Al Kabi writes.[20] The people of Baghdad cling to their homeland; they are desperate and will never leave her, but she cannot gather them in her arms to protect them. The poet views this national development as shameful because a city is meant to be a place of safety. Khawla recalled clutching her children, the desperate desire to keep them safe. In the poem, this maternal city is "vainly reaching" to "gather her little ones" (8). Carved into this city is a family intimacy: a common kinship for the city's children.

Drawn to images of Iraqi motherhood, Khawla also appreciated poems that imagined Iraq as a working woman. Hashem Shafeeq imagines Iraq as an industrious weaver, who must start over, for the threads have been lost. In "The Spindle," the social fabric of Iraq has been destroyed, so Iraq must reweave its distinct patterns in an image of hope. Iraq, also embodied as a woman with no wealth, begins mending "the hem of her homeland," and the larger rent in the social fabric.[21] Unlike Eurocentric narratives, where women are helpless objects in need of masculine state protection, these Iraqi icons are determined to heal the broken state. Feminine resolve at the center of the homeland stitches together a senti-mental, domestic, and political weave.

Khawla adored these poems. But Marwa regarded these images of a torn Iraq with ambivalence, since she did not want to talk in educa-tional venues with Americans about current tensions in Iraq. Even amidst Iraqis, she said, people did not want to address the recent sectarian con-flict. Preferring poems written by exiles, Marwa chose "The Last Iraq," by the well-known poet Fadhil al-Azzawi, who left Iraq following his three-year term in prison after the Ba'athist coup of 1963.[22] The poem personifies Iraq as a naughty but beloved child. Written during the Iran-Iraq War, the poem articulates anxiety about the young soldier: for the war will shoot these "angels," who flee the front (72). Both women loved the image of Iraq as a childlike but ghostly presence who sits in the center of everyday life for exiles.

The majority of the poems selected detailed the desperate plight of exiles. "I don't remember how long they walked under the sun or how many died," Dunya Mikhail writes in her poem, "America."[23] In this poem, the Iraqi refugee asks America to desist on the questions and open the gates to other refugees. Time passes, and the refugee arrives without her father. After her father dies, this refugee is haunted by the dead floating past her in dreams, surfacing over the houses of her youth. Being granted refuge in America, while her family members are not accepted, is like a photo album, filled with "loneliness" (37). After reading the poem, Khawla began to cry, speaking of her elderly father, who was vulnerable in the small city of Babylon.

Both Khawla and Marwa responded to the poems by narrating their family experiences. Reflecting on the poem, Khawla was drawn to the lines about all the questions and the fingerprints; she had her own traumatic experience crossing borders. Since Khawla lived for two years in hiding, she related to the poem's emphasis on inquiries. She always had to be secretive, use code names, report to security that her husband was dead. Told to leave Iraq, Khawla faced the difficult situation of performing the death of her husband and her own infirmity to get the family across the border.

Marwa chose poems that compared Iraq to a lover, expressing her longing for her homeland. As in Adam Hatem's image of the nation as a shackled lover, this difficult love symbolized an exile's relationship with Iraq, and for Marwa, alone in a nuclear family, she wished for her adoring grandmother and community of aunties.[24] This desire for Iraq was heightened because she attended a public high school where she was the only covered woman in the school. On her return to Iraq, she reveled in being in the country of her origin. Having grown up listening to descriptions of her father's wealth and houses, Marwa remarked how her father's hair had turned gray since he came to the states because of his work in a local store and their limited means. Exile disenchants: for there is limited assistance for refugees, and the change in income or job status is daunting. The loss—the people, their homes, their jobs, their schools, their family members and friends left behind—is a dream deferred. And in the poem "A Country Out of Work," economic problems are also illustrated in Iraq: unemployment links the police, factory, and field workers in a nationalizing image.[25]

Khawla responded to poems that emphasized trauma, especially as she considered her relatives, who were still living there. The poem "We Are

Not Dead," by Munthir Abdul-Hur, suggests that Iraqis are like "paper boats," floating in a traumatic state.[26] These fragile boats are "pushed to the waves by the hand of a trifling child"; eventually, "fold after fold, the sea takes our dreams" (36). The image of helplessness, of flimsy boats floundering in water, reminded Khawla of her uncle, who had lived in Jordan for almost a decade. Her uncle and aunt finally returned to their house, which they had not lived in for several years. A man knocked on the door, claiming some past grievance, during the days of the Ba'athist regime. Then this man stabbed her uncle to death.

Living in another country while your relatives are experiencing violence creates anxiety. When I brought an excerpt by Heather Raffo, Marwa read about a father who tries not to weep while watching the televized war. He recognizes the neighborhoods where many friends and family live. His daughter also watches television. Unable to find the right words to pray, she says the names of her relatives out loud, "Sati, Zuhayr, Huda, Zuhira," repeating the names and imagining their faces.[27] The phones do not work, so they can't get any information, and the television shows pictures of people burying the dead in their backyards. After Marwa read this piece, she started to cry. "This scene is exactly right," she said. "We have to include it." Then she gazed down at the table. Joining the conversation, Khawla expressed how painful it was to watch the war on television; in fact, sometimes she turned it off because it felt unbearable. At the next workshop, Marwa insisted on including this excerpt in the upcoming educational venue, which was held at Seattle Pacific University in 2009. It wasn't until after reading this scene that Marwa told the story, in front of two hundred students, of her mother's breakdown during the war.

Marwa protested the refugee crisis and highlighted the challenges of exile, but only later did she speak of a divided Iraqi population, because it connected to her maternal history. It's a "hot topic," she said. "Not even Sunnis or Shiites want to talk about this. And we can't talk about this because it is too complicated." When I voiced my view that the postwar U.S. plan to rotate nine sectarian leaders through the presidency encouraged segregation, they nodded in agreement. Unfinished negotiations over how the federal government would divide oil profits, especially since the Sunni state had few resources, further created sectarian division, I added. Then Marwa, who had been hesitant to talk about this several months earlier, now told her story about her grandmother. Having lived through the bombing of Baghdad, her grandmother was later displaced, needing to leave her house, which was in a Sunni area. Marwa found it a painful topic. The reason that Sunnis and Shiites did not want to discuss this division, according to Marwa, is that this division didn't exist before the war.

Continuing her story, Marwa spoke of recent civil unrest and attempted reconciliation. She explained how various Sunni and Shiite families would swap houses so that both families had shelter. Initially reticent, Marwa oscillated between her Iraqi patriotism and her concern over her grandmother. But at a later workshop, she gently informed me that her grandmother died. Then she wanted to talk about these politicized divisions. Responding to Marwa, I tried to integrate poetry and political perspectives. We discussed how this unrest reflected how Iraqis have felt torn by so many diverse state and global forces. For instance, the poet Mahmud Al-Braikan was murdered in his house in Basra in 2002. His case was never solved. In his poem "Of Freedom," he considered how many advantages, like wealth and power, were offered in exchange for one's loyalty.[28] This reconsideration of freedom was not the American rhetoric of freedom from dictatorship, but rather freedom to express ideas. After the onslaught of bombing in Iraq and declared victory, Paul Bremer disbanded the army, and many people were desperate for employment. The war shattered the economy; families had no means to feed themselves. Militant and political groups took care of the poor, but they asked for loyalty and votes. The poem states, "you have offered me a house, decorated and comfortable, in exchange for a song that sticks to instructions" (54). Amidst these pressures and territorial fighting, refugees flee. Khawla said that recent refugees did not want to talk about why they had left Iraq. This desire not to speak was due to the trauma of the deaths, which impelled these families to leave their property. As their translator, Khawla was overwhelmed at times. She described one traumatic story, which the Iraqi woman had never told another person. "For ten years," Khawla kept repeating, "it had been ten whole years."

To protest the plight of these recent refugees, Khawla selected the poem "Flour Below Zero."[29] While the desperate conditions spoke of the limited ration coupons during the past embargo on Iraq, the "thieves" stationed just "behind the door" reminded Khawla of the present brutal attacks refugees described in raids by local militias and by hostage-taking gangs. For Marwa, the poem encapsulated what she called the "whole history" of Iraq. She selected the poem so that university students would understand how much we have in this country. She spoke of her cousins in Baghdad, who had to wait until the electricity turned on to use the computer or even to run the washing machine. When the hot water turns on, the electricity goes off, so you end up showering in the dark. The poem details how a family ran out of food and there is no public safety. What is left are "whizzing ghosts" and children whose tragic "inheritance is war" (46). In response to the poem, Marwa declared that the "children in Iraq have no childhood." She emphasized, "They have not been children." Khawla added, "children cannot play outside because it is not safe." They have heard the sound of bombs; they have seen the dead. What they have not seen is a childhood.

These impressions of children were detailed, based on recent visits to Najaf or Babylon. For the al-Mtowaq family, there were intergenerational differences in their experiences in Iraq. Visiting Najaf, both Marwa and her brother spoke with the American soldiers and joked around with them until their extended family warned them not to. Their Iraqi relatives feared that they would be accused of being American spies, and they warned them not to disclose where they were from in public situations. Their parents constantly reminded their children not to speak at any checkpoints—not English, not Arabic. They were supposed to remain quiet while their father dealt with the situation. When a gunshot rang out or a helicopter chopped above their heads, her mother panicked. Her mother still suffers from post-traumatic stress disorder, especially after living through the American bombing alone in her house with her small children. In contrast, Marwa felt galvanized by her visit, despite her concern about the safety of her relatives.

After recent visits to Iraq, both women reconsidered their American identities. Seeing an American soldier in the small city of Babylon,

Khawla said hello to him in English. He did not look at her—just mumbled hello. In English, she asked him how he was doing, but he didn't respond. In her charming, feisty fashion, Khawla responded, "What, aren't you allowed to talk with me?" And the young soldier, not much older than her own eighteen-year-old son, said, "I'm sorry, but we are not supposed to speak with civilians." But she continued to speak to him, asking him where he was from. He responded with his regiment number, and she said, "No, what city are you from? I'm from Seattle." At that point, his demeanor completely changed, as he smiled and asked, "Really?" Smiling back, Khawla proclaimed, "Yes, I am an American." She took out her U.S. passport. But as they started talking, Khawla's sister joined them and pulled her by the sleeve of her abaya, hissing in her ear, "you shouldn't talk to him. People will think you are an American spy and you could be killed." There was identification with the American soldier and affiliation with her Iraqi sister, alongside recognition that in this terrain there could be no safe dialogue.

Border crossings intensified bi-regional identifications. When Khawla's son talked with a soldier in Babylon, her son professed his identity as an American. "No way!" said the soldier. "Yes way!" retorted the son, repeating his slang. After they laughed, the soldier asked Alaa to work as a translator for the military. At this point, Khawla stepped in. She told the audience of university students that she wanted to bring her son back home alive. So even as the claim of an American identity was fully felt within the country of Iraq, where there was empathy for the stiff, young soldiers, there was also sadness about the violence and vulnerability of the city's inhabitants. Their claim "I am an American" has several meanings, which were further complicated when Khawla returned to Seattle. While withdrawing money from an ATM, she heard a man on a motorcycle, who yelled at her, "Go home, terrorist!" During the 9/11 decade, this man may have imagined himself as policing culture, associating the female body of Khawla, not as one who has sought refuge, but as one who has come to destroy his home: an estranged "economy of fear," to use Ahmed's language for distorted views of refugees as terrorists.[30] While telling university students about these two experiences—one in Najaf, one in Seattle—Khawla gently informed the audience that the man did not stay long enough for her to explain: "This is my home." At home in an American city, Khawla knew that her son was welcome to join the U.S. military, but she has experienced a limited social invitation—racist attacks because she wears a veil.

Khawla has changed since she left Iraq. In Iraq, her sister was always adjusting Khawla's veil, telling her not to speak to American soldiers. Khawla's use of English, her proclamation of Iraqi and American identity, and her clothing all speak of an altered identification. Her American outfit was no longer acceptable in the small town of Babylon, since the pressure for a certain form of female dress was an anti-Western reaction—a change after the fall of the fairly secular dictatorship of Saddam Hussein. In contrast, when considering outfits to wear for their testimonies at the university, Marwa suggested that they both wear a full black abaya, but Khawla declined, stating that she would wear her usual American clothes. Marwa wore her new scarf of the Iraqi national flag, while Khawla chose a gossamer cream scarf to wear over a navy blue dress. At the second performance, Khawla asked if she could wear her abaya, and I reiterated that she could wear anything she chose. Arriving in a black jacket and long skirt, she pulled out her black abaya with pretty sequins on the sleeves, and dressed in it right before the students came in. Afterward, she took it off and said, "Now I have my American clothes on again." The lines of identity were as fluid as the flowing azure scarf she took on and off while chatting with me.

Unfortunately, most American students really did not understand the subtleties of these two very different styles of dress; they saw only the head scarf. But for Khawla the two outfits marked two cultural identifications. Initially, students from my three classes reported that they viewed Khawla as more "foreign": a covered older woman who read the poems in Arabic. Marwa, in contrast, translated the poems into English and began the performance with online images of Iraq from her photo collection on Facebook. Yet, by the end, many of my students expressed admiration and affection for Khawla, while they were overwhelmed by the passionate fury of Marwa, who is the same age as my students. In the question-and-answer period, following the testimonial stories of *Iraqi*

5. Khawla Hadi, Marwa al-Mtowaq, and Kimberly Segall. Photograph by Luke Rutan. Courtesy of Seattle Pacific University/Luke Rutan. Reproduced with permission.

Voices, the questions were often answered twice: first by Marwa, then by Khawla. The answers often shifted depending on their intergenerational perspectives.

These two narratives of national identity, with their generational splits, challenge the stereotypes of endless warfare between Shiites (as if they are all one simple group) and Sunni (who are equally culturally diverse and variegated). Confronting the simplifications of "centuries" of Shiite and Sunni divide—as if Alyia was still a military general fighting over the rights of succession after the prophet—these testimonials by Marwa and Khawla showed divisions in intergenerational perspectives. Their complex affinities are hybrid: gendered, generational, diasporic. In current Shiite divisions in Iraq, many responses have been generated by the Western invasion—a full spectrum of reconciliation and revenge politics, by leaders like Al-Sadr and Al-Sistani. Also, various local Shiite sheiks have become more powerful because of the American alliance; they have offered to help fight the foreign influence of al-Queda, which brutalized their communities and only emerged in response to the Second Gulf War. Historically, the Ba'athist party persecuted Shiite communities: draining the southern marshlands, eliminating political dissidents, declaring Shiites to be disloyal Iranians during the Iran-Iraq War, slaughtering communities after the First Gulf War. However, these massive sweeps of ethnic cleansing have also included Sunni Kurds and Marsh Arabs, since the dictatorship was not targeting religious identity as much as political resistance.

Bonding the Shiite community, local militias have been needed for security. Rituals also connect Shiite communities: recording the historical loss of Mohammad's relative mourns suffering, both ancient and present. But any simplistic attempt to render recent history through sectarian or terror paradigms is insufficient. Any "ethnic model" or "republic of fear" icon, to follow the political analysis of Eric Davis, does not encompass the resistance of many members of Iraqi society.[31] While the public protest of these two Shiite women demonstrated how unresolved loss passes to second generations, it also rejected mythic views of a homogeneous Shiite narrative of loss. As I hope to have shown in this practitioner's chapter on alternative spaces of history, and in the upcoming sections on poetic protests, creative forms not only suggest how people imagine healing, but also how such cultural expressions disrupt globalized gender stereotypes and complicate mass media's depictions of protest, sectarianism, and violence. Resistant springs pour forth in a plethora of national identifications.

3 | Sectarian Media, Nine Women, and the Stage

Transregional Identities

> I intended to write a piece about the Iraqi psyche, something
> that would inform and enlighten the images we see on TV.
> —Heather Raffo, *9 Parts of Desire* website

Given that Western media initially missed the multiple signs of ongoing
resistance, recently characterized within political transitions as the Arab
Spring, are we still missing important signs of protest, namely, variegated
voices and gendered perspectives? This chapter analyzes a resistant performance of politics called *9 Parts of Desire.* When the playwright declared her
protest against the "images we see on TV," she also attempted a "dialogue
between east and west."[1] The play begins with a call to prayer, marking
the play within an Islamic space. But when a single actress performs nine
different roles, the various characters are located in numerous regions:
the site of the play constantly shifts between Baghdad and Britain, from
Basra to New York. These powerful post-9/11 female characters articulate
female histories within diverse sites of personal agency. Analyzing these
sites of memory also offers a nuanced understanding of how recent conflict is embedded in multiple forms of social loss; in effect, contesting
media portraits of the Islamic world, dismissed or simplified as a religious
quagmire of extremist or sectarian politics with silenced—or stripped and
violated—women. Premiering a few years after September 11, the play was
first performed in New York City and then expanded on and published
in 2007. While the play performs both resistance and mourning in its

inception in New York, the political lament is not over 9/11, but rather for nine Arab women. These nine voices proclaim diverse political identities and protest violence—an Arab Spring—staged in urban space, shadowed by absence, the missing Twin Towers.

To understand Raffo's protest against televised images, it is important to begin with the idea of television and the press as stripping and selecting. Even in the most exciting footage of the Arab Spring, where a woman is resisting a police officer in Tahir Square, it is a mass media image of liberation alongside substitution and stripping. Quite literally, the woman is stripped of her clothing by the officer, who strikes at her with a wooden club. While women's roles as protester are an important inclusion, her voice is stripped—we do not know what her specific reasons are for protesting. Uncertain what happens to her, we do not hear her story. When another Egyptian woman speaks to CNN, a substitution of identity occurs. A second woman speaks for the first. Remaining glued to my television, I wanted to know her story too, but the short newsflash gave me no historical location or personal experience for the second speaker. I do not assume that these two women have the same stories or political desires. We are told that many people in the city are disturbed by the violent treatment of women by the military; in effect, the stripped woman has become an important site of collective identity. But the global film clip records the political voicing of the Arab Spring with a visual portrait of victimization. Thus, the female figure succeeds as an icon of protest, but the woman's story is lost. Specific memories and the numerous stories of women—what I call intimate landscapes of political sites—are absent from the filmed version of the Arab Spring.

This legacy of media stripping permeates our 9/11 heritage, especially as simplifications of religious identity occur within Western portraits of sectarian conflict. In 2006, David Gritten in the *BBC News* proclaimed that for over "1,000 years, Iraq has served as a battleground," with skirmishes that have "defined the schism between Sunni and Shia Muslims."[2] After Gritten's long article on ancient religious divides, patterns of Sunni rule, and demographics of Shiite predominance, only a few lines at the end suggest that Iraqis do not agree with this simplification: "Many Iraqis would argue that their society," especially urban areas, such as Baghdad, are very "cosmopolitan and that class and social status are of greater significance than religion."[3] While violence, pulsing across territorial lines in political, gendered, sectarian, transnational networks, has horrifically marked this transition into democracy, this violence, flashed on the screen of media, is rarely situated in nuanced histories of crossnational dynamics, transitional politics, economic tensions, past recollections of atrocity, and female experiences—instead, it is seen through a single lens that is focused on ancient sects. While Iraqis complicate how these developments have recently emerged, what dominates in this article is the imposition of Western knowledge over local ways of knowing.

Similarly, in 2011, Thomas Friedman argued that the "lessons" learned from Iraq focus on the need for the United States to be a foreign moderator and to recognize sectarian rifts.[4] Published in the *New York Times*, Friedman's article claimed: when the "authoritarian lid" was lifted, then groups exploded as "each faction tested the other's power" in civil war.[5] Unfortunately, the author cannot distinguish tensions within sects, nor does Friedman associate the policy or military action of the United States with this localized violence. In Iraq's foundling democracy, recent territorial fights by political groups about power and the distribution of oil profits—often simplified by Western media as a long-standing sectarian feud—are identified by the press as ancient patterns, absolving the United States of a legacy of violence and lack of postwar planning. There is no mention of the American construction of Iraqi states, leaving the Sunnis with few oil resources. No mention of the American decision to select nine rotating presidents, based on sectarian lines; a change from before the war, when sectarianism was "not very important politically," according to research by Nir Rosen.[6] Unlike mass media, Raffo's play stages multiple memories of violence, set amidst transnational connections. Thus, this play establishes the diverse perspectives of Iraqi women, elucidating the losses of several communities in Iraq and in the diaspora, and, in effect, foreshadowing the complex fractures in Iraq not filmed by the media lens.

Instead, this sole performer—acting out several voices—protests the televised ideas of stripped histories and battered images by enacting social injury in multiple regions. Unlike the Western media's location of a woman's body in a crowd as its historical icon, this political performance locates nine voices with diverse protests on historical events and female experience. Staged after the invasion of Iraq, Raffo does predict turmoil; in her production notes, she describes the "psychic civil war," because of the trauma of violence, and her character Huda imagines a civil war over government power, not because of ancient sectarianism.[7] While the success of this play is documented—it ran for nine sold-out months at Manhattan Ensemble Theater—Raffo's political intervention has not been critically noticed, her protest against both mass media and violence and her nuanced female histories largely forgotten.

Raffo's research and informal interviews with Iraqi women, her experience as an Iraqi and as an American, and her relationships with her extended family members in Iraq all influence her "dramatized" characters, each based in research, what she calls "composite" figures.[8] Given this book's focus on performing memory as a site of protest, it is important to elaborate on Raffo's innovative framework for historical events and experience. She writes about the amount of time that she spent collecting material. This process began with garnering relationships of trust and befriending the women that she met. Her self-position mattered: she was the "right mix" of insider, from an Iraqi heritage, and a safe outsider, who lived in the West, so that women felt that they could "express fears or secrets" that others in their community might judge severely.[9] As Raffo further describes, it was not about "formal interviews," but rather an unfolding of life stories within relationship.[10] And as she created various characters to depict these viewpoints, none of the stories, except for rare intervals, were described verbatim.[11] These voices were created as part of a multitongued history.

Indeed, unlike social science with its more precise transcription of voices, Raffo's performance imaginatively locates historical events and experiences in nine diverse roles—symbolic sites of memory and multiplicity. Arguably, these composites are not just selective transcriptions, nor imaginative fictions; instead, they dramatically record where historical events have emotional impact. All of the female characters reflect on traumatic memories; in effect, they record social wounds of the past. None of these historical injuries are based on sectarian grudges, echoing the case study of my previous chapter, which suggests a recent emergence of sectarian politics. In fact, studying Raffo's play suggests how multiple losses have created fragile zones in today's young democracy, not to be dismissed as ancient hatreds.

Unlike the newsflash with its limited history and lack of female perspectives, Raffo's play explains multiple fractures and artistically collates these losses into a *feminine nationalism*. Since her play records women's experiences even as it remembers thousands of dead civilians, it participates in a memorial of mourning even as it forms a monument to recollect diversity, women's losses within various communities. Indeed, Raffo protests the traumatic effects that have accumulated because of violence from *diverse* time periods. Depicting a young Iraqi girl, for instance, who remembered the loss of her father and brothers to the Ba'athist regime, Raffo exemplifies how disappearances in Iraq form a vast social wound—an aching, collective memory. As a child in primary school, the young girl publicly repeated her father's words to her classmates: "Saddam put his name on the bricks of Babylon, but he cannot put his name on the stars over Iraq" (27). Then her father disappeared. As an adolescent, years later, she finds his journal, where he writes about her public speech as a child in school, which was overheard by authorities. He is concerned that he will be arrested because of his daughter's treasonous rhyme. In his journal, he writes, "I am sure to die" (27). Alongside sadness over the disappearance and death of her father, the teenager now feels a horrified guilt.

This unresolved loss is complicated by global media. During the American invasion, this young girl watched television and saw Saddam Hussein captured, taunted, and shamed on television. She wonders why she was frightened of Saddam all her life, especially when she sees him in a hole, surrounded by Americans. The Iraqi dictator killed the girl's three brothers and father, so when she sees the former president on television, she is shocked by the power dynamics: the soldiers "make fun of him" (25). While watching television, she notices that he looks like a fragile, elderly man, even though she had long imagined him as larger than life. She cries not only because the dictator "stole my father," but also because her father has been killed by a dictator, and this dictator has been globally framed as weak and then ridiculed (27). Her searing self-criticism is not only because of her unintentional role in her father's arrest, it is also a re-evaluation of herself and her former fears of the regime, in light of foreign intervention, which creates ambivalence about the media spectacle beamed to multiple countries. She cries out, "I am stupid!" (27). This social injury is not sectarianism; nor is the historical wound only about a dictator's violence. Rather, the televised site of loss re-visions the former regime because of an occupying power—a crisis of identity, in effect, redefining her collective memory of tragedy after the fall of the dictatorship.

Another characterization of collective memory focuses on torture. The tortured woman, the figure of Huda, is a disturbing site of historical memory. Afflicted by the Iraqi state, Huda details her experience, where women were chained and naked, lined up together like "sardines" (52). All night, the women heard disturbing sounds of rape and pain. Reflecting on mass rape in prisons, Huda compares Iraq to a tortured woman. Tortured sites of Iraq intertwine as citizens connect multiple traumas— the former dictatorship and the temporary occupiers—to torture and sexual abuse. Torture leaves a civil residue. And when Huda imagines the war-torn body of her country, she does not suggest a civil war based on age-old sectarianism, but rather a conflict, after repeated experiences of trauma, of not being able to trust state government to protect or care for its people. Iraqis have lived together for thousands of years, so the conflict is for whom the people can "trust" after excruciating experiences (40).

Echoing Huda's perception, sectarian tensions are a recent identity claim after U.S. occupation, say two experts in international politics, Eric Herring and Glen Rangwala, emerging because of current sociopolitics of an enfeebled state government.[12] In fact, in polls taken in postwar Iraq, a majority of Iraqis (70 percent) embraced "one unified Iraq with central government in Baghdad," as opposed to decentralized regional governments.[13] These polls did not list sect or religious group as a central component in voting.[14] So despite emergent violence and wars over limited resources—exacerbated by scarce job options and failed postwar reconstruction of water, sewage, electricity—there is also national sentiment.

In terms of national images, Huda looks like the poster child for the Iraqi War, since she has experienced oppression and is a pro-war Iraqi who fights for women's rights. But in Raffo's hands, Huda's historical perspective is more convoluted than the American screening of a war for women's rights. Unlike televised portraits of women's oppression in the Islamic world, Huda complains about recent upheaval in gender identifications. She speaks of a "backward" movement: young Iraqi women are "shell shocked" and fearful; they are "afraid to speak up." Their grandmothers were more "liberated," she claims, than this anxious generation (38–39).

The shell-shocked state of feminism was influenced by U.S./U.K. decisions to place exile parties in power, who were not popular with Iraqis, and according to Nadje Al-Ali and Nicola Pratt, for "failing to include women in the political process."[15] Despite initial rhetoric about developing women's rights, American policies, which fostered ensuing violence, have "forced the majority of women back into the home," and made the survival of their families their central, daily preoccupation.[16] Gendered losses influence both men and women—especially as families adjust to psychological and economic repercussions of changed gender policies.

Also, the pro-war Iraqi is uneasy about war because of two powerful collective memories: two forgotten Arab Springs. Huda details the central problem of this war. The United States supported Saddam Hussein throughout his rise to power and war against Iran, and recapitulated on their initial support of Iraqi resistance during the First Gulf War. Huda expostulates that the problem is not because of the war; rather, the problem is an earlier "mistake" of "supporting Saddam" for his entire life (40). Moreover, the military support by the United States and United Kingdom should have occurred years ago, during the First Gulf War, she insists, when the people's revolution in Iraq was not supported, even though sixteen of the eighteen provinces fell. When the promised military support from the United States never came, Shiites were massacred in the south and sanctions crippled the revolutionaries and the middle and upper class.

6. Tank deployed against uprising (1991). Courtesy of William Segall.

This political uprising—for Iraqis in the south and the north—is remembered as a period of betrayal because promised U.S. air support never arrived. The Arab Spring turned into a massacre in the southern regions, as tanks and soldiers from the modern state churned people's bodies into mass gravesites. Afterward, a no-fly zone was declared, across the northern and southern lines, to prevent another atrocious political cleansing of the Kurds. Intriguingly, history forgets this experience; for instance in *Inventing Iraq*, Toby Dodge argues that the level of resistance in the south, despite their hatred of Saddam Hussein, "surprised U.S. Central Command" in the Second Gulf War.[17] This "problematic" form of "militant and aggressive Iraqi nationalism" has developed over "three wars" and sanctions, Dodge claims, but he does not list the Western political betrayal of their Arab Springs as an important part of this nationalism, a response to a traumatic legacy. When the Shiite resisted the Ba'athist regime, thousands were killed.[18] In fact, Huda's memories mirror the militant and the nationalist, described by Dodge, thus, complicating her position as a pro-war Iraqi. So while she does not protest the

Second Gulf War, she does voice her ambivalence, detailing overlapping memories of Western betrayals and Eastern violence.

And there is another historical event, which Huda narrates as an invasive betrayal. Watching the televised screening of Americans entering Iraq, Huda narrates the Western invasion in the 1920s, when Britain forced out the Ottoman Empire. Detailing historical battles during the British takeover of Iraq, Huda condemns the decimation of highly populated areas, like Fallujah and Najaf, which she refers to as the "cycle, repeating" (40), since these regions were battlegrounds in the Second Gulf War and British-occupied Iraq.[19] Huda's nationalism builds on these memory zones: a double body of collective injury.

So despite her condemnation of Western influence, as in British colonization, Huda desires this war because it will crush the hated regime that has killed so many of her friends. Since she herself has been imprisoned and tortured, she reflects on her life and her country as a painful journey toward recovery: for her own horrific experience and for her homeland, it takes a "lifetime to be liberated" (53). After being tortured, Huda describes a loss of self, which has taken a lifetime to reclaim, and she imagines this same process on a national level. Iraq is imagined as a tortured body, which must rediscover its identity and heal, especially after the trauma of being violated by those in power. The traumatized body recovers slowly, not by cataclysmic change. After years as an activist, she states that she does not "believe anymore in revolution" (40). Instead she points out the need for a measured and thoughtful process; like a plant, it must be deeply "rooted" (40). Her language shifts from the tortured body to a gentle hope for a gradual growth of national development, a model for an Iraqi Spring.

Huda is also part of a vast political diaspora. Huda has fled to several locations—from Baghdad to Lebanon to Istanbul, then returning to Baghdad, and finally relocating in Britain. Her loss is positioned in objects of memory, namely, pictures. After her husband dies in London, she cannot move and refuses to change anything in her house. Keeping her husband's portrait in the same spot, she is unwilling to leave her house in London because it is a site of shared loss, familiarity, and identity. In Raffo's staging, Huda's "disheartenment" combines several factors: displacement, her husband's death, multiple historical events, and the desperate state of Iraq (39). Fearing civil war, as the invasion will "hack," not "sculpt," the nation, she reflects on the thousands of years people have lived together, and her own family intermarriages, Shia, Sunni, Kurd (39). Unlike the media's one-time, flat image, the role of Huda suggests multiple locations of historical loss and national identification—a network of tortured histories, transnational identity, and tangled hopes.

Another transregional site of Arab protest is New York. For an Iraqi American, watching the news and talking on the phone, she is anxious for the welfare of her extended family in Iraq, and remembers another set of collective memories. Television shows her the "mass graves" and the desperate claims on bodies, where family members carry the skeletons of their beloved home in a bag (35). The Iraqi American also carries figures home, but hers are from Western media. Transfixed to the television or telephone call from Iraq, she cannot function outside this war realm. Ensconced with her television, she refers to herself as a "cave"—a term for the space of globalization where things are hidden out of sight (48). Staying in her apartment as much as possible, when she does walk down the streets of New York, she sees not only pedestrians but also bodies in the road. These imagined casualties inscribe New York City as the site of war—an American lamentation of its war-caused casualties, not its Twin Towers.

War memories and public life become enmeshed. The Iraqi American wants the constant bustle of the city of New York to register the horror of the war. Amidst the shopping malls, the bars, the exercise club, the war permeates the televisions; however, despite the global media, the city continues to move and remains unmarked, void of one hundred thousand corpses of Iraqis, except in her mind. When she is talking to a woman about the number of Iraqis dead, she notes her own frivolous activities: she is speaking of the dead while getting a pedicure. This dislocation between her life and the war becomes a social loss, and she states, "I cannot carry it" (48).

Responding in protest, she rejects America's selective forms of compassion. Everything comes to a halt when a small group of Americans are in danger: engineers are sent to "save everything," movies are produced, talk shows are featured. In American media, when a traumatic event happens, the talk shows question whether people can ever "move on" (45). In contrast, violence in Iraq is not placed in this American psychological frame. Raffo's character protests televised segregation and detachment about the war. There is silence, even though people in Iraq witness their children "kidnapped trying to get to work or hacked to death or there's a tank in my ammu's front yard" (45). Her sentences run together in a traumatic fusillade as she explains how people survive extreme loss "over and over and over again" (45). Protesting the limits of American imagination, this young woman falls into depression and becomes physically ill: "I can't breathe—I'm sick" (47–48). Unable to leave her apartment, she watches the news. Searching for the location of her family amidst the footage of American bombing, she imagines a city of graves.

Unlike the Western media's select sympathies, Raffo's female characters produce new and disconcerting questions. First of all, what happens when the Iraqi woman lives in Baghdad and Britain, Basra and New York? The play challenges boundaries, as social injuries are not limited to Sunni or Shiite or Kurdish divides; but from Britain to Basra, the play maps out altered borders of the West versus the Rest—new territory for histories of transitional violence, diasporic ethics, and international politics. For instance, a startling effect is produced when these characters are all linked through a single actress in a common body—and then, one of these central characters is killed by an American bomb. The performed protest is not just a staging of multiple historical losses. If so, the play could have staged nine different women, each with a distinct role and set of collective memories, and unity could be suggested if these nine actresses joined hands; otherwise the embodiment would show separation. Instead, Raffo's play has one actress become nine different characters. A single actress suggests the infinite flexibility within religious and national identifications even as she performs transregional entanglements.

Each of these women is marked as Muslim because each of them holds onto the veil. However, only a few characters wear the veil as a sign of their religious identity; many of them transform the veil into an intimate use object. Across global lines, there are many Islamic regions that allow women to choose whether or not to veil. The few political states that force women to veil are creating their own identity markers through women's bodies. But Western political states that force women not to veil in certain locations are also ushering an embodied control society. In contrast, Raffo's women selectively choose how they want to clothe their sense of modern Islamic selves. Transitioning between nine characters, a single actress performs these voices, and these transitions disrupt any singular view of an Islamic persona. Each woman faces unresolved issues and narrates her survival strategies, challenging stereotypes of silent Muslim women, locked in harems and fixed political identities, as Suha Sabbagh and Fatimah Mernissi trace.[20] Instead, Raffo's intimate stories interrupt generalizations. By describing themselves, women resist what Brinda Mehta terms the "negation of identity" in orientalist and patriarchal frames.[21] Because there are multiple women speaking, strong women stage, not an exceptional woman adrift in a tide of passivity, but rather an associative norm.

In terms of diverse national identifications, performing multiple voices in a single body not only collates a collective portrait, but the single actress also splits the dichotomy of self and other into pieces. This multiplicity parallels some of the playwright's notes about her own experience. On al-Jazeera, Raffo describes herself as Iraqi and American, a position that rejects self and other.[22] Her characters—creative constructions, based on her research, experience, and imagination—show compound loyalties. In her notes on the play, Raffo describes a double identification: both Iraqi belonging and an American longing. When she went to Iraq as a child, she remembers her grandmother's house. Sleeping on her grandmother's flat roof, looking at the stars in the sky at night, she refers to Baghdad as a "magical place" (ix). Years later, when she travels across the border, Raffo describes how her identity is delineated by border guards in Jordan, "to them I was classified as other," but this changes when an Iraqi guard welcomes her to her "father's country," a place where she can feel at "home" (ix). As an adult in Baghdad, Raffo is called "daughter," and all fifty relatives desire to host her. Her sense of self relates to location, especially her father's childhood home and the buildings that her grandfather built with marble. During the violence, she locates herself in these imagined sites. She associates Baghdad with the "gut-wrenching war," characterized by her anxiety about her relatives (ix). Her identity shifts between Iraqi "daughter," linked by sentimental and blood bonds, to "orphan," disconnected from her family's experiences during the war (ix). She is also orphaned, because her ancestral home is being destroyed by her current homeland. The nostalgic magic of childhood contrasts the idea of a territorial orphan or an alienating experience of the war—all descriptions of multifarious nationalisms.

The bi-cultural orphan, claimed in Raffo's self-description, also mirrors the trope of the orphan throughout the play. The orphan—a site of historical loss and religious ethics—emerges when the doctor fears for the next generation, genetically orphaned by the war. The Iraqi doctor delivers children deformed by the uranium-tipped American weapons, and she mourns as a misformed child is born and the mother dies in childbirth. Plus, she suffers a brooding transference, for the doctor herself is pregnant. As war's horror grows in cancerous sites of human bodies and inadequate health care, this orphaning of citizens is because of deficient living conditions and ravaged medical sites. Across regions, the heinous nature of war also spreads to Americans, as in returning soldiers, who now have the war embedded "inside you, like a burden, like an orphan" (34). Through these images, two countries are married via displacement and emotional attachment: a nation pregnant with the violence of war, a nation that gives birth to a displaced child. But the orphan is not just an image of loss, since Islamic history and practices regard the orphan as a central site of social justice. Orphaned of his parents, the Prophet Mohammed expressed the need to care for the traumatized and defenseless. These ethics of social justice characterize Islamic policies of tolerance and economic concern for the poor and orphaned. Thus, the image of the orphan speaks (simultaneously) of extreme loss, transregional ties, and the adoption of ethical responsibility.

This orphan image was present at the beginning of this project. Raffo's inspiration for this play started when she saw a painting in a museum in Baghdad, created by a female artist. The artist was killed by an American bomb, and she left behind a daughter—orphaned and blinded by the bombing. In researching this artist and interviewing other artists in

Baghdad, Raffo created a portrait of Layal as a woman who draws the unresolved losses of other women. Secretly painting injustice, using symbols, she sublimates the stories "living inside" of her and draws her naked body or stark images of trees (9). There is a covert sketch of a university student, brutalized by Saddam Hussein's son, and then killed by his Dobermans: re-created in a symbolic form, this female victim is painted as a fragile blossom on a tree, out of reach of the barking dogs (9). The art composes violence, "transcending" death by commemorating Iraqi women; indeed, while brushing against tragedy, this artistry ingests loss, a form of mourning (8). In a similar manner, this play enfolds collective losses into a protest that participates in a healing memorial and a feminine nationalism.

Using these stories, this play contains a collective protest, to change the mind of the politically powerful. Indeed, Layal compares herself to Scheherazade, who spins stories to change the views of a political leader. Scheherazade sleeps with the unstable king, who is decimating his country with violent gender killings and infuriating its population, taking the daughters of his nation as brides, murdering them at dawn. Scheherazade's choice to marry the king and confront this series of gendered murders makes her a "political hero"—what Mernissi terms a "liberator in the Muslim world."[23] In similar terms, Layal, aggrieved at the devastation of women, sleeps with a political leader, and begs this official to protect her and all "daughters of Muslims" (10) when American bombs shatter civilian houses as well as military targets. Persuading him to safeguard residential areas, she cries out after the conversation, "Shahryar," the king's name in the *Arabian Nights*. If her arts of persuasion do not succeed, then she will use her painted art to deliver portraits of murdered women from oppressive hands to an animated form of life—a reviving symbolic tribute (10). Similarly, this play uses an icon of conscience to lament the death of women. Protesting the violence, this play, embedded with an American audience, publicizes a nuanced history of the fractured state in Iraq, embedded in local and foreign violence.

These dead bodies map out Iraq, not through its nation-state territory, but rather through its women. These body mappings cross between national and regional spaces—a protest movement that marks how political groups from both East and West have claimed women's bodies within their violent demarcations of power. Revolting against these gendered losses, Layal paints vulnerable and yet powerful portraits of the female body, which she refers to as a "map of me" (62). It is also a charting of the war, especially the numerous American bombs that dismember Iraqi women:

> without my legs
> buried in the backyard
> they're making their own map of
> me anyway—sure after every / bomb (62)

The violence of the language's repetition, like an alliterative bomb, keeps falling in the broken sentences. As bomb after bomb becomes a group narrative and a collage of death, the language shifts from single injuries into a vocalization of collective protest. At the same time, external destruction turns to rage as Layal destroys her studio and creates a political mosaic to humiliate the American president. She beats her body and calls out in Arabic before she dies—a national protest that reminds the audience of its political culpability. As Raffo explains in her play notes, Layal, close to death, "explodes under the weight of the many women" that she has depicted (69). In this drastic subversion, the play revises history. Unlike the powerless death of the artist, killed by an American bomb, Raffo's artist explodes with fury and passion as she protests the stories of suffering from multiple sites of Iraq and its diaspora, highlighting the East/West entanglement of violence.

Layal's explosive death is staged through her cries, and these cries reiterate the voices of many women in the play. When multiple voices intersect, they reflect certain social classes; it is a "collision" between different viewpoints—what M. M. Baktin terms "heteroglossia."[24] These hybrid voices reject simple constructions of nation or gender. Linking these women through repeated words, fused speeches, shared objects, or one character completing another's sentence, Raffo desires to show the "complexities of nationality" alongside the "universality" of women (70). Many Iraqis who watched Raffo's play commented afterward that it was an extremely "emotional experience" and that they could identify with

the various voices: an empathic identification, even if they would dis-
agree with a certain character's perspective, a recognition of their "fellow
countrymen."[25] Not just national, it is also a transregional voicing; not
just the artist's voice, "it is all of us" (8). As the actress shifts into various
voices, the play presents a feminist nationalism across transnational lines
through its Arab and American actress and author: in effect, the Iraqi is
American; thus, the American is also Iraqi.

While the Iraqi has been held up as the "other" for American society, the language and embodiment of this play suggests that there is no
distinct self and other, by intersecting these women in a single body with
syncretic ties. The fluctuating body on stage suggests that the American
can present the voice of an Iraqi, and the diverse Iraqi personas are easily shifted into by the Iraqi American actress. Unlike categories of dis-
similarity that are often invoked, James Clifford delineates how cultural
differences are part of an "inventive" system, woven with a blended "syn-
cretism," especially since cultures influence one another.[26] If there can be
a crossing between American self and Iraqi other, it is a double challenge:
rejecting both Western and Eastern identity politics. To quote the play,
"why do you look at us as if we have two hearts?" (64). The play protests
against antagonistic divides, gender-mined polarities, unmourned losses,
and televised icons of violence and victims.

This form of protest also crosses between languages—intentionally
resisting the domination of the Western tongue. When Arabic is spoken
by various characters, the non-English language evades the majority of
the American audience. These Arabic allusions may evoke special meaning for Iraqi audience members, such as the popular Iraqi song in the play
about the country being consumed. Originally created when Iraq was a
"battleground" between the Ottoman Empire and the British, this song
mocks the British claims of liberating the country in 1917 (75). This song
re-emerged during the Second Gulf War in 2003, as this protest song
calls for national unity against foreign interference.[27] Diverse languages
are part of a larger "insider versus outsider" dynamic when staged in theater, states Marvin Carlson: a "site of otherness" and a "site of resistance"
to official power.[28] Perhaps political power is located in language and
violence; for while many Iraqis speak English, very few English speakers

remember British colonization in Iraq, marked by the very first air bomb-ings of civilian populations, including night bombings of people's homes, leading to terror-filled mass exodus. When Arabic interrupts the flow of English, this shift disturbs the dominating discourse, and while in New York, proclaims the value of Iraqi culture and history.

But inserting untranslated Arabic in this play is not necessarily polar-izing; it is a specific type of cultural crossing. The Arabic lines suggest that the American audience will not fully understand the meaning of the words even as they ingest the emotion behind the phrases. When Layal beats at her face and chest and cries out, *Yaboo, yaboo!* before the fourth call to prayer preceding her death, it is a desperate cry—more powerful than had she cried out, "Tragedy, tragedy!" (63). Loss is felt—even if the exact nature of the words is not known—in a cross-cultural claim. And Arabic names intertwine with English as the names of Iraqi relatives woven with the words "I love you" cross in a telephone link between multiple countries. Sentimental bonds travel between countries and lan-guages; linguistic attachments of loss cross Western and Eastern lines.

In *9 Parts of Desire*, language does not mark the insider or outsider. Arabic is spoken by characters who reside in multiple regions. In effect, it *challenges* the "outsider" label through a global nationalism for Iraqis throughout the world. The English entwined with Arabic and the Iraqi English coded as American are all valued as legitimate voices, important tongues. Traveling words, spoken into telephones, connect these women. The telephone is handled by multiple characters, and the term, *hallo, hallo*, an Iraqi-English marked phrase, travels across national territories. The phone crosses regions, but it is also dropped onto the stage, when Layal cannot convince her daughter Sabah to stay in the safe region of England. Faulty telephone lines parallel broken economic lines, when one lower-class woman cries out this greeting while selling everything she owns to survive. As traveling linguistics—a combination of Arabic, Eng-lish, and Iraqi-marked English—it is a "broken English," carried between places (65).

Like the words on the telephone, other shared objects and phrases link these regional women. These shared objects for these nine characters are often used to document their multiple experiences. Books, journals,

pens, pictures, and portraits all witness to their political and social experiences. For instance, the witness book, detailing the truth of an American bombing of a women's shelter, becomes the hidden journal, read
by a teenager to find the reason for her father's death. These witnessing
objects protest the erasure of women's histories. An old woman remembers being forced to erase a portrait of her mother because she was not
allowed to draw the female body. A young woman protests the erasure of
Arab suffering in the media coverage of war. In these two forms of erasure neither of these women's perspectives (or emotions) is validated by
others. Despite their distinct nationalities and class, this parallel creates
an interesting merger: both American media and Islamic fundamentalism erase their stories and eviscerate their identities. Political reactions are
situated on the physical site of women's bodies. But Raffo rejects these
erasures of identity with her collective props of protest.

The object crossing between women does not highlight sectarian
identifications that emerged in response to the occupation and during
the civil war; rather, writing instruments symbolize diverse sites of loss,
across national zones of economics and international lines, which contributed to fracturing fault lines. After Umm Ghada, a mother, who
lives in a yellow trailer, details how her eight children were killed by an
American attack on a bomb shelter; she holds an imagined pen for the
audience to sign her registrar of witnesses. Then Layal, an upper-class
painter who has one daughter, transforms this pen into a paintbrush,
to paint and commemorate women murdered by the Ba'athist regime.
Through transitional objects, there is a space of exchange between
these two women and their ideas. Both women serve as commemorative
agents, telling stories of the dead in political protest against national and
transnational violence.

Another shared object used for protest is the veil, which defines religious affinities and postwar doubt, in the liaison of an Iraqi girl and Umm
Ghada. When the young Iraqi clings to the black fabric, it is wrapped up
like the body of a doll. After the girl has read her father's journal, she
realizes that her own words led to her father's death, and the black folds,
wrapped in the embracing shape of a doll, symbolizes her lost innocence.
The seven-year-old lost her father, and later the teenager loses her ideas in

a world where there is no safety. This enfolded doll-veil is dropped to the floor, so that it falls like a great black hole. Descending to the ground, the veil hollows out the charred area where the American bomb dropped, the civilian shelter that housed Umm Ghada's family, and as she stares into the veil's black abyss, this mourning mother struggles with a personal and social crisis and cries out to God; she cannot understand why she is still alive when all her children have died. Protesting the American bombing on February 13, 1991, she records how 403 people died in the bomb shelter. Pointing to "charred handprints and footprints" of desperation, she condemns the United States, which had tested a new bomb (29). American explanations that they thought it was a military communication center are rejected, and she asks the audience to sign her witness book (31). Thus, as a visual tool, the veil suggests the complexity of postwar belief, and the veil protests the blackout of media information about these events; indeed, this traveling veil connects two female histories, which are publically erased. Not just the Western military's erasure of violence, but also the young girl's emotive response to both the former regime and the televised portrait. At the same time, the veil sympathetically ties characters together: the Iraqi mother and the Iraqi girl—the mother with no children and the child, orphaned of her father. As such, this veiled protest performs a feminine bond and female relocation of histories, alongside fluctuating sites of religious identity, suggested in the fluttering shifts of the veil, held in different ways by each female character.

To understand how the veil is, at times, a site of personal identity, at other times a form of public protest, it is helpful to have some background. Women select to wear the veil or unveil—not just as a sign of religious faith, but sometimes also for political identification or resistance. When women are forced to veil or unveil, the clothing erases their choice to select their own political or religious vestments. In various contexts, the veil is not only a sign of individual faith, but also a symbol of respect, garnered within a religious community. After Western violence, the forced veiling of women becomes a public sign of rejecting Western practices or an attempt to create national identity through gendered locations. An Iraqi woman, a member of the Da'wa party, might choose to wear the veil during the secular Ba'athist regime; not because she is forced to veil, but rather, as Al-Ali and Pratt claim, as a sign of revolt against the national government.[29] Similarly, the veil has become a symbolic protest against the West; part of a "rejection of things western and rage at the western world," as Leila Ahmed argues, because "Arabs have suffered and continue to suffer injustices and exploitation at the hands of colonial and postcolonial western governments."[30] The forced veiling of women maps out a political territory, not unlike the territorial mapping of sects, which show a contestation over power, and, at times, a backlash against the West. In contrast to the idea of veiling as protest, Western iconography locates the veiled woman as an oppressed figure. In this Western mediation, the veil not only symbolizes backward practices but also creates a racist hierarchy: the oppressed in contrast to Western freedom.

Moreover, the veil, during the period of the Prophet Mohammad, symbolized associations of class. The veil, as Ahmed further expounds, was only later required by Muhammad for his wives, assimilating the customs of some of the conquered neighboring territories that practiced veiling as a sign of the elite upper crust of society.[31] In all these instances, this clothing piece becomes a traveling symbol with distinct cultural capital. In *9 Parts of Desire*, each woman decides to use and to change the meaning of the veil, upending any simple orientalism. As a use object, the veil ties diverse female identities together, some religious ties, some not, in a sympathetic web—communal bonds, female histories, braided into a collective protest.

But the final object of protest is not a veil, but a picture. The show ends with this artistic portrait, painted by Layal. This picture, called "Savagery," protests the violent erasures of women from both Eastern and Western sources. When the elderly merchant picks up the portrait and the other remaining sentimental objects on the stage, it is a meager gathering, from the wreckage of Iraq. Layal's other pictures from the museum are "burned dead"—a parallel between the destroyed art and the dead artist (67). The play protests how the female survivors lose everything, even their objects of memory. And the image of the picture is reminiscent of other portraits: the photos of the American soldiers who have tortured Iraqis, the picture of Huda's dead husband, or the photos of Umm Ghada with "emissaries" from across the globe who have witnessed the tragic deaths at the bomb shelter (29). But why leave this final portrait in the hands of the street seller? This epilogue discomforts the viewers, because it sublimates female histories into an object, which Nanna offers to sell to the audience. The theme of erasure is evoked again with economic loss, as Nanna sells her own portrait, for only two dollars. In most tragedies, after the protagonist dies, the ending is a final dirge. In this play, however, the mourner's lament, followed by the street seller who sells off the property of the dead, heightens the tragedy. It is like a merchant selling the crown of the dead king in the final scene. This final act protests against the commodification of Iraq, a protest located within decimated cities, selective images, tortured bodies, and gendered space.

It is a "secret" that we are being told (68). After witnessing the death of Layal, this secret changes the viewer; it is an association with the dead. And there is another secret. Nanna tells the audience that the United States military did not protect the historical treasures of Iraq. The American pronouncement of freedom is reframed as freedom to destroy "national history," because if the shared objects of history are destroyed, then it is "easier to finish" off a once-wealthy and powerful nation (43). After this decimation of shared history—for Iraqi Shiite, Sunni, Kurdish, Jewish, and Assyrian Christian groups—the play protests the erasure of national unity and female histories. Disrupting an entire society is social trauma, according to Erikson; it is "damage to the tissues" of communities, a dark, "communal mood" that can "dominate a group's spirit."[32] In the stories of Iraqi women, many losses are not fully worked through. Their pain transfers onto objects—shoes thrown into the river, relics sold by a street vendor, the ever-present abaya, prayer beads incanting war survivors, unfinished spaces on a canvass, honoring the dead. Each symbol of loss rejects cultural amnesia. These objects appear, again and again, obstinately refusing to forget—a map of social loss. Protesting the forgotten site of devastation, the precursor to civil war, Raffo performs a monument to the Iraqi dead in the midst of 9/11 wreckage—in effect, an Arab Spring on American soil.

But this play extends beyond a mapping of collective loss, because these Muslim women—painters, doctors, dreamers, merchants—sculpt images of diversity, potential, competence.[33] Not just a mirror of violence, this feminine protest is a diasporic claim. The United States and Britain are now Iraqi homelands, because of the diaspora that the West helped create—a claim for *merging Western and Eastern identities*. In fact, these female journeys offer an alternative map of national identities—as the doctor, medically trained in the West, returns to Basra, as Huda flees Iraq and lives in London. This construction of transnational identity is a global site of ethics, after the violent failure of 9/11 nationalism.

In contrast to the Western media's portrait of Iraq as other or Iraq as ancient feuding grounds of sectarian violence—with no complicated shading about the history of Iraq, reasons for economic division because of the federal system, nor the influence of occupation—this protest responds to the many social losses that help us to understand violence, critical to conceiving any forums of reconciliation; at the same time, the play dares to imagine a syncretic affinity between women and nations. This transnational affinity makes a political claim on its Western audience: the destabilization of Iraq by foreign occupancy has led to militant groups, displaying their power to disrupt the state government and American forces by taking over various neighborhoods. These bloody power dynamics have led to clearing out interreligious neighborhoods, such as urban sites in Baghdad, as these reckless militants declare areas as Sunni or Shiite to the detriment of mixed marriages and communal bonds of multisect neighbors. Like the words of the mourner's song, women are not being protected by the state; instead, they are "hunted."[34] Protesting against the unsecure state of civilians, rejecting polarizing divisions between countries that calcify the current site of conflict, Raffo not only protests violence, but she also asks her audience to map out *transregional bonds*.

Where does this Arab Spring lead us? Political springtime requires us to hear new stories and consider the Muslim woman as a site of political heroism, not the site of female oppression, and to view the Arab as a site of American and transregional identity. If these transgressive spaces of cultural spring are accepted, it offers a relocation of global identity and ethical responsibility. In effect, Raffo's protest, a performance of American and Arab identity, offers not only a striking double consciousness, but also new locations for transnational thinking. This Arab Spring creates an imaginative space of multiple women's voices—a shift between languages and locations—to protest against the forgotten histories of Muslim women and the erasures of media iconography. Given its initial inception, a protest in New York City in 2004, the performance of *9 Parts of Desire* is an altered site for America's post-9/11 imagination, overall, a critical intervention, just three years after the violent crash.

4 | Baghdad Blogs and Gender Sites

An Iraqi Spring for Youth Culture?

Who knows? Maybe I'll start a tribal blog and become a
virtual sheik myself.

—Riverbend, *Baghdad Burning*, 2005

While Western media are interested in blogs as a form of personal protest, not much is written on the identities of these bloggers, nor on
the types of blogs that are being produced.[1] In August 2011, a group
of ninety-eight bloggers from fifteen different countries in the Middle
East and North Africa responded to a Harvard University survey. Most
of the respondents were young, in their twenties. Overall, 81 percent
blogged in English, 90 percent had university degrees, 30 percent had
been threatened. Who are these young twenty-something bloggers and
how do their blogs contribute to protest? Blogs offer an important form
of onsite testimony—a mapping of public and private space. Not just historical documentation, blogging records changing political emotions. In
the two blogs examined in this chapter, both were republished as books:
one in 2003, one in 2005. While both bloggers, using the code names
Salam Pax and alternate listings of River or Riverbend, integrate wit and
witnessing, they face distinct pressures at work because during the violence of a political transition there are gendered experiences. One has
not been paid for two months at his architectural firm, and he fears an
extremist backlash during the political upheaval, a potential threat to this
twenty-nine-year-old gay architect. The other, a twenty-four-year-old

female computer programmer, is no longer accepted at work, a backlash against women after the Western occupation. Savvy users of a youth culture lingo, both "River" and "Pax" create forms of self-expression that mix Western media and personal experience—a hybrid national location that communicates political desire.

Before diving into these blogs, which witness street politics and protest, I want to highlight how the voices of River and Pax, with their diverse national affinities, challenge the limited parameters of Arab identity within the Western lens. Take, for example, the self and social description that emerges in Pax's blog. An intelligent, secular, gay architect, he defends his national history and Islamic culture, boycotting political misperceptions. One of his parents is Shiite, the other Sunni, and his family has lived abroad and in Iraq. And in River's blog, we see the importance of her work as a computer programmer and writer, alongside her reliance on faith, during the bombings and urban upheaval that she records. Her story, far from the Western lens, details her urban identification and her Sunni feminism. So while many critics treat blogs like an alternative form of journalism, these texts as personal stories are also replete with dark humor, challenging the media's metanarratives. And unlike press reports, these blogs are also coping mechanisms during a time of violence. These blog sites—with their creative expressions and gendered voices—give us a new sense of protest movements and chart diverse political identities, vocations disrupted by violence, post-upheaval sectarianism, and democratic desires.

Moreover, as counterhistories, both blogs protest assumptions of the Western press. Emotive reactions, not just cognitive arguments, were often the focus of the media. At this time after 9/11, the emotion of American "morale," claims Ben Anderson, was being surveyed on the home front.[2] But I want to extend this idea of emotion, arguing that the media idea of a moral war was being determined not just by the mendacity of weapons of mass destruction or by the changing list of women's rights, but also by the morale of Iraqi reception. Pax's blog challenges how the Western press depicted Iraqis before the war. He quotes an article in *The Guardian*: as with "so many Iraqis, after 20 years of war," the doctor, who is organizing his hospital for inevitable bombings, is a "fatalist" who "smokes heavily, loves high-cholesterol foods."[3] With wit, Pax responds to insinuations about Iraqis: he asks if this doctor's love for high-cholesterol food is one more "violation against UN sanctions?" If the United States intends to "demolish all high-cholesterol food production plants," then Pax plans to resist. "Fight for your right to have a heart attack!" (5–6). Using satire, the blog separates the sentimental embrace of political rhetoric and populist generalizations of fatalism. As counternarratives, these blogs resist Western sentimentalism, which circles around emotive 9/11 images and perspectives on Arab identities. This Western sentiment casts a challenging atmosphere for these authors to bear witness to their own democratic desires and to their experiences: as in devastating chemical weapons and cluster bombs, in places like Fallujah, and in urban spaces changing in the midst of war.

The press of the war, interested in how Iraqis on the street would respond to the fall of the regime, focused on the portrait of a young boy, slapping the dictator's statue with a shoe. Repeated on televised screens with a shock-and-awe proliferation, evidence of the celebration became more profound as Westerners were told that shoes are a great sign of disrespect—cultural evidence, the truth about Iraqi morale, is initially interpreted as a signature of an advanced society's moral war effort and occupation. In contrast, Pax protests how these media frame Arab identity, and refuses to wave pop-national flags for celebration, contesting the Western lens by envisioning an alternative scene. It is a "bad remake" of an earlier movie where Britain comes in to "rescue" Iraqis from the Ottomans, around 1920; now, an "even worse movie," the "civilized world" enters Iraq to give the "barbaric" Arabs a "better living" (14). These two metanarratives erase the history of those who have fought and died to liberate their own country. "I feel sorry for every revolutionary Iraqi," any person who fought for democracy or who wrote a poem or book and was killed for it. If they had known about the foreign invasion, they might not have "bothered" (14). The blog positions democracy, not as emotion or a Western idea, but rather as an Iraqi ideal that Arabs have died for—an *Arab Spring*.

Protesting misconceptions of Arab identity, Pax defines himself through his blog. This blog of an urban identity receives twenty thousand hits a day—causing Gillian Whitlock to call Pax a "cyberlebrity."[4] Not only are there mugs and T-shirts celebrating this Paxian persona, but the allure is also in his syncretic English—what Whitlock calls his techie lingo, alongside "codes of the gay subculture" and pop culture.[5] Pax locates himself through his family, his political perspective, and even a hybrid Arabic language—a counternarrative to the press, a subversive language of economics and experience—what he calls "Arablish." With darkly comic language, he describes his "emergency list" of snacks, wine, and good books to get through the horrendous onslaught of aerial bombings, reminding us that civilians in political transitions are defenseless. Using Arablish, Pax shows how life is on hold—on "ba3deen"—which means after the bombings (6). Asking his boss about his broken computer, the boss will consider it "ba3deen" (7). His house is also on hold: an occupation of family members who flood into his home, a safe urban location not near military compounds. As the teenagers invade, one young cousin plays video games, another watches WWF videos, a third studies in Pax's bedroom. There is even a young girl on his computer reading discussion boards from Saudi Arabia about "what does the man of your dreams look like?" (15). Situating his prewar house as a multimedia site of teen energy, he escapes with an older cousin to find some illegal alcohol, and as a witness to war, he situates his identity within a modern family, vocational blues, and the ensuing violence.

Resisting the media's persona of an Iraqi, Pax crafts his own political voice, rejecting dictatorship and American policies alike. Not loyal to the regime—which demoted his parents for not joining the party and enforces policies of "no-trial-just-shoot-them" (25)—he also rejects an invasion by foreign armies. Avoiding polarized encampments, he criticizes Western sanctions as the "noose" around civilian's necks, when they were already "hostages" to a regime (120). And as the dictator stages last-minute elections before the bombing of Baghdad, Pax decides that these elections are "more funny than tragic" (5). In effect, the blog charts out private and public spaces of experience, constructing a new form of nationalism, one not loyal to the state government.

In the published form of the blog that began in 2002—titled *The Clandestine Diary of an Ordinary Iraqi*—the author positions his self-portrait in both global and national terms. While traveling in Europe, Pax describes how his life was "enriched" by travel, but also "transformed" by these experiences (63). Before the war, he was content with not being particularly "rooted" in a specific place because he feels at "home" in multiple locations (63). However after 9/11, travel became more difficult: when the authorities look at his passport and his name, he is associated with foreign concepts and stereotypes. Troubled by a loss of acceptance, Pax feels pressured to "identify" with values that he does not really believe (64). Pax poses a question in his blog: was he previously deceiving himself about not needing to connect with a single homeland? In the past, "cultural heritage" was not a concept that could be betrayed, because it was not "how I saw myself" (63). Am I just an adept "chameleon," he questions, blending in to multiple places without having any true color? (64). Posting questions about cross-cultural identifications, the blog forces readers to consider current policies of exclusion in Western nations; moreover, Pax's blog suggests a shifting site of identification—a transition after 9/11 and in the midst of war—an emergent nationalism.

So even as the blog records street politics, this writing also constructs a national affinity. In contrast to the Western press, Pax crafts a site-specific geographical identity that wanders from the living room into the streets. Detailing the tragic sedimentation of feeling, after watching footage of the bombing on BBC and al-Jazeera, he watches his favorite building in Baghdad burn and weeps. To watch "your city" as it is "destroyed before your own eyes" is a painful experience, beyond words (148). A second piercing spectacle follows the bombing—global images of looting reveal the city "undone by your own hands" (148). Watching the media is not a detached experience. Attuned to BBC, the family views the military surrender. "What a shame," his youngest cousin whispers. While the family knows the Iraqis must surrender, the media sight of them lifting up a "white flag" makes "something deep inside of you cringe" (129). Knowing it is a global image is excruciating.

Pax's national identification also centers around psychological locations of death that haunt the streets and the media.[6] When Pax leaves his house, he walks near the front door of a building. As two American military vehicles pull up, the soldiers run forward with drawn weapons. Pax yells in English not to shoot. It is a near-death experience, where he barely avoids becoming a "statistic" (160). The next day, he sees the burned door where he was almost killed. Describing familiar places lambasted as militarized space in media coverage and on the streets, spaces become redefined. Even his favorite ice cream shop has three tanks parked in front (164). And when a taxi driver complains about current conditions, Pax challenges him. Indignantly, Pax asks the driver if he wants the terror of a dictator back? At the same time, the devastation of war creates strong patriotism. The Red Crescent petitions people to help them remove the corpses off the street and bury them. The place where they will bury the corpses? The hospital—usually a place of healing—now grounds for a cemetery (163). Documenting violence, the blog shows convoluted responses to political change.

By recording experience, the blog cuts across the identity lines of war. For instance, the blog details how Pax tells his best friend, Raed, that he is the "product" of Islamic culture (55). His friend laughs, reminding him that a few minutes earlier, he was talking about how delighted Pax was while "watching MTV Germany" (55). The blog restates this quandary: this "mess I am in really bothers me" (54). Despite his "talk of Anti-Americanism," Pax constantly writes about American music, movies, and culture; in short, it feels like the "embodiment of cultural betrayal" (54). Speaking across divided lines of war identity, Pax's blog integrates regions. Given the strident march of war divisions, the blog, in some ways, enacts a measure of healing as it integrates the author's diverse self and social affinities. But, at the same time, it is a political act: a witnessing forum, a cultural liaison, a revisionist history.

In many ways, it is a political confrontation that cuts across religious lines. Using testimonial experience, Pax challenges how Western readers view religion, suggesting that Iraqi extremism is a contemporary identity shift, due to material conditions and American military involvement in Afghanistan, Israel, and Iraq. American policies are continuously poking "sore spots" (38). And by "demonizing" religious beliefs, Western media are aggravators, even for secular Iraqis, since the continuous "verbal bashing" against Islam is discomforting (39). Distinguishing between politicized Islam and Islamic culture, Pax positions his own web identity through cross-cultural identifications, sexual orientation, and the diverse religious practices of his family. Although Pax is not religious, he views himself as belonging to an Islamic culture. Clarifying cultural, political, and spiritual beliefs in Islam, the blog works toward cultural translation across Western boundaries.

The blog functions as a vehicle of translation, not just for language, but also for cultural practices. Resisting the Western media's description of Iraq, Pax quotes a *Los Angeles Times* article in which the journalist contends that tribal leaders mediate in civil matters, failing to consult with the Iraqi courts. Giving an example of an individual killing another, the local sheik asks the perpetrator to give the "victim's family $7,000 in blood money" (17). Commenting on this article, Pax predicts his Western readers will respond to this information with "rants and flames and angry disgusted emails" (17). So Pax explains that negotiators are hired to resolve local disputes. He stresses the importance of these rural practices, since they are not attended to by federal law—a critical strategy in this local schema. It is a "deterrent, not a pay-per-kill scheme" (17). The *LA Times* article presents tribal leaders without explaining Iraqi customs, making Pax feel like "a bargain basement person" (18). Using wit to overcome cross-cultural misperceptions, Pax proclaims, "I hope no one hears we come that cheap per shot" (18). He vows to contact his tribal leader, informing him that he needs to get his "pricing policy up to date and fast" (18).

Protesting the demolition of public space, Pax documents the violence. Why should people use cluster bombs in neighborhoods that are full of civilians, then "refuse to clean up the mess!" (185). This protest emerges from his ideals of human rights and actions of a democratic nation. Both Western military tactics and the number of civilian deaths—one hundred thousand killed—are foreign denials of human rights. Unlike Western rhetoric of democracy, Iraqi definitions of human rights and democratic responses are counted in terms of violence. As Frederic Shaffer argues, those who define democracy as a singular ideal or a homogeneous practice "risk ignoring how local populations understand their own actions."[7] Pax posits human rights as essential—part of an *Iraqi Spring*. But despite the "shock and awe" campaign that destroyed the infrastructure of his beloved city, Pax remains hopeful for the new democracy in Iraq. Yet when the postwar political vision turns myopic—grave miscalculations across Western and Eastern lines—Pax chides, why did you not bring along "*Democracy for Dummies* books" (179).

Similar to Pax, River protests political rhetoric in the media, but she also graphs an inventive nationalism in her intimate portrait of a woman in war.[8] Eager to return to her job as a computer programmer after the bombings, River describes how she received equal pay, wore whatever clothes she wanted, and was well-respected. But after the American occupation, she walks into her office and instantly notices a change. The shabby room is "sadder," the red carpet "spoke" of being trampled on by thousands of people, and the objects are personified as carrying a "burden" (23). War has brought a "strange new nightmare" of broken lights, kicked-in doors, and clocks dismembered from the walls (23). External spaces reflect the altered attitudes she sees on people's faces. Describing "strange new faces," not many of the former ones, she realizes that there are no women, and all the men seem "sad and lethargic" (23). About twenty men stand around, wrangling over who should be the new director, since the old director had a heart attack during the war. The office suffers from its own "power vacuum" (23). She finds one familiar face—familiar because he is "welcoming" (24). The directors refuse to make eye contact with her, and she is told that they cannot keep her safe. When River asks for clarification, one director bluntly states that she cannot work there. She returns downstairs in shock, abruptly realizing that the people downstairs were the same as before the war. All at once, these faces were not foreign, they were the "same faces" of employees, but there was an unfamiliar "hostility," which shocks her (24). The reason that she is not welcome is not just a matter of security; it is a hostile response to female workers after the U.S. invasion.

Iraq, as one of the most progressive countries for working middle-class and upper-class women, and one of the most educated countries in the Middle East, changed after the Second Gulf War.[9] There was a backlash against Western occupation, staged in reaction against women. Gender divisions are policed during war, and in Iraq women lost constitutional rights to inherit property that had been guaranteed in their former constitution. While they did get to vote, women also became the targets of territorial fights for political and localized power.

So what does a computer programmer do when she is fired from her job? She starts a blog. The self-proclaimed computer geek humorously suggests that she will become a "virtual sheik" (91). Rejecting Western attitudes that Iraqis are backward, tribal peoples, she reclaims the term "sheik." A twenty-four-year-old university graduate, she positions herself as a female leader in the electronic world. Starting to connect to a host of international readers, River uses her "stubborn voice—the one that blogs" (230). It is a creative form—a "beginning"—and she is surprised at the massive number of readers who respond (5). In front of this witnessing community, River protests the loss of public space—both at work and on the streets. Not only is her office a space of estrangement, but the American soldiers also fear taking ice in their water that is given by the "strange Iraqis" (15). During checkpoints, she feels humiliated when "angry, brisk" soldiers search her and her family (14). Public spaces become militarized. In an area of heavy fighting, her friends attempt to flee the area, and a tank hits the family's car. Many members of the family are killed—the husband, son, and daughter, who is just a small toddler. All die. Public spaces become estranged, hostile, terrorized.

She combats the stress of her life through blogging. At night, she wakes up panicked, as explosions and gunshots go off. Other times, she wakes up, feeling as if she were suffocating. When the electricity goes out, the 120-degree heat envelops her. The calming effect of blogging—contrasted to the valium that many Iraqis consume, according to River—is that the postings transform the horror into witnessing words. Violence is modified—a very limited form of control—through language. There is also a small measure of control because the blog is dated, so the entries posit a beginning and end point of incidents of violation. The blog works as a cathartic, political voicing.

Since everyone in her community is undergoing extreme stress, the blog is also a healing form of communication with people outside of the war zone. With the trauma of war, individuals seek solace. Under usual situations, people can discuss problems with their family or friends or a therapist; but in violent transitions, people are besieged with problems—not just family deaths, but also explosions, thefts, kidnap-pings. Given the saturation of violence in public space and private lives, the blog is a survival mechanism, a witnessing other, an integral, capital-ized "SOMEONE" (II 9). In effect, international readers are her wit-nesses, because reading communities learn about the war and respond. They are not flooded by the atrocities of war: the terrors of kidnapped family members or midnight raids of their home. The blog as a coping mechanism provides multiple responses.

River writes about gender in times of war, despite many constraints. During this war, women are seen as in need of rescue. This Western lens is in danger of stereotyping half the population as "sexually constrained" and "uneducated," to use Chandra Talpade Mohanty's words.[10] Extend-ing this idea, Amal Amireh contends that focus on the "Arab woman" ignores issues of class, culture, and rural-urban diversity.[11] If River speaks of injustices against women, during the Second Gulf War, it becomes problematic, for Western media assume that such injustice is a sign of a backward society in need of rescue. Gender challenges are not only from Western media. On al-Jazeera, false assumptions are projected by Iraqi exiles. Having left Iraq at age fifteen, Shatha Jaffar tells the interviewer that during the Ba'athist regime only females belonging to the party were educated (66). River retorts that she was not part of the party; yet she was accepted into a great university because of her grades. Her friends were doctors, translators, lawyers. River's political act of blogging inscribes her experience, highlighting that gender oppression is not a traditional response in a Muslim country, but rather a recent change.

Moreover, when the Western press frames the war, as recent research proves, it ignores local women's groups in Iraq.[12] Further exacerbating gender coverage, the press about Abu Ghraib, as Jasbir Puar decries, restricted roles of gender and sexuality. The exposition of male prison-ers who were raped at Abu Ghraib became part of a larger media pat-tern, since the most circulated Arab representations are men, despite the numerous photos of violated women. These photos are part of a larger discourse about masculinity—what Puar diagnoses as an American ori-entalism about a repressed sexuality that hides a deeper "perversity" in the Islamic world.[13] Western stereotypes entangle gender: caricatures of sexually repressed men and sexually oppressed women are tied together in a torturous dance.

These global discourses make writing as a woman of religious or political affiliation a complex act. It becomes difficult for women's organizations to speak of equal rights, because the idea, evident in the provocative work of Valentine Moghadam, is linked to Western culture, and this rhetoric is viewed as a way to control Arab governments, as Eyad El Sarraf explains.[14] Even the term "feminist" has no perfect translation, for the word *nisai*, as Miriam Cooke argues, also denotes "womanly"; yet despite this translation, many critics claim that the term is essential for referring to ways people have been oppressed and have acted to bring change.[15] How to steer through the split between Western and Eastern language and power divides? To begin with, activists must not ignore these binaries, but rather confront assumptions buried within the debate, placing challenges of injustice into what Nicola Pratt calls a more global context.[16] But for River, her strategy as a computer programmer in Baghdad is to reframe equal rights, not as a Western concept, but rather as an Iraqi experience.

Media stereotypes of Muslim women are further challenged by River's sense of a spiritual self: "I am female and Muslim" (17). Writing about the difficulties of the war, River details the importance of her faith in surviving traumatic events. Without faith, "I would have lost my mind"; without a "God to pray to, to make promises to, to bargain with, to thank—I wouldn't have made it" (19). While religious affiliations are stereotyped as submissive roles, the potential of prayer, as R. Marie Griffith argues, elicits both personal and political desires.[17] In this blog, prayer imagines a larger communal network of Iraqis surviving with divine comfort. It is a personal and religious nationalism that does not associate the divine with violence.

River remembers how faith was a survival mechanism on the first day of the American invasion: her mind was "numb" as she flinched during the explosions, and she would give "thanks" to God when an explosion was distant (248). In moments when her mind cleared, she would complete housework. In effect, her beliefs formed part of a narrative of survival, a therapeutic description of coping during trauma. Faith—often described by the West as a sign of women entrapped by patriarchy—was inscribed here as a bright young woman's belief in a higher power, an ultimate meaning. Hope in the midst of war.

Even as she proclaimed her religious identity, a powerful inscription on the blog, she taught her readers about spiritual identifications. Before the war only about half of Baghdad women wore headscarves, and it was "my business whether I wore one" (17). In prewar Baghdad, she used to wear jeans and shirts, and chose how to dress. River explains how her friends and family members had various preferences. The scarf was a personal choice, a sign of devotion to God. After the occupation, there was a policing of women's clothing by extremist groups. River cannot leave the house in pants; instead she wore a long skirt and long-sleeve shirt. As a translator of gender and war, River blogs to her international readers: "Don't blame it on Islam. Every religion has its extremists. In times of chaos and disorder, those extremists flourish" (19). Most people in Iraq are "moderate Muslims" who consider faith a personal matter (19). The blog critiques the split between personal belief and select groups that militarize faith, reacting to U.S. policies and practices in the war.

As a subtext here, there needs to be a distinction between American feminist ideal visions of "individualistic fulfillment" and women across the globe who are fulfilled by communal affirmation in spiritual communities, establishing what Kelly Chong describes as diverse "moral and cultural" goals.[18] Wearing the headscarf, when an individual's choice, can function as a sign of an honorable status that commands respect: the religious role can be a form of cultural capital, offering possibilities for spiritual leadership within feminine circles, extended families, and the larger community, especially through religious charities. Of course, forced veiling strips women of this personal authority. Moreover, participation in a Muslim community does not mean that these women all hold the same "norms and values," a correction pointed out by Miriam Cooke's research.[19] The complexity of women who claim religious affiliation is evident in River's work: the blog lauds faith even as it protests the loss of religious freedom in public space.

River never claims that she is a feminist. Rather, she positions herself as an educated young woman, a computer programmer, a woman of faith, and a nationalist who is against dictatorship. In *Gender Trouble*, Judith Butler suggests, too, that the "feminist" collective is always a "phantom construction." While serving a purpose, the term cannot capture the complexity of women; some groups will be excluded.[20] Scrutinizing this phantom feminism shows the complexity of women as spiritual, vocational, intelligent actors who reject any simplified international screening.

Gender is also inscribed in media memory. For instance, American politicians cite problems with al-Jazeera's biased viewpoint, especially because they show dead women and children. Al-Arabia and al-Jazeera are criticized for interviewing civilians and showing corpses in embattled areas like Fallujah; indeed, these presses are accused of the "spread of anti-Americanism" (253). Western journalists, embedded with the U.S. military, accused the al-Jazeera journalist Ahmed Mansur, filming live in the center of the bombing, of bias in his reporting. He reported that more than "seven hundred" people died (254). American rhetoric of the biased Arab news station is a cover-up, defies River, covering over the number of civilian deaths.[21] But River prefers al-Jazeera, which presents several forums for contested views. Unattached to a particular Arab state or any political institution, al-Jazeera's debate style is described by Lynch as part of its drive for democracy.[22] Visibly contrasting this perspective, American forces bombed al-Jazeera's office in Kabul in 2001, and in Baghdad in 2003, killing reporter Tareq Ayyoub.[23] Clashing perspectives on the Arab press as anti-American or as pro-democracy suggest monumental divisions in paradigms—arguably, an imperial lens versus an Arab Spring.

Even without the press, animosity toward American military action would be there regardless, stated River, since several families of Fallujah refugees had fled to Baghdad, so Iraqis were hearing firsthand testimony about the war. Fleeing out of this densely populated neighborhood, the refugees told stories of "mass graves" (II 23). Residents were "shot in cold blood" as they tried to cross the streets of neighborhoods; then they were "buried" under concrete (II 25). Embodying their traumatic experiences, refugees had "tear-stained faces" and appeared to be in "shock" (254). Witnessing to these testimonies, River reported that civilians in Fallujah were being "murdered" (II 25).

Pax also wrote about events of Fallujah. Two hundred thousand Iraqis, many of them Shiite, protested the occupation of Iraq, after the initial siege of Fallujah.[24] Responding to this protest, America proclaimed that we will "kill or capture" Moqtad al-Sadr, a Shiite leader who contested the occupation, and shut down *al-Hawza* newspaper.[25] Salam Pax's blog questioned American policy in stirring up this hornet's nest. He was concerned about the targeting of certain political leaders and astonished at the deck of playing cards that the United States was distributing. The faces on the cards were not kings and queens, but rather the most wanted on the hit list of the U.S. government, like Moqtad al-Sadr. Posting a photograph of this political game of assassination, Pax displays the cards on his global site.

River described the initial conflict in this urban site of Fallujah as a massacre. After American soldiers occupied a school, then parents and children held a "peaceful demonstration" (15). When some children threw rocks at the troops, the soldiers "opened fire," and several children died (15). Anger increased within the Fallujah community. So when four Blackwater agents, private mercenaries hired by the United States, drove into the community, the American military called the mercenaries and told them to leave the area. The Blackwater agents refused. Known as Rambo teams, these guns for hire were under an amnesty written by the United States, which was not revoked until 2009, so they were not subject to American military courts or any national laws during the post-9/11 war decade. The Blackwater vehicles were targeted by the Iraqi resistance fighters in an ambush and the four agents died. During this incident, a crowd of almost three hundred people in Fallujah joined in, hanging the charred American bodies from a bridge. This "iconic image," as Jeremy Scahill writes, was televised across the world.[26]

Responding that this group of "killers is [*sic*] trying to shake our will," President Bush promised to respond "aggressively."[27] The United States reacted with a vengeful strike, which U.S. military leaders disapproved, comparing it to an attack on civilian areas in Vietnam.[28] In this instance, American military memory deviated from the administration's policies. Recklessly disregarding past history, the administration ordered

American troops to lay siege to this city of four hundred thousand people.[29] In the end, the city's hospital and many civilian houses were destroyed. At least sixty mosques were decimated. Over seven hundred civilians were killed.[30] Even though a truce was proclaimed by Baghdad military leaders, the United States continued to bomb this residential area with 500-pound bombs.[31]

There were many protests, and one prominent sheik declared, "We hated Saddam for punishing people collectively. We will not tolerate whoever we thought was our friend to do the same."[32] In Iraqi collective memory, these events were remembered as a massacre. During the attacks, because this wide area—this Fallujah neighborhood—was locked down, there was very little to eat: no food entered the urban area and water was shut off. River viewed these American tactics as "collective punishment," since the entire area was under attack. There were dead bodies in the street. No one buried the corpses for fear of being shot, claimed River (II 26). The blog showed disjuncture between global media and testimonial experience.

Sometimes the violence overwhelmed the bloggers. At times, Pax stopped writing. "I had lost my bearings," he remembered, and needed to "re-orient." He was too "burnt out" to write (55, 143). Witnessing the changes in public space, River claimed that there was too much happening; it was impossible to condense in a "meager blog" (255). The violence in Fallujah became a traumatic site of national memory in Iraq; in contrast, many Americans remain unfamiliar with this highly populated city and its losses. In response, River protested how "American long-term memory" only includes "American traumas"; everyone else is expected to "get over it," forget, carry on (48).

These visual dislocations of Western media and horrific civilian deaths became uneasy sites for bloggers. Given this disjunction, River personified the computer as condemning her for avoiding the documentary images of Fallujah that she had downloaded. She ignored the computer for several days. When she switched it on, the file would "call out": sometimes "begging to be watched"; at other times, "condemning my indifference" (II 139). Why did River avoid this testimonial media? She had already heard stories of "people burnt to the bone" from America's chemical weapons. But she did not want to watch the film clip because it would confirm how "lost" her country was under occupation. She finally watched the footage and described it as an "invasive experience," as if "someone had crawled" into her psyche to illuminate her worst dreams (II 139). So disfigured are the people by the chemical agent that River could not identify which corpses were female or male, child or parent; the only way to tell was by their clothing. As she watched the film footage, she realized that the clothes were "eerily intact"—as if the corpses were burned, then the skeletons "dressed up lovingly" (II 139). The image that haunted her was of a dead child, a tiny girl, who wore her pajamas and had tiny earrings still dangling on her skeleton.

After witnessing these civilian deaths, River retreated to her identification as a writer. Creatively resorting to a computer metaphor to change loss into language, she desired to "completely shut down"; to place herself on "standby" (8). After a year of occupation, River described her desire to delete certain recollections (248). Personifying the computer as a powerful witness, she felt rebuked by it when she did not write. Blogs suggest purpose and meaning during the stranglehold of atrocity.

Blogs provide a global witness to civilian deaths, even as these losses are denied in public forums. In River's blog on Fallujah, November 10, 2004, she reported on the bombing with cluster bombs and "forbidden weaponry." In response, she received a "barrage" of American responses, emails that accused her of lying (II 140). River processed the e-attacks, not only about the forbidden weapons but also a continual false reference to 9/11: the jarring claim that "Arabs brought all of this on themselves" (46). She must teach readers that 9/11 was first linked to Afghanistan, and Afghanis are not Arab. The miscegenation of history and lies continued in George Bush's speech on 9/11, four years later in 2005, claiming that American military were battling a "global war on terror," which "reached our shores on September 11" (II 102). But Iraqis had nothing to do with September 11, 2001, River disputes.

Lack of Western comprehension creates local reactions. Pax received indignant responses, especially when he posted on the use of cluster bombs in civilian areas. Attempting to cross borders with Western allusion, Pax quoted Graham Greene's work, *The Quiet American*: a man "incapable of imagining pain or danger" to others or to himself (83). Also, a young Iraqi engineer is quoted by Pax, before the war. She said, "I hope they see us as people" (107). Another Iraqi woman responded, "Why should we be sitting here trying to convince you that we are ok? Why should I have to make you feel like we are people worth living?" (108). Within these blogs, their protests suggest reactions to violent screenings of identity and selective memory.

Public images of American suffering are global memories via media; meanwhile, Iraqi national losses are not remembered in substantial ways. River stated that the 9/11 losses of three thousand Americans was constantly projected by media. Yet she was expected to forget the "8,000 worthless Iraqis we lost to missiles, tanks, and guns" (46). While initially she pitied Americans when the Twin Towers fell, the decade-long use of victimization to spur invasion bothered her. This "mainstream news" felt "far-removed" from "reality" (II 76). River viewed Western media as ideological, but also emotionally sanitized: the news was "clean," like "hospital food"; the coverage "organized and disinfected" (II 75). The sincerity of the speakers sat beside the monstrosity of the bodies devoured by war. The spokesperson tried to appear both "concerned" and yet "uncaring" (II 75). Globalization is often criticized for allowing hostile or anti-Western views to inflame non-Westerners. But rarely is globalization viewed as a striking force because it constructs split views: the contrast of passionate concern versus detached American professionalism.

What happens when 9/11 was projected as a central identity and history marker in Western media, and at the same time, Iraqi collective memory was forgotten or misremembered by the United States? What resentment built when multiple sites of collective memory—like al-Amri-yah and Fallujah—were not registered by American popular memory? As Western theories that Iraq and Islam were incompatible with democracy were gaining favor in the Western world, the early model on the street of Western democratic conduct was economic and military support of dictators, and later in Iraq, of raids without warrants, disappearances to unknown prisons, torture, and bombed-out neighborhoods. While a public loss of identity was reflected in the mirror of global media, the blog was a forum for reclaiming identity.

The media, with its apparent transparency, manipulate for "socialization," as Jean Baudrillard recognizes; thus, the 9/11 media's focus on invasion was a spectacular portrait of its own power.[33] When the American media filmed the military entrance into Baghdad, they showed Saddam Hussein's statue being pulled down, and then they showed the Twin Towers falling. While not explicitly linking these two sights with words, the media was complicit in associating these two visual images.

Western media—as global interventions—are critiqued in these Iraqi blogs. While Western media imagined Iraqis continuing their lives before the bombing, Pax and his family were standing in lines for petrol, putting duct tape on their living room window, and gathering food for relatives who had fled to their home. Globalization, as Arjun Appadurai connotes, creates a "crisis for the sovereignty of nation-states."[34] Western media beam out scenes of wealth, health, rights, and products that others watching the media may not be experiencing: global "disjunctures."[35] While watching reality television, River struggled with the random flux of electricity. More alarmingly, her family had to gather a ransom to save her kidnapped uncle. In contrast, River critiqued the show *Survivor*: were their lives "so boring" that Americans had to watch "conjured" lives? (II 76) Her own reality show imagined a group of Americans in a suburban house in Fallujah. The show would reveal them struggling with electrical outages, water shortages, checkpoints, midnight raids, and bombings. After their possessions were burned in a bombing that struck their house, they would return to the site as refugees and attempt to rebuild the house with $150. The American media created severe gaps with Iraqi suffering and shortages: a war identity versus American extravagance.

America's long-term memory of 9/11 contrasted its short-term memory and hasty forgetting of the civilian afflictions of Iraq's 2/13. In 1991, Iraq was bombed by American missiles that struck a civilian bomb shelter: this civilian refuge allowed only women and children. She recalled the images of distraught people, grabbing at the fence that enclosed the shelter. They were pleading, weeping, desperate to find out what had happened to their children, to their wives. River went to the site, her ground zero, honoring the four hundred children and women who were burned to death. She remembered a family friend, who "lost his wife, his five-year-old daughter, his two-year-old son, and his mind" (47). The Pentagon offered an initial excuse for Iraq's 2/13; later, they called it a "mistake" (47). Global memory has forgotten the event.

Both of these blogs also contended with the growing sectarian warfare, arguing that this was a recent event, since each blogger has relatives representing both Sunni and Shiite faith practices. Both blogs emphasized the U.S. role in creating sectarian division: nine puppet presidents, each ruling for one month, position sectarian identities. Failed reconstruction encourages Balkanization. River was concerned with the enhancing of sectarianism by the news media, especially in a "hostage crisis" that turned out to be a false situation. In this 2005 situation, the media recorded Sunni aggression. River's blog referred to two reports: "Dozens of Shia hostages" captured by Sunni fighters in Medain, and "Sunni guerrillas capture 60 hostages," to be murdered unless "all Shia do not leave the town" (II 78). Watching this broadcast, River was uncertain of the town. Searching Internet and news channels, she found a Yahoo news article locating the town of Medain, where Sunni and Shiite have peacefully cohabitated for years. Most families were related to the Ashayir group and had more familial than religious conflicts, and Shia demonstrators from Medain protested the false report (II 79).

Later, Iraqi officials claimed that this hostage situation was "under control" (II 79). While the BBC estimated the number of hostages at 60, media of al-Arabia escalated the numbers to 150 Shia hostages. Though the Iraqi National Guard and the American military were ready to raid, many people in Baghdad did not believe the reports. River discovered that a "high profile" Shia politician was the source of the information (II 80). Eventually the Associated Press acknowledged that these were exaggerated reports. Yet they claimed that these inflated reports signified how fast "rumors spread" in a nation of "deep ethnic and sectarian divides, where the threat of violence is all too real" (II 79). River disagreed with the media because rumors come through local people. This Shia was an Iraqi official. River felt he should be exposed because the false report dangerously incited sectarian anxiety, both creating and mirroring an endless simulation.

While there are sectarian identities, there are many intermarriages and diversified neighborhoods of Sunni, Shiite, and Kurdish composition. Pax's blog is also placed as intrasectarian identity, since his parents are from different religious backgrounds. With typical comedy, he wrote about the distinct prayer traditions. Should you "cross your arms or let them dangle by your sides," when you pray. "Who cares? Just get on with it!" (43). Given that Pax has a Shiite and Sunni parent, what is he going to do? "Hang on to my belly with one hand and let the other dangle?" If you have to choose, continues Pax, "go for Shia. Very dramatic" (43). Not only do they appreciate "ceremonies," but men can also "cry, wail," and be "drama queens," while others consider you quite "devout" (43). On a similar track, River wrote, "Don't blame it on Islam" (19). People coexist as Muslims, Christians, Jews, sects of Sunnis and Shi'a: we "intermarry, we mix and mingle, we live" (19). Churches and mosques were built in the same neighborhoods, and children attend schools together. In short, it was "never an issue" (19).

Media as a form of authority simultaneously record sectarian fighting, suggest division, and produce more sectarian anxiety. The spectacle of media, as Baudrillard visualizes, creates a reality effect.[36] As Nir Rosen wrote in his insightful report on Iraq's *Aftermath*, this violent civil war was a case where brigades of informal militias—the most marginalized people under Saddam's regime—took to the streets, taking power from the educated middle and upper class. Considering ways that class—for instance, the 1.5 million-person slum of Sadr City—even more than religion became the defining point in this civil conflict, how did media tropes organize violence or restrict ways of knowing? Did these beliefs add fire to local forms of struggle and international misrepresentation? Starting with an *imperial spring*—amidst widespread political desires for an *Iraqi Spring*—the final upheaval was a form of *class warfare*.

In 2006, River blogged about the ethnic cleansing occurring in Iraq, as various political groups claimed certain regions and used their religious affiliation as a measure of control and a show of force. There is an "ethnic cleansing in progress and it's impossible to deny. People are being killed according to their ID card. Extremists on both sides are making life impossible."[37] As violent conflict consumed Baghdad neighborhoods, Pax took a hiatus from blogging.[38] Having previously given a warning about Moqtd al-Sadir, he now detailed the hit list and thuglike actions of the untrained militia in 2004, disenfranchised young men paid by al-Sadir. Pax warned, be quite "careful about what you say about al-Sadir," for at this point their influence was spreading, and you had to avoid being on their "shit list," since even the government in Iraq was cautious when it described this informal militia. This group was not just a problematic political group. "They are thugs, thugs, thugs," he concluded. In a mock letter to the U.S. government, Pax reminded readers of his earlier postings: American attacks on civilian areas, press censorship, and assassination attempts of al-Sadir would create vast problems. He wrote:

> Dear US administration,
>
> Please don't act surprised . . . planning to go on a huge attack on the west of Iraq and provoking a group you know very well (I pray to god you knew) are trouble makers. Oh and before I forget. Help please.

Neighborhoods in Baghdad became violently divided in gangster-like turf wars. Reporting from civilian neighborhoods, Rosen renamed the civil war in Iraq as a "victory of the slum over the city, or the periphery over the center."[39] Families had to pay protection fees to these thugs, or they would be threatened or abused, and only certain religious identities were allowed to stay, causing families of two-faith denominations to flee. Pax and his family had to escape, because their neighborhood was claimed as a Sunni region, and his mother, a Shiite, was threatened. Displacement, as a national narrative, matched a devastating refugee flow, internally or across national lines, evident in statistics by Refugees International—a total of over 4 million Iraqis fled their homes since the U.S.-led invasion in 2003.[40] Very different paths of exile existed for these two bloggers: because of his family's political influence, Pax left for Europe; in contrast, River gathered her belongings in a suitcase and headed over the border to Syria as a refugee.

But instead of the helpless image of "refugee," River's blog battled to claim her identity as a writer. In 2007, she titled her October 22 entry "Bloggers without Borders," on a site that charts out her exile.[41] To cope with her dispossession, she used her website to document the objects that she had to leave behind. She remembered the family's dining room table, the site for meals and homework, and other sentimental objects. When she looked at an object, like a "stuffed toy," it was like a "chapter of memories." As a way to combat her dispossession, she created a storage of virtual memory, and these listed objects constructed an emotional mapping. She said farewell to the "ghosts," the walls emptied of pictures, and while the possessions were mere "items," overall, her home was like a "museum" because it spoke of a specific "history." River's catalogue of objects within this virtual museum commemorated a historical site—the flight of the educated class from Iraq.

While Pax's online blog ended in 2004, River's electronic link continued during her time of displacement until 2007. Anxious about her future, she used the blog to reposition her identity. Continuing her October 22 entry, she recognized that she was "suddenly a number," even though she was well-educated and middle class; still a "refugee is a refugee," a person who was not "welcome in any country—including their own." Since it is illegal to work in Syria or Jordan if you are a refugee, she was even further displaced. Even though she knew that there were a million and a half refugees fleeing Iraq into Syria, she did not initially think of herself as one: since refugees "sleep in tents," transport their possessions in sacks, not "suitcases," and do not own "cell phones" or use computers. Refugees are often seen in the media as desperate, uneducated, poor people. For River, declaring her skill and education through her cell phone and global site, it is another globa-*lies*-ation.

Rejecting desolation in this October 22 entry, River narrated her journey in order to further define herself. Fatigued after traveling, she pulled her suitcases up to her room and responded to the knock on the door from a young boy. There were Christian and Kurdish families in the building, and one family "sent over their representative"—a boy, only nine years old, missing two front teeth, carrying a "lopsided cake." They lived just across the hall, he said, and "mama says if you need anything, just ask," since "we're all Iraqi too." Before he left, he called out, "Welcome to the building." And with this national gesture—a welcome dessert—there was hospitality across all ethnic lines. It was an inclusion, outside of national borders. Within all the precarious limitations of being in short-term refuge, River wrote about her altered national identity. She cried her first night because she felt the "unity" that was "stolen from us in 2003." The loss of unity in her country became sublimated into the altered nationalism of a refugee community.

Narratives of refugees are often despairing because of the dire lack of resources and opportunities, as in Jordan and Syria; yet exile narratives can foster alternative group identities.[42] What group identities are emerging in Iraqi communities of exile? How are these displaced youth and families being supported (or neglected) by Western and global aid in this refugee crisis? What is happening to Iraqi refugees, during the political turmoil of Syria's Arab Spring? What hope has feminist discourse in the face of a political backlash? In what ways is democracy being imagined as engendering equality across class lines in Iraq? Are creative sites attempting to redefine national reconciliation, as in River's blog?

These two popular bloggers, who have attracted extraordinary attention, are part of a youth culture. Educated, urbanites, middle class; yet one is secular and the other professes her religious faith. And both were displaced when the Sadr Brigade, a motley group from the slums, alongside the protective response of the Sunni minutemen, the "Awakening" brigade, carved up Baghdad and its civilian bodies. In 2011, while Baghdad was still a place where people disappear, Prime Minister Maliki, as a secular Shiite, had battled the militia of Moqtad al-Sadr, who had run wild because their leader was in exile, forced there—as Pax reminds us—by an American death warrant. While today some of these street militias have been incorporated into security forces, others turn toward crime, as in extortionist kidnapping; yet, despite the lack of security in Baghdad streets, the political graffiti is gone. The only sign of youth culture, notices Rosen, is an inscription of "Long Live Barcelona!" on the walls: a rally around football fever—a hopeful sign.[43]

The two popular blogs, as examples of youth culture, position alternative nationalisms, separate from dictatorships or imperial rhetoric; yet, unfortunately, these blogs with their youthful inscriptions of gay Iraqi nationalism and feminist Iraqi nationalism are paradoxical identifications. They mark sites of nationalism and erasure—the removal of one-fifth of the population, many of them educated and wealthy enough to flee the country. These virtual forces of youth culture perform an Iraqi nationalism from outside the country. While Pax was working on a film in 2011 called the *Baghdad Blogger*, of River there has been not a trace since 2007. Still their global imprint continues—a lasting legacy through politicized e-identities and virtual desire—with a hope for Iraqi democracy, despite ongoing rifts. With the strength of their wit and witnessing, their blogs continue to nurture aspirations for an Arab Spring. Using their blogs as a political force, they have taught their readers about the virtual muscle of testimonial sites. Or to evoke River's words—"tanks and guns can break my bones," but my blog cannot be "deleted" (10).

5 | Media and Iran's Forgotten Spring

Intergenerational Politics in Persepolis

> [Iran's] old and great civilization has been discussed mostly in connection with fundamentalism, fanaticism, and terrorism. As an Iranian . . . I know that this image is far from the truth. This is why writing *Persepolis* was so important to me.
> —Marjane Satrapi, *Persepolis* (2003)

Closing the orange door of the taxi, my friends and I drove to the border of Iran and Iraq. In the distance, I see the border guard: he is a young Iranian, looking bored, gazing out, automatic weapon loosely held in his hand. It is a checkpoint. So many times, stories of my friends in Iraq all end up here, or at least cross here, over this border. Sometimes because of war—as in a million Iranians, a million Iraqis, killed in the Iran-Iraq War—or sometimes in search of safety—as in massive diasporas from the violence of bombings during both British colonization and secular dictatorship. In Western media, Iran is a primetime location; indeed, the uncanny 9/11 discourse of weapons of mass destruction hauntingly pervades—across this altered historical site in republican and democratic lines. More insidiously, the dark potential of Iran—for an Islamic Spring—forms a constant subtext, a shadow behind Western press coverage of the Arab Spring.

In fact, even as media narrate tender hopes within political protests, these Western citations often include fearsome enemies—religious parties with whispered allusions to Iran. In recent discussions of a political

102

springtime across the Arab world, the Western press often asks a series of building questions: What happens next? Does political protest continue on and on? After political springtime, what groups vie for power in this transition? And then, even as crowded bodies flood Western media screens, these blooming spaces of protest are eventually conceived against the dark antagonist of a Religious Spring. But much is forgotten in the Western media's whispered subtext, their particular construction of Iran. What emerges and circulates is skepticism, woven into the media, through doubts about religion and democracy, wondering if the Arab Spring will turn into the Islamic Revolution. These emergent layers, padded with a historical allusion to Iran, are an intriguing staging of place and politics—a relocation of knowledge within the Western press—stuffed within sites of transnationalism.

From the start, there must be confession across this Persian border, in my American inscription. Iran is an imagined location for me. Not necessarily a cultural bogeyman. Having been to its borders, I look across to territory that is unfamiliar. Perhaps I have witnessed Iran through public spaces, in an indirect fashion, through terrain that emits the continued presence and aftershocks of war. While living in Kurdish Iraq, I traveled to the explosive sidelines of the past, the borderline with Iran. Bringing medical supplies to Doctors Without Borders, I saw the amputation of legs that mark a Western site of destruction. The landmines are designed, constructed, and sold by the Western world. While the Western powers and territories are rarely unsafe or situated with landmines, the terrain between Iran and Iraq is a no-man's land that defies the geographical imagination. Imagine what it would be like to live in unsafe space, to walk on property where mudslides moved your backyard into a space of death. These former zones of war reject any political understanding that war is over. Iran, for me, is an imaginary space, which I populate with a small boy, who uses crutches.

But this imagined terrain cannot just be a site of victimization. As Iran continues to dominate the Western media, usually in negative forms, I want to write about an alternative set of memories, an innovative mapping of Iranian protest. My guide will be an illustrated history of Iran, memoirs published in two books titled *Persepolis* and *Persepolis 2*, which were later combined in a film version of *Persepolis* by Marjane Satrapi.[1] These books have become cult texts in my hometown, where it was the "Seattle Reads" choice of the year. I went with my two next-door neighbors, who identify themselves as Persian, to hear Marjane Satrapi speak. Many university and high school students were assigned these texts, and in my class, some students misread the series as pop genre: the tale of Islamic persecution of women, followed by the author's saving flight to Paris at the end of the book. But this spectacular lens misinterprets not only Satrapi's ideas about her geographic and generational position, but also her depiction of her faith in Islam.

The film version of *Persepolis* was also making a global circuit, creating distinct responses. For instance, right before Tunisia's first democratic poll in October 2012, the film version of *Persepolis* was televised, leading to public protests in Tunis against the broadcast film.[2] This protest, located around the capital of Tunisia, spun around the Islamic revolution in Iran, and then, recaptured six months later on Western newscasts, traveled across multiple imagined territories. This chapter begins with NPR's description of *Persepolis* and political conflict in Tunisia, then relocates to the controversial cultural site of Iran in Satrapi's illustrated memoirs. Contrary to Western press spin, Satrapi's work is not limited to the Islamic Revolution; rather, it charts out dual protests—against the Shah and then the Ayatollah—a record of several points of Iranian history and a diasporic movement from Iran to Austria, back to Iran, and then to France. After the textual mapping of protest and land masses, moving back and forth in a Euro-Middle Eastern patterning, the latent version as a film form crossed to Tunisia, where NPR framed the film within its 2012 series on the Arab Spring.

In terms of Tunisia's protest, the Western media recorded a religious response to the film version of *Persepolis*. The uproar was framed around the depictions of the divine, not permitted by legalistic Muslims. However, the graphic memoir and film version also depicted sites of identity held sacred by the author, not just spiritual beliefs but also sites of social loss. Part of the battle is over who gets to define what is sacred within political terrain, since Satrapi claims that she wrote these texts to defy stereotypes of an Islamic Iran, which is limited to "fundamentalism, fanaticism, and terrorism."[3] Such media and criticism ignore Satrapi's beliefs, sketched within this multiregional text, since her illustration of her experience presents both social loss and sacred locations, tangled within Iranian family histories—what I call an intergenerational spring.

At the beginning, we are invited on a "Revolutionary Road Trip" (via National Public Radio) to see how nations that participated in massive uprisings are attempting to "remake themselves" and their "political systems."[4] Specifically, on June 4, 2012, Morning Edition considered how "Some Taboos Vanish in Tunisia, Replaced by Others." In this report, Eleanor Beadsley considered how political censorship, common under the dictatorship of Ben Ali, was being replaced by "religious censorship" in a post-dictatorship state. Interviewing the founder of the most popular television station, the show focused on Nabil Karoui, and what he termed his "political choice" to air the film *Persepolis*. His purposeful choice was designed to show others what would happen if Islamic groups were voted into "power."

In response, hundreds of protestors, affiliated with an Islamic group called Salafists, ransacked the television station, took the television owner to court, and protested in public spaces. Unlike some examples of the press, NPR is commendable for its included interview with an Islamist. Offering another voice to this situation, we hear a brief quote from Seif Eddine Makhlouf, one of the lawyers against Karoui and his popular television station. This Salafist lawyer spoke of the fine line between free speech and national turf, delineating how citizens in Germany are not allowed to post swastika symbols. Or in the United States, limits have been placed on civil liberties through the *Patriot Act*. In startling contrast, Makhlouf detailed the freedom within Tunisia to speak freely against the president or the government, but attacks on God or on beliefs about "what is sacred," were unacceptable limits. In effect, the broadcasting of the film was a "symbolic violence against the people." What is extraordinary about this geopolitical statement is that the lawyer gave three locations for tension between freedom of speech and the confines of what is sacred space within the nation. In short, the lawyer stated that he is for free speech, but all societies operate within certain limitations and noted exceptions.

While this reporter's coverage overall was excellent, unfortunately, with her sarcastic tone, Beardsley did not listen to the subtle argument about the painful limits created by historical injuries, resulting in political controversy and restricted national parameters; instead Beardsley derided how the fundamentalists were furious at the illustrations of Allah, ignoring completely the critique of the difficult balancing acts of freedom for all and nationalist legacies, or of the challenges of legislating when one group feels attacked by hate speech. Nor was there any reasoning about why certain beliefs have become sacred sites of national identity in Tunisia. Obviously, the use of the swastika is engaged with a historical location. The Patriot Act is invoked by its supporters as a historical response to 9/11. But there was no imagination about why the national courts have given a symbolic penalty ($1,500) to the television owner in Tunisia. What historical losses have created sacred space in Tunis? Given the history of Tunisia, where Salafis were imprisoned and tortured by the last dictator, and where European powers have meddled in colonization and long-term domination of politics and economics, including France's last-minute offer to send military aid to Ben Ali, certain religious identifications have become, for a few, regarded as sacred, national spaces.

But NPR did not frame its response to *Persepolis* as national politics: what Makhlouf has called a symbolic violence that injures the respectability and rights of others. Rather, the majority of the article frames religious extremism, as if speaking of Islam "makes them crazy." No similar analysis of the fanatical belief of the Patriot Act, no interrogation of America's sacred spaces and human rights violations, no translocation of political boundaries for Western violence—a selective mapping. So while conflict between secular and religious parties indeed exists, NPR's framework mirrors the violent edges without reflecting on historical wounds that various groups evoke. These injured parameters need to be understood to build greater civility across regional lines (and perhaps even between these emergent political groups in newborn democracies).

Islamists are a modern political entity; indeed, there is great controversy between the moderates and Salafists in Tunisia. In a recent 2010–2011 survey called the Arab Barometer project, findings on Tunisia suggested that despite the Islamist Ennahda party's success in the October 2011 elections, the majority of Tunisians do not support political Islam; indeed, 79 percent believe religion is a private matter. Yet many, 49 percent, trust the Islamist party, which mobilized quickly to care for the recently released political prisoners, visited many provinces to pledge moderation, and have consistently protested the regime; indeed, Mark Tessler, Amaney Jamal, and Michael Robbins argue that Tunisians wanted a change from the elitist regime, evident in their voting patterns.[5] While Salafi militants have pressured for more spiritually inspired policies, the winning moderate Ennahda party has formed a coalition government with two secular parties and has vowed to keep the largely secular constitution.

With its numerous assumptions, Western media highlighted the cultural site of *Persepolis*—depicting Iran and its revolutionary bodies—in an intriguing location of political negotiation. But instead of static, fanatic identifications, this chapter considers political protests and shifting locations of religious identity, which cross between Satrapi's depiction of Iran and another site of NPR's road trip. Even as Tunisia was placed within this journey, so too the news on June 12, 2012 focused on Egypt, where interviews with potential voters suggested their frustration with the presidential candidates: a former prime minister under Mubarak—Shafik—and a candidate from the Muslim Brotherhood—Morsi. But there was one NPR interview, which I especially appreciated, conducted by Soraya Sarhaddi Nelson, heralding multiple voices.[6] In this broadcast, we hear an Internet game sound in the background with sharp bleeps. In this Egyptian game, shoes are thrown into the air against Ahmed Shafiq, which land with catcalls of the Arabic word for "remnant," a tie to the former political dictatorship. What a creative e-form of democratic fury! Then we hear the sounds of a web video with chanting protesters. We learn that the former prime minister accused his opponent of stirring up sectarianism. But, beyond this dual antagonism, by far my favorite part was the quote from a driver, who, like many others, "plan to change their vote." The driver stated that after voting for Morsi initially, next time he will vote for Shafiq. Voicing discontent with the recent political performance of the Brotherhood, this driver will choose a different candidate next time. What I would love to hear next on NPR is a narrative of the success of democracy! The driver changed his mind. Political stances, sometimes with religious ties, are still expected to perform; indeed, the public votes them out if they do not succeed. No religious bogeyman. What was suggested was a desire for change, a need for economic opportunity. Moreover, would the West have responded differently to the 2013 military coup in Egypt if Shafiq, not Morsi and the Muslim Brotherhood, had been ousted? It is a reminder that in Egypt, like Tunisia, sacred and political sites are not necessarily fixed locations, but rather contested zones with transnational tremors, changing sectors.

In Tunisia, returning to NPR's special feature on the broadcasting of *Persepolis*, we hear background sounds of the film, during the interview of Karoui. This section in the film was not of a political revolution, but rather the scene of a little girl talking with God. After her beloved uncle was killed by the state, she directed her anger to a safe place, a religious location. She yells her despair at God: "Get out! Get out!" The statement of religious and political crisis is an intriguing gateway to cross to this well-known text on Iran. So while one political group in Tunisia protested Satrapi's depictions of the divine, another group used Satrapi as its political claim for the young democracy. Amidst this contestation, this chapter protests how Western media framed the debating voices as an easy polarity between religious versus political beliefs, but was also a nonhistorical rendering of Islamic politics, on top of a refusal to visit the allegations of international locations and sacred sites of political belief. What happens when we shift from religious frameworks—especially since Satrapi depicts herself as "modern and avant-garde" and "religious" (6)—to a conflict resolution approach, reconsidering sites of historical loss and healing as central to political navigation. Indeed, what I propose is an alternative road trip; it is a journey of social loss at the site of Satrapi's Iran.

Social loss, religion, politics, and healing are not isolated spheres. For instance, at the beginning of the illustrated memoir, *Persepolis*, Satrapi clearly delineates her religious belief with a cartoon of a smiling baby marked with a small halo, and the caption, "I was born with religion" (6). In her funny sketches, she recalls her childhood theology; she imagined herself becoming a "prophet" alongside a "few others," like Mohammad,

Jesus, Abraham (6). Locating her body in an Islamic tradition, the child protagonist—who I refer to as Marjane, to differentiate from the living author Marjane Satrapi—rejects gendered extremism and writes a "holy book" in her spiritual campaign against suffering and injustice. Concerned with class division, because the maid does not eat with the family, discomforted by economic inequity, as her father drives an expensive car, and even concerned with the pain of others, health concerns for the elderly, her treatise embraces three rules to "behave well, speak well, act well" (7). Humorous sketchings—religion through a child's eyes—are nonetheless important choices for inclusion within this historical depiction of Iran. But when autocrats force women in the society to veil, Satrapi depicts a break in the society between women who desire or who protest this legislation.

On a surface level, the graphic memory does not explain why one group of women protests for the veil and the other group does not. While Satrapi's text shows modern women calling out "Freedom! Freedom!," thus rejecting the stereotype of the oppressed female who accepts this state proclamation, the text fails to situate why a group of women would protest, shouting, "The veil! The veil!" (5). Missing from this scene are reasons why women selected the veil as a political practice. The fury against Western dress veiled the anger at Western intervention in Iranian politics. But glimmers of this ire spill into Satrapi's text, especially her historical introduction, which relates how Iran's democratically elected leader, Mohamed Mossadeq, was overthrown in a Western coup. In fact, the United States and United Kingdom participated in overthrowing a democracy in Iran. This forgotten memory, outlined by Satrapi, was spoken in public during President Obama's speech in Cairo. In his groundbreaking address in June 2009, this U.S. president remembered what many Americans had forgotten. "For many years, Iran has defined itself in part by its opposition to my country, and there is in fact a tumultuous history between us," announced the president. "In the middle of the Cold War, the United States played a role in the overthrow of a democratically elected Iranian government."[7] Prior to President Obama's statement, very few in this last decade of U.S. politics and media admitted how the American winter has crushed the spring bloom of democracy in Iran.

Western intervention in Iran is delineated in the introduction to the first memoir, *Persepolis*, and the later film version shows a puppet show in which the politics of Reza Shah and Mohammad Reza Pahlavi are depicted in scenes with marionettes whose strings are pulled by the oil-hungry West. Both the memoirs and the film record protests against these dictators through crowds, sketched in public spaces, and close-ups of family members, detailed with stories of political revolts. For example, the memoir shows Marjane as a little girl, enraptured by her uncle's tales of political resistance. After her uncle was arrested and thrown in prison by the Shah, he told his young niece to remember his story, for "our family memory must not be lost" (60). In Satrapi's historical account, she details how the Shah came to power. After Mohammed Mossadeq, then prime minister of Iran, nationalized the oil industry in 1951, Great Britain—which controlled the profits through their British petroleum company—organized an embargo on all oil exports from Iran. But their economic retaliation did not stop there: Satrapi explains that the "CIA, with the help of British intelligence, organized a coup against him. Mossadeq was overthrown" (ii). After this demise of democracy in 1953, the Shah, with the support of the West, held power until 1979, then "fled Iran to escape the Islamic revolution" (ii). The illustrated narrative visualizes for Western readers why a modern family in Iran—political democrats, who hold faith as a private affair—protested against the Western-backed Shah.

In the midst of this history, Satrapi locates herself within several generations of her family members who have fought, and even died, with aspirations to return to democracy—a heritage of protest on behalf of an Iranian Spring. When the Shah was finally overthrown, Satrapi's uncle was released from prison. Afterward, the nation voted for a more Islamic model, rejecting Western influence, which led to her uncle's second arrest, under a new leader—the Ayatollah. While the Western world repeatedly chants the term "Islamic Revolution," what is forgotten is how this political backlash began because the West overthrew democratic leaders who wanted more than a 16 percent handout on their own oil reserves.[8] Satrapi speaks her history and depicts her own faith beliefs, protesting against the Western erasure of her history (the Western-backed coup that placed the Shah in power), and resisting the autocratic bureaucracy in Iran that claims to be Islamic (the dictatorial leadership of the Ayatollah). In re-mapping Iran, she must battle "orientalism": stereotypical views that Muslims are not responding to "policies or actions," but rather, as Edward Said argues, what they are "fighting on behalf of is an irrational hatred of the secular present"; as if backward Arab countries were destined to be inferior, fueling continual resentment against the West.[9] In contrast, these graphic memoirs construct a modern self within her family's political legacy and her private faith—a particular response to the Western-backed coup, the Islamic revolution in Iran, and later, the Iran-Iraq War.

The extreme shifts in regimes—one Western-based, one reactive to Western invasion—are mapped in experiential terms of loss. Under the Ayatollah, Marjane's uncle was in prison. He was allowed to see only one visitor; he asked to see young Marjane. Visiting her uncle in the jail cell, the little girl was scared by the prison. He called her the daughter that he had always wanted and gave her one last hug. But the next image is a drastic catapult.[10] It is a newspaper caption: "Russian spy executed" (70). The beloved uncle was executed because of his leftist political idealism by the Islamic state. The text is a form of public mourning: *Persepolis* remembers, names, and honors Satrapi's uncle, and Marjane cries over her uncle's death. In the next section, when God comes to see her, young Marjane shuns God, remonstrating that she never wants to see him again. Visuals of blackened space enfold loss—an interpretive atlas of the event—as Marjane floats in the backdrop of a dark universe, "lost, without any bearings" (71). The space of loss and political execution are contoured within geography of spiritual pain, traumatic imagery, and entangled political protest.

The losses of the family are often set within religious frames. Chatting with God, the child Marjane has a divine relationship of visible intimacy. Often the little girl is enfolded in God's arms like a cradled baby. But when she overhears her parents speaking about a massacre of four hundred people under the Shah, then she tells God that she wants to be part of the revolution. She asks her parents if she can participate, but her father refuses, saying that the protest is dangerous; the soldiers "shoot people" (17). Returning to her room, she cannot find God; she goes to bed and cries, "God, where are you?" The child hears the story of atrocity, which contrasts the religious intimacy and security she feels with the divine. The graphic reads, "That night [God] didn't come" (17). The sketched image shows the mortified child, who feels the absence of God when faced with the unbearable nature of political massacres.

The portrait of the divine—in itself a rejection of Islamic legalism—culls an image of God as a grandfatherly presence. It is an interesting choice, since her own long-dead grandfather suffered as a political prisoner. When Satrapi narrated how her grandfather and her uncle both suffered in prison, she changes intergenerational losses into sacred spaces, ending these jail scenes with the presence of the divine. When Satrapi's mother was a little girl, she visited her father in prison, and in the jail cell, the little girl wanted to play, asking her father for a ride on his back; as a child, she did not realize that prison conditions had caused rheumatic back pains and ruined his health (24). Later, as an adult, her mother realized that her father's health had been destroyed by the state. She felt guilt over her childish antics: not just part of the mother's loss of childhood innocence, it was a crisis of illumination. As Marjane watched her mother weep, she witnessed the trauma of history through stories. Responding to her mother's story, young Marjane sits in a bath, to reenact the painful dampness of the enclosed jail cell that destroyed the health of her grandfather (25). God sits next to her. This divine presence, staying with her in her imagined wet cell, is the only one that accompanies her in this reenactment of trauma as political history. This scene—an activation of a mother-daughter bond alongside a child's Islamic faith practice—is also a baptism into a political heritage.

Stories of violation become part of a family's social fabric, and political losses become communal sites. When Mohsen, a family friend, returned from prison, he described the horror of incarceration, and spoke of his friend Ahmadi, who was tortured, then killed. Graphics depict Ahmadi's back scarred with a whip, his open wounds urinated on. Then he was burned with an iron. Suggesting more than individual loss, these graphics show collective loss, because local events are disseminated as stories among families, unpacked in living rooms. Indeed, we receive a child's view, as Marjane peeks over at the iron, shocked that this item could be used for torture (51). Gazing at the iron in the kitchen, she becomes a communal witness. With the death of Ahmadi, it was not just the loss of one person, but—as Peter Homans reasons in his Holocaust research—in times of atrocity, "symbolic loss" also occurred as communities work through their frayed "attachment to a political ideology."[11] After hearing about torture and decapitated bodies in the adult world, the child Marjane begins to imagine torturing another child, whose father worked for the secret police under Reza Shah. When Marjane gathers a gang of friends and they arm themselves with nails, Marjane's mother puts a quick stop to their dark antics. When Marjane looks at herself in the mirror, she projects her fantasy of torturing others and taking revenge and envisions herself with small devilish horns on her head. But this feeling does not last long and she cries (53). Overwrought, she returns to her mother to talk about justice and forgiveness. Afterwards, Marjane returns to the embrace of God, who urges her to be forgiving. Similar to her earlier holy book, Satrapi values justice and recognizes the importance of forgiveness, part of her attempt to resituate herself after atrocity. Indeed, people who have been traumatized, in Kai Erikson's studies, "calculate life's chances differently. They see the world through a different lens"; it is "not only a changed sense of self and a changed way of relating to others, but a changed worldview."[12]

Social loss is also passed on through stories between generations. Satrapi herself does not remember her own grandfather, but hears stories of his life, part of a second-generation trauma. When Marjane asked her grandmother about grandpa being sent to prison, the grandmother responded by asking her how her day at school went. While the grandmother mentioned the poverty of the past, explaining how she boiled water so the neighbors would not suspect they had no food, at another point, she changed the subject, and Marjane noted, "She won't tell me about grandpa" (28). The silence speaks volumes to young children. In another instance, there was "the same silence as before a storm" (30), when the family waited for Satrapi's father to return home after photographing a protest against the Shah. Young Marjane imagines a black screen of death with her father and image of God that looks like a grandfather.

They feared the father had been arrested or killed, and to represent loss, Satrapi uses silence and black background to enshrine the language of unfinished mourning within extended families. But more than loss is imagined. This black screen, repeated throughout the book, symbolizes a paternal political bond between grandfather, father, and child of continuous resistance, in this instance, part of an intergenerational imagination, a populist record of Iran's thirst for democratic rights, continuing in the Green Movement.

Indeed, this alternative history of Iran with its entwined politics, spirituality, and family histories constructs a rite of passage, embedded within what I call "collective loss." By this term I mean to suggest not that everyone has a similar experience, but rather that such tales of violence pass between parents and their children in a way that encloses family groups and communities within a collective bond, distinct from an individual level of traumatic symptoms and personal grief. Transferring loss into a political and spiritual bond of identification for a child, the memoir twists the usual autobiography: the record of lost innocence also graphs a powerful political witness. This loss, with all its intergenerational dynamics, is a form of mourning, creating sacred spaces that inform a collective protest for an Iranian Spring, for which so many have died.

But not all loss fits within political and spiritual frames. Unlike her earlier navigation of trauma, where the presence of God allows Marjane to have agency, to speak back and to respond to political violence, the horror of a child's death cannot be piloted within this safe spiritual frame. After an air-bomb attack on Tehran, Marjane saw the rubble of her friend's house. When she noticed Neda's bracelet, scattered in the debris, she picked up the trinket, then realized that part of her friend's arm was still attached to her jewelry. The pictures show her expression of horror, of covering her eyes. Then a black screen with the words "no scream" could offer relief (142). Rejecting the Ayatollah's vision of Iran, this map of grief, to use Judith Butler's theories, "interrupts the self-conscious account."[13] Years later, in June 2003, Satrapi reflects on this crisis point on NPR's Fresh Air: after seeing her thirteen-year-old friend die, "you realize you can die." She expresses a gnawing disquiet: "Why should she die and you survive?"[14] It is unreconcilable, beyond spiritual and political frameworks; but even so, perhaps there still is a traumatic frame, because the text commemorates her friend through pictures: the rubble of the little girl's apartment—a monument of cement blocks— forms a visual tribute to the dead.

Amidst all these losses, there is a constant record of political protest. But this protest takes changing forms. When Marjane challenged her teachers about revisions within class history books, her parents received phone calls from the principal. Fearing Marjane would be arrested, they sent their teenage daughter to boarding school in Austria. Unlike her confident identity in Iran, in exile Marjane felt lost. She tried to assimilate; for instance, "out of solidarity" with her peers she started smoking more often (II 38). But such acts of assimilation created a sense of cultural betrayal for the protagonist: a sense of cultural distance, "betraying my parents and my origins" (II 39). Like an East-West atlas, these spaces of identity loss crossed nation-states, pervading her graphic images as her small figure was forced to relocate far from the safety of her family.

Within *Persepolis*, the extreme loss recorded in Europe implodes a popular metanarrative: the Western myth that the oppressed Muslim woman must be rescued and relocated in white civilization. In fact, the experience of the Western world led to extreme alienation and homelessness, dislocating how Western myths perceive gender rescue. Within a series of dating experiences, Satrapi reflected how crossing to the Western hemisphere was a journey of xenophobia. As an exile, Marjane was uncertain about fitting into the dating scene, especially since she faced racist reactions from older Austrian women, who did not want her to date Austrian men. When she was in a relationship with Markus, his mother came into his room and ordered Marjane to leave her and her son alone (II 66). The mother called Marjane a "witch" who was only interested in getting an Austrian passport (II 66). Another instance of racism occurred at her boardinghouse: the owner barged in on Marjane and her boyfriend and accused her of "secret prostitution" (II 67). When her boyfriend Markus slept with an Austrian woman, betraying her physically—just as he betrayed her by not defending her against his mother's xenophobic attacks—Marjane experienced not only rage but also an identity crisis. She abandoned herself to despair—charted out in the text as an urban nightmare—two months of sleeping on the streets.

Satrapi described the complexity of this breakup: it was not just a "simple separation"; she had lost the only "emotional support" that she had in Austria (II 79). But the graphic images suggest a collective consciousness that ties the betrayal of the son to his mother's attack on her racial identity. Satrapi writes, "I was going completely crazy" (II 83). Reflecting on her homeless experience and her entire history, Satrapi wondered why it was that after all her suffering in wartime, it was a "banal story of love that almost carried me away" (II 87). Considering the intensity of the rejection—the triple combination of Markus's amorous betrayal, his mother's cultural rejection, and the agony of exile while her parents lived in a war zone—the splintering fascination and rejection, projected by some Europeans onto those viewed as foreign, while probably common to many, was anything but banal. The fascination with foreign war and violence, which many of her friends, like Momo, ask her about, and moments of rejection because she is seen as foreign—not Western, not Austrian—this unresolved conflict, where one feels anger and desire for an accepting love, can lead to an internalized self-crisis, argues Freud.[15] However, when racial issues are part of this rejection, Anne Cheng diagnoses the mesh of politics and experience thus: it happens that "political domination is reproduced at the level of personal experience."[16] Traveling from Eastern to Western terrain, a dynamic of oppositional identity was projected onto her, leading to an urban melancholy—a space of depression.

Social loss crosses transnational borders. After the broken relationships in Europe, followed by her own near-death, Satrapi returned to Iran. But when Marjane learned of the many deaths that occurred while she was away, she felt guilty for not being present. The father detailed how the government became paranoid that the Iraqis would free all the political prisoners, so the state executed thousands of people; overall, the victims of the war numbered over a million. The strong father-daughter bond in this story became a haunting presence as the father's stories of war took up residence in his daughter's mind. Walking down the streets of Tehran, she relived her father's words by imagining corpses in her city. Many of the streets had new names, in memory of martyrs. Satrapi felt like she was walking in a "cemetery," it felt "unbearable" (II 97). In the illustrations, Marjane enters a city where the skeletons of the dead thrust their heads out of window frames, doors, and streets. As she hunches over in despair, Marjane is surrounded by seven embodied skeletons that all appear to touch her, reach for her, look at her—an urban map, a location of terror, a space of war, even after the bombings had stopped.

In contrast to her "father's distressing report," Satrapi viewed her "Viennese misadventures" as unimportant and decided never to tell her parents about her experience (II 103). Only the Iranian experience could be publicly plotted in this painful chart of history. In Europe, Marjane had purposefully avoided televised coverage of the news, since she felt a sense of "betrayal" as she integrated into the punk culture in Vienna while they were "bombed every day" (II 39). Feeling "guilty," the protagonist changed the news channel when it covered the Iran-Iraq War because it was "unbearable" (II 40). Avoiding media, she still relived traumatic memories from previous political suffering—dreaming of the execution of her favorite uncle. In an interview with Dave Weich in 2004, Satrapi discussed how the ongoing war increased her desire to forget her homeland: when she reflected on her country, it became harder to "integrate." Especially since she was furious about the "lack of knowledge" and "all their judgments." To survive, she had to "forget about it."[17] Because of the intergenerational bonds of parents and children, Satrapi never told her parents about her suffering as an exile, since her parents had made a great economic sacrifice to support her in Europe and they endured much greater trauma during the Iran-Iraq War. In fact, her parents did not learn about her exile until 2002, when they read about her history in Satrapi's second book.

Marjane internalized her alienation even as she immersed herself in the war stories of her father and of her war-wounded friend Kia Abadi, a veteran who lost his right arm. Displaced by exile and from familial bonds by the war itself, Marjane enveloped the losses from her exile and her community's suffering. Eventually, she attempted suicide—but fails. The dark screen background returns, but this time Marjane floats near-death, and a familial image rescues her: the grandfatherly image of the divine enfolds her in his hands, compassionately chiding her—it is not her time—sending her back. After her crisis of identity—a devastating near-suicide—Marjane has a political and spiritual awakening; in the film version it is informed by funny sketches of both God and Marx. Satrapi weaves political and spiritual icons that resemble a grandfather she has never met—resistance figures, supportive bodies, and a political projection (13). Like the early picture of a child in her pajamas holding the scales of justice, then a sign for peace, and finally a warrior's pose as a young "prophet," the adult Marjane still holds compassion and justice as sacred sites.

The figure of the grandfather also emerged when her grandmother chides her. In order to distract the police from noticing her lipstick and apparel, Marjane suggested a man nearby was leering at her, redirecting the police in Tehran. While she found this encounter humorous, her grandmother was furious: "Have you forgotten who your grandfather was? He spent a third of his life in prison for having defended some innocents!" (II 137). Marjane looked closely at herself in the mirror, deciding it would be the final time her grandmother chastised her. This mirror scene of identification focused on Marjane's relocation of her identity along an intergenerational line of relatives who died for their beliefs.

Social loss is not empty space; it wraps around intergenerational political trauma, tying remembrance, identity, spirituality together. Maurice Halbwach claims: "We ask how recollections are to be located. And we answer: with the help of landmarks that we always carry within ourselves, for it suffices to look around ourselves, to think about others, and to locate ourselves within the social framework in order to retrieve them."[18] Being grounded in intergenerational stories of both loss and political action is a bit of a psychological paradox: the alternative destruction and construction of self occurs because of traumatic experiences and stories. A (de)construction of self occurred while in exile in Europe: a desire to avoid recalling the pain of loved ones and a divorce from stereotypes projected by many Europeans. By the end of *Persepolis II*, then, there is a measure of relief, since this double alienation of war trauma and identity exile transformed over time into intergenerational bonds—developed through family stories and spiritual locations into Marjane's own self-assurance and political authority. Such bonds, simultaneously intimate and globally interconnected, portray *continuous* democratic desire—Iran's forbidden wells of political life.

Given that her time in Europe was the cause of two near-death experiences—homeless rupture and suicidal disconnect—mass media and practiced stereotypes leave a lot to be forgiven. Again, the purpose of writing this book, according to Satrapi, is to reject the Western world's extremist views. In her introduction, she questions why the country should be "judged" by the violence of a handful of "extremists." She protests that the Western world has forgotten the many brave men and women who died in prison and "suffered under various repressive regimes." Why allow these freedom fighters and those who "flee their homeland to be forgotten"?

While these books are problematically filled with war, torture, and caricatures, which, in effect, reiterate some stereotypes of extremism, Satrapi complicates stereotypes in several ways: by presenting how political violence responds to specific grievances against the West and local leadership; by presenting multiple Iranian views; and by historicizing xenophobia, thus censuring myths of Islamic women galloping behind a Western hero, the pale horse of rescue narratives. In fact, Satrapi shows the political and religious fault lines created in Iran after historical violence. We see what Erikson terms the "mood" of social trauma that can create a common "kinship," but often points out division within traumatized communities.[19] So while the *Persepolis* series caricatures bureaucratic extremists, these memoirs also show factitious political positions in Iran, resonating with Mansoor Moaddel's argument that there are multiple reactions to the Shiite religious movement, which has always been "diverse"; indeed, religious scholars are "politically heterogeneous." Moreover, critiques this Iranian scholar, many of Ayatollah Khomeini's theories were his own invention, part of an ideology that is inconsistent with Shiite political theory.[20] Manifold positions, dissimilar religious practices, pervasive political protests debunk any generalizations about Islamic politics in Iran—an altered national guide.

How to reconcile with this legacy of media and social violence against Iranians like Marjane Satrapi? The Iranian writer asks her readers to remember political protests. Such political hope for Iran, as Satrapi envisions, alludes to the political changes in other countries, and she quotes the first president of South Africa. His words left a landmark on global history: "we will forgive, but not forget." After a lifetime of fighting for the right to vote, Nelson Mandela emerged from his twenty-seven years of incarceration to speak of remembrance and forgiveness. As in Mandela's historic statement, Satrapi begins her introduction to *Persepolis* in 2003 with a desire for history not marked by forgetting. Rejecting stereotypes of never-ending cycles of vengeance, Satrapi writes: "one can forgive but one should never forget."

But there is much to forgive. Not only those Iranians who have created a bureaucratic structure of repression and called it Islamic, but, perhaps, also the West for overthrowing a democracy in Iran, then forgetting about the Iranian Spring. Finally, contemporary violence—mediated in Western ways of knowing, social judgments and displacements, which almost killed Marjane, as evidenced in her near-deaths—continues on as mass media lynch her history with a rope of monstrous shadows, its modern screen entwines places like Tunis, like Cairo. These violent spaces record past injury, but the lens of the mass media simplifies the violence of sacred spaces, forgetting historical contexts, omitting the protests, the deep veins of contesting voices in a democracy—all part of the beating pulse within recent political springs—embodied in such diverse political vessels as Iran, Egypt, Tunisia, and even Mandela's young democracy in South Africa.

6 | Guerrilla Fighters, Televised Testimonies

Democratic Miracle or African Spring?

> The child is not dead, where he lies with a bullet through his
> brain. . . . The child is present at all assemblies and law-giving.
> —Nelson Mandela, first "State of the Nation" address,
> reading from the poem "The Child," by Ingrid Jonker

In the *New York Times*, hope in democratic reform after the populist movements of 2011 is imagined through a certain kind of political leader—what Thomas Friedman coined the "Arab Mandelas."[1] But after the Arab Spring, is the next stage an Arab Mandela? While the transition to democracy in South Africa is often remembered as extraordinary, and their progressive constitution defends human rights, there are problems with converting powerful leadership—in this case a former prisoner turned president—into an icon. Any attempt to change democratic eras into the single story of a star, branding Nelson Mandela as miracle, as in the film *Invictus*, is also a selective form of forgetting. It is an omission of thousands of public performances after the elections in 1994—an African Spring. I want to reclaim these forgotten voices, and at the same time rename this historical epic not as a miracle, but rather as the growing and grassroots work of everyday men and women in South Africa who came forward to tell their stories on state and popular stages. And again, mass media matter in these innovative protests: before democracy, the press filmed the killing of black youths on state channels to show the deaths of terrorists. And then after democracy, they filmed thousands of stories,

121

told from perspectives not heard during the white-dominated regime. Mass populist and popular protests, on stage and in state commissions, were essential even after elections, an ongoing flow watered by African Springs.

To start, there must be some conception of the truth and reconciliation commission and its location in public spaces. Naturally, every critic who has taken a stab at this momentous and vast vehicle of the commission has come to a wide range of conclusions: some laudatory, some critical.[2] But instead of offering an exhaustive portrait of the state commission, I hope to honor a very small group of survivors who participated in the commission and serve as guides in this chapter. All of them are guerrilla fighters and resistance leaders, and they asked me to facilitate a drama workshop, five short years after the democratic dawn of Nelson Mandela's presidency, in order to produce a protest performance called *Khumbulani*—the Xhosa term for remembrance. In order to rethink how this young democracy developed various public venues for healing after atrocity—an African Spring of voices—this chapter details my work as a facilitator, using performance as a collaborative medium to witness to their stories. Analyzing mass media, multiple locations, and local inspiration, this chapter considers the protest of these trauma survivors alongside press and poetry of the state commission.

Here again my concern is with the politics of healing after atrocity. In the simplest terms, I want to question what happens to guerrilla fighters after war, and to societies that must transition after thousands of people have been imprisoned, tortured, raped. In early protests, a heap of stones, mass voices, a handful of rifles and protest songs in a fight against a regime with a legion of tanks and superior weapons characterized militarized spaces and urban protests. But these street performances started to change into a latent process for finding one's democratic voice when the South African state, negotiating a compromise for elections, also set up a public commission, which over twenty thousand survivors of human rights violations participated in, coming forward to have their voices recorded, a process that performed democratic space.

South Africa abounds with public venues of protest. In cultural forms, protest is often sung, as in community performances of protest songs accompanied by dancing and swinging of imaginary rifles to shoot at the regime's military tanks—and the songs tend to enact the past: survivors weep and cradle their memories of dead infants that were asphyxiated by the army's tear gas, professional actors change classical tales of tragedy into local histories, and musical extravaganzas enact legendary war scenes between the British and early Dutch farmers, or the sweeping war movement of Zulus. Nearly all of them, however, push the boundaries of collective memory, as they also creatively add personal testimonies, physical movement, and commemorative objects to show the forceful violence of the past. Even the world-famous venue of the truth and reconciliation commission has been described as a commemorative space for controversial histories: since around twenty-one thousand survivors and eight thousand perpetrators came forward after the regime agreed on a date for democratic elections. Their public stories mapped out multiple views.

This extensive state commission involved lawyers, journalists, translators, audience members, and applicants, who petitioned for amnesty or reparation: a vast and "syncretic" instrument for "national instruction," to use Loren Kruger's performance terms.[3] It was also a compromise between groups like the National Party and the African National Congress, who were debating between Nuremburg-style trials and a blanket amnesty.[4] This compromise was not only an important condition for democratic elections, but as the research by Catherine Cole suggests, these stories of the past also contained the "effects of atrocity," even as the vast effects of the past "exceeded" the commission's ability to manage this damaging legacy.[5] South Africa's political compromise—land courts, conditional amnesty, and human rights hearings—became a national event. Commissioners, applicants for amnesty, and witnesses of human rights violations told their stories in the specific region where people had been murdered. Traveling to local areas from 1996 to 1998, the commission created an alternative space for speaking of the past, which received wide media coverage and literary responses.

My introduction to the truth and reconciliation commission came through a public protest. In 1997, I visited my mother-in-law in Zambia, who was working on a health project during the first onslaught of the AIDS crisis. Taking several public buses, I continued to travel to South

Africa, where I saw the play *The Story I Am about to Tell*. On stage, a woman cried about the death of her son. He had received a parcel bomb in the hidden shape of a set of earphones, a gift from the apartheid police. It was an unimaginable, messy death—the killing of a youth who desired democracy. Before her involvement in the stage production, this woman had given her testimony at the truth and reconciliation commission. As the lines between theater and therapy, trauma and testimony, completely broke down, I was undone, unraveled. In theater, we speak of a fourth wall, an invisible barrier between stage actors and audience, easily demolished by entering into the audience. A fifth wall, uninscribed in theater, between actor and trauma survivor collapsed. The effect for me as an audience member was speechlessness. How can she tell her painful story again and again? Is this healing? Is this retraumatizing? Why tell her story in theater after speaking at a state commission? To investigate the politics of loss and healing, the following year I returned to attend truth and reconciliation hearings in 1998. Then I wrote a grant proposal for a study of culture/performance and moved to South Africa for almost two years. After witnessing this unique space—merging populist and political, artistic and therapeutic, state commission and creative play—I, too, crossed boundaries, first in 1998, and then after moving to South Africa from 1999 to 2001.

Riding an all-night bus into Umtata—a largely black city that received no funding from the apartheid government—I stepped off the vehicle at six in the morning. It was July, so the winter darkness was only broken by small street fires lit by vendors to keep warm as they slept near their stalls. Entering a small hotel, one of the few buildings on the main street, I asked the white owner where the hearings for the truth and reconciliation commission were. The owner questioned why I wanted to attend. Rolling his eyes at my next question about private taxis, he offered to drive me to the town hall. Entering the town hall, I saw row upon row of plastic chairs; most of the seats were taken. If you didn't count the lawyer, near the front of the stage, I was one of four white people in the crowd. When the police led a black man into the room, they ushered him to his seat in the front so he could give his testimony. As he told his story, the crowd laughed, and the amnesty applicant looked nervous. I was perplexed. At the break, I asked the Xhosa woman next to me about the laughter. She said that the amnesty applicant, a Zulu man who was not from Umtata, was a police spy—an *askari*—who was confessing his murder of a twenty-year-old student leader from Umtata. While he testified that he was forced to kill the youth by the police, he did not find an appreciative crowd. She leaned closer to me. "He had a choice," she hissed firmly. As the testimony started, she affirmed this information again with a firm nod to me, a welcome witness to her community's history. This time her repeated yes was in Xhosa. "*Ewe!* He had a choice!"

After Umtata, I attended other commission hearings, several theater performances and festivals, read local reviews in newspapers of the plays and hearings. But it still did not feel like enough, especially as women like Thandi Shezi were coming forward with their testimonies. Shezi had been silent for a decade. When the truth and reconciliation commission offered state reparations to victims of human rights violation, she decided to apply. At the commission, she spoke for the first time of prison and her gang rape. Then she attended a joint program, working with a therapist at the trauma center and collaborating with a theater practitioner in a separate venue on a testimonial project: *The Story I Am about to Tell*. During this play, she related her traumatic experience: "in body, I am a woman. But inside, I am dead."[6] Witnessing at the commission "has helped," Shezi claimed, and "forming the theatre group and relating my story to people I didn't know was also a process of reconnecting" (129). Returning to the horror of the past, she remembered how she found the "courage to stay alive" and the strength to envision her mind and soul as separate from her "body" (129). Because of the silence and splitting trauma, Shezi began working on healing through the testimonial play, in her rejuvenated faith in God, through therapy, and in healing relationships with her children.

While the commission formed a critical part of acting out the horror of the past, cultural performances, in contrast, were played out multiple times with varying audiences and locations to bring healing over time. Wanting to understand this process, I set up an interview at Cape Town's trauma center. I drove over to the center, located near District 6—a former multicultural suburb, later declared a "black spot" during apartheid's dismal urban destruction of its national landscape. While there are many wealthy neighborhoods in Cape Town, the area of the trauma center was not one of them. The first day I met with this South African psychologist for an interview, I arrived early and walked down the street to get a diet coke. No sooner had I entered the small convenience store than the psychologist came running in, telling me that I couldn't just walk to the store by myself; this was not a secure area.

Sitting in his small office in a plush chair, I explained my project and my training in performance studies. The therapist, excited about my research, spoke of an opportunity for his clients to tell their stories through theater, similar to the trauma center in Johannesburg; it was a chance for us to collaborate on a public venue. Immediately, I said no. Given that I am the daughter of a therapist, I understand the fragile state of survivors of trauma. But the psychologist was not finished; since the clients were all in therapy with him, my role was merely to facilitate the play that they wanted to perform. Yet there were other reasons I refused to help the trauma center—my reluctance as a foreigner, a white-skinned American, conscious of my country's history, my privilege. But the psychologist kept explaining that many of his clients were telling their same traumatic moments over and over, like so many bullets to the brain, and that these crushing memories invaded their psyches, completely taking over their ability to interact with others and live out their lives. The psychologist felt like a precedent for collaborative work had been modeled by Johannesburg's trauma center and testimonial theater.

My phone rang two more times after this interview. The first one was almost bearable; it was a resistance leader named Shirley Gunn, whom the apartheid government had imprisoned, also incarcerating her infant in the next cell so that she had to listen to her hungry baby scream. This activist, with an assured air, spoke of her work with former resistance fighters, all of whom had testified at the state commission. In some ways, her work was more political than mine; she had been organizing street protests, calling for restorative payments from the state for survivors of political trauma. But she claimed that testimonials would be a powerful witness, a political tool. Again, I declined, but this time I went to a week-long workshop for practitioners of reconciliation and asked several Xhosa directors to take up the task. Unfortunately, since the trauma center had a minimal budget, there was no money—hence, no director. So the play needed to be directed by a willing volunteer.

Another phone call. This time the call came from the shantytown, where a million and a half people live below the poverty line. A Xhosa woman, who had been imprisoned as a resistance leader, spoke to me, again asking me to be part of their newly formed theater group. "Why do you want to do this play?" I asked. There was a short pause, and then she answered. So many people refuse to speak of the past, since they are ashamed about what happened to them in prison. To break the shame, people must speak of the past to heal. After hearing her words, something broke within me, a tearing of my protective self-humility. I knew that I would do anything for this group, and taking up this task, I have been marked by these women and men who wanted to tell their stories. Over the ensuing weeks with this group, I recognized that I was viewed as an important facilitator, and that understanding the politics of race does not mean that one's color should blind one to the reconciliation work that must be done. The color of my skin—my whiteness—was regarded as an important international witness to their protest history.

So I set up another meeting with the psychologist on a crisp, autumn-drenched day in 2000; this time to establish possible ideas for a drama workshop. It would be a place where survivors could share the stories that they wanted to tell. As the facilitator, I would give options for staging the testimonies and the group would work together on selecting or adding to these ideas. Many of the clients of the psychologist had expressed interest, but Erik Harper stated that he would select from his clients the ones he thought would benefit the most and were ready for a group venue. Even after this meeting, I was nervous while driving to the trauma center. There was a guard, who showed me where to park my car inside a locked gate. Then the psychologist arrived, greeting me warmly. We walked down a cement path to the shell of a church and entered into a spacious room—plastered and plain, a few lonely tables, some scattered chairs. I circled the chairs in front; perhaps the old altar had been there. As apartheid cleared out black South Africans from the city, in areas like District Six this ghostly church had watched its congregants flee. Now this religious edifice formed one of the two trauma centers in a country marked by torture and disappearances. Cement walls, high ceilings, no heat, apartheid ghosts—I shivered.

A tall man, the first participant I met, approached me and looked down at me with intent eyes. Then, after his assessment, he pronounced, "I will be your translator, since I speak English and Xhosa." After the others arrived, I brought this proposal to our small group of fourteen. Although all of them spoke English, they liked the idea of having Monwabisi translate, especially if they wanted to give their testimonies in Xhosa. After the first few minutes of introductions in this group, I acknowledged that each of them had come with a story that they wanted to tell. I would be a facilitator, I said, but no more; it was they who must make the final choices—direct their own stories. It was their chance to perform their political voice in a newborn democracy.

Before the workshop, I called my father, who has worked with traumatized people in his therapy practice for forty years; he advised me to listen, to create a safe space. My introductory activities were extremely safe, but given the way that the participants seemed molded into their hard-backed chairs, a certain silent wariness of one another and our new forum, I decided to add physical movement and role-play, perhaps brave choices for working in collaboration with a trauma center. It was a simple movement. We would start on one side of this spacious room and walk to the other. Once the physical embodiment began, then I started the role-play, asking them to hold in their hands a petition for reparations, to walk to the envisioned courtroom, slapping the paper down on the government's desk. Many had protested at the state legislator for reparation, so their strides showed furious intent, adding more energy in the room. Then, I played with pace, asking people to walk across the room, carrying something heavy, a large package. One more time, we claimed this abandoned space with movement, walking as if we were in a hurry, and many participants smiled at me, enjoying the playful exercises. Returning to our circle, I set up safe venues for creatively expressing testimony. With arms full of paper, pencils, crayons, I asked them to draw a picture or write a scene from the story that they wanted to convey to the audience. Since these thirty-somethings—the so-called Lost Generation—had boycotted schools, protested the military, and changed the political tide instead of attending school, only a few in the group were literate.

Even though they had recorded the story they wanted to tell, we did not yet move directly to shared experiences. When therapists talk about safety, it is not just that there needs to be a mood of kindness or validation; it is much greater, there needs to be a patient space open to creative expression. Before being integrated into the public terrain, safety must grow from the very roots of activities that develop self-confidence. To enhance this creative safety net, members were asked to share songs that were important to them, then to explain what memories the lyrics invoked. Since such songs have been creative weapons in the battle for human rights and democratic opportunities, even dating back to British colonization, the melodic expressions have been integral to political struggle against economic racism and repression. Upholding the security of a protest song, even as participants integrated their personal details, this performance activity encouraged trust and shared political identifications.

Later in this workshop—in contrast to the group that was seated in a circle above me in chairs—I sat on the floor, again physically modeling my role as a facilitator. As each told me the main event that they wanted to share with the group—arrests, township burnings, protest in court—I created a three-act forum to accompany the events they selected. Having attended a conference with African directors on conflict resolution, I followed advice for role-playing the past. A few people volunteered to play the police, while a few performed the arrested. But for people who had been tortured, realistic enactments with the police fueled aggressive roles and rage, so I was concerned that some of the survivors would be retraumatized. Quickly cancelling this idea, I moved to the individual testimony as an important safe space. What was needed was a different enactment; it was unacceptable to empower some survivors at the cost of others.

The next day, survivors told their protest stories in small groups. Then, the group began speaking of injustices on stage. I asked for volunteers, and I was taken aback by the first story, given by the man who offered to translate. As Monwa spoke of torture, he detailed his fifteen

7. Monwabisi Maqogi (Trauma Center, Cape Town). Photograph by author.

years in prison, during which time he had been shifted to six different prisons. Not allowed contact with his family or his friends; restricted from having a lawyer. For years, he was tortured. His words were painfully belabored as if each sentence was its own lifetime. His final words wandered out with a small, unbearable stillness: "They tortured me, beating and electrocuting me everywhere, even my private parts." No longer standing tall at six feet, Monwa seemed to have collapsed; dropping his eyes to the floor and hanging his head, he suffocated in the memory of pain and shame. The silence afterwards was deafening.

None of the members of the group moved. My intentions to be a fairly nonintervening facilitator began to feel completely unethical in the face of this man's drowning in traumatic memory. Eventually, I walked a few steps closer to the open stage and said, "Thank you for your story." The group broke into applause. Then I asked him, "What were you doing before you were arrested?" He described how he fought with the military wing of the African National Congress. I asked him if he wanted to extend the scene by showing how he fought, before being arrested. Appreciating this idea, Monwa and the group extended the timeline of their narratives. Guiding through questions, I used improvisation as a strategy to preserve control over narratives even as I assisted survivors in bridging the time frame over the abscess of traumatic memory.

Conceiving the police in a framework that did not retraumatize survivors was an important tactic of conflict resolution. Having studied works on drama and healing by Roger Grainger and Robert Landy, I knew roles were important for acting out the past.[7] The survivors were eager to play the part of the police, to embody their former perpetrators. As a group, we performed two policing scenes that I imagined, and they voted on the one they wanted. The following was the final choice: I hid two men who wanted to speak of their torture behind the audience and asked them to enter as resistance fighters. Holding invisible weapons, they entered slowly toward the stage, their bodies crouched, their military knowledge and intensity fully displayed. Then, I suggested that the actors playing the police look for the fighters, but fail to find them.

Breaking the fragile fourth wall of theater, the police began to circulate among the audience, demanding to see their identity cards. The police arrested four audience members—actors in our group, planted in the audience—for it was important not to scare the audience with police aggression. The acting police lined the actors up with their backs to the audience, like bars in a prison, and then departed. Crouched on either side of the stage, these fighters rose of their own volition and stood behind these human bars to tell their prison stories. Unlike torturous descriptions of the body pummeled by electric currents, this transfigured scene included political resistance. In performance terms, the plot asked the fighting soldier to stand next to the fallen body of the tortured man—an embracive form of memory.

After these extensions, I still felt the entrapment of the jail cells was dominating their voices, strangling their stories, and from a performance perspective, their voices seemed muffled behind the prison bars, even though the bodies that created the jail structure were spaced far apart.

So I asked them if they wanted to push past the human bars, to articulate what happened in prison and what happened after they were released. Wanting to try out this option, the narratives of these two men and their more liberated tones and expressions broke from the original staging. When Monwa pushed through the staged jail bodies, he looked at the other group members and at me while telling his story, the first time that he spoke of his experience and made confident eye contact. "Now I have been released, and I am free because of the CODESSA negotiations." When he was first released, it was a difficult adjustment, he recalled. "I considered suicide when I was released. Since I was tortured and electrocuted all over my body, I thought that I would never be able to have children." But there was a change in the narrative, in terms of length, performance manner, and stage presence, as he made his concluding statement, "Now I am married and have a son. And I am free."

The other change that Monwa added was a final song of resistance at the end. The group joined in after the first stanza, and this spontaneous song transformed this scene and the play process. After this, songs became an improvisational tool for the actors. Since songs to celebrate the resistance guerrillas were well-known to this group, these inserted songs greatly influenced the survivors' collective identifications: a public performance that protested former and present injustices. These public venues of song and story were also healing. While survivors only occasionally inserted songs at the end of their story, songs were also added when survivors broke into tears during the storytelling. When a storyteller wept at the remembrance of a traumatic event, a member of the group would begin a song, and the rest of the group would take up the song, circling around the one who wept and the one who comforted. Unlike the first time a story was told, when there was silence afterward, the addition of songs changed the individual tale of grief into a collective protest of state oppression.

Within this young democracy, songs moved from individual trauma to collective identity. For instance, "We the Nation Weep for Our Land"—in Xhosa, *Thina Sizwe*—provided a simultaneous elegy for the dead and a hopeful hymn for God to bless the young democracy. These songs—a lyrical voicing of collective loss—cushioned the individual's tears and heart-wrenching stories. Unlike the individual "I" of testimony, the creative construction of "we" had an envisioned commonality. As in songs that link the past and present in Zulu collective images, it forms what Veit Ehrlmann views as distance from past pain and the "chaos and isolation" of current politics—a form of post-traumatic consolation.[8] After one of the songs, one survivor approached me to discuss how important this performance was to her. She spoke passionately of how meaningful the songs were, especially as reminders of the courageous battles in the past and the continual protest in the young democracy against poverty. The songs previously sung in funerals, marches, and rallies to spur on comrades in a battle against apartheid also symbolized present struggles—political desires for more economic opportunities within this democratic springtime.

Many of the other therapists sent their clients to the workshop to observe and to join in the singing of songs, valuing the link between the past, the present, and the strength of a communal bond. These songs were sometimes divided into harmonies; sometimes they led to spontaneous dancing. What a contrast from the depressed group members, clinging to their chairs, in the beginning. While trying to facilitate the performance, I would find that several additional survivors had joined our group. Like a forty-year-old man in a wheelchair—his right arm raised in a fist, up in the air, above his amputated legs—he sang, teary-eyed, as if his life was occurring through song.

These songs and group experience taught me a simple lesson: there was no single story. The initial stories told at the truth and reconciliation commission focused on traumatic events, human rights violations, which were recognized and honored as part of South African history. But, the group context of Khumbulani further developed support, which was helpful for narrative development, especially creative activities that imagined ways to tell the story that were not limited to the victimized state of horror. And the very form of staging with a beginning, a climax, and an ending added resolution—wrapping the embodied wound in a wider social understanding. When told to several audiences in the township, in downtown Cape Town, and in performances at the trauma center, shared emotion and common threads of collective experience—all part of communal healing—also became a political statement of alternative histories, detailing the heroic actions of community members.

And stories developed within these creative venues. Later, Monwa told me that after his father died, he dropped out of school when he was young and searched for employment in order to help support his family—an extraordinary contrast to the first time he told our group his story, when he spoke only of being tortured and his desire to commit suicide. Involved in protests against the apartheid government, Monwa eventually fought with SWAPO, as the South African war moved into Angola. Tall and stately in appearance, as he grew up his friends nicknamed him "the general." When the apartheid secret police heard his nickname, they assumed that he was an important military commander, and he was arrested and tortured to find out political information, which he did not have.

Upon his release, he took a public bus to a small town in order to kill the policeman who had tortured him. Arriving at the policeman's house, he found there was no one home. Waiting for hours, until it was dark, Monwa decided that he would return the next day to kill the man who had slaughtered both his youth and soul. But when he returned to the shantytown of Khayelitsha, he stayed the night with some friends, who urged him to apply to the truth and reconciliation commission, since the media publicized how survivors could receive reparations if they told their stories of human rights violation. He decided to apply, and put off his trip to the policeman's house. When selected to tell his story in front of a large audience of community members, Monwa detailed his torture at the hearings for victims of human rights violations. After telling his story, a public acknowledgement of his extreme suffering and a respectful admission that his sacrifice was part of the nation's movement toward democracy, an important change occurred in Monwa. After the truth and reconciliation commission, he decided not to kill his torturer.

Perhaps this commission could never fulfill the miraculous forgiveness that the country hoped for, but in this case, it was a transformative example, since there was a measure of conflict resolution here. For the survivor did not seek individual revenge; instead, he chose to participate in a massive uprising of thousands of witnesses and audience members who agreed to testify in a state forum. We will never know how many acts of vengeance were deferred; all I can say, in the most straightforward terms, is that this particular policeman is not dead. Unfortunately, the struggle with the past does not end there, for Monwa, upon returning to his home community, began to despair and flashback to being tortured. He became suicidal and started seeing Erik Harper at the trauma center. At times, the difficulties of finding a job increased his sense of alienation and helplessness. Also the final reparations, suggested by the commission, and the original impetus for Monwa's participation, were not ratified by the state legislators. Through the trauma center, Monwa discovered a political group that protested the ungranted reparations; it was the group Shirley Gunn coordinated, called *Speak Out!*, or in Xhosa, *Khulumani!* These final reparations were granted later by the state legislators, but the amount was much less than the commission advised because the government was overwhelmed by the rebuilding of the two-tiered economic structure of their formerly racist state.

Such desire for revenge is understandable, of course, since torture creates unimaginable suffering. Excruciating pain also forces the victim to play out roles imagined by the torturer, as Elaine Scarry details, because pain drives people past the edge of language, so you cannot tell your story; indeed, you are at the whim of your oppressor, who repeats his bullying power and beliefs.[9] Since body and identity are forcibly robbed from you, retribution is a normal reaction, Teresa Godwin Phelps contends; after all, how can the state be trusted to act as the agent of retribution if it has supported the network of terror and played the role of terrorist?[10] While retribution appears to be forgotten with reconciliatory justice, Phelps rationalizes that since victims lose the ability to use language when tortured, public commissions—allowing victims to speak—are forms not only of retribution but also of restoration.[11]

While Phelps explains part of Monwa's story, the struggle over what kind of narrative and identity the survivor constructs, both at the commission and in other cultural forums, has not been fully addressed. In bearing witness, Monwa's story was heard—a critical transition—a story that promoted respect, regained language, decreased alienation. Overall, the stories provoked assonance and dissonance in the audience's public soundings of acceptance and rejection. When many members of the audience, in a sympathetic mood, acknowledged the injustice, it created a shared understanding of the past. The commission elaborated ideas of ethical or political purpose, according to Hilde Lindemann Nelson; indeed, the categories of "perpetrators" and "victims" created a clear moral vision to condemn oppressive practices, the "boundaries of me and not-me," in the terms of Mary Duggan and Roger Grainger.[12] Because this state forum did not deny or forget Monwa's political experience, the interaction informed Monwa's decision to not take revenge. The narrated story changed his social and national role, short-circuiting a cycle of revenge. In the case of Monwa, a new relationship between individuals and the state was established through civic roles of witnessing. This primary stage—an extraordinary emergence of mass participation in public spaces—was followed by other transitional stages, creative integrations of this African Spring.

Undulating waves of emerging testimonies flooded the media—radio broadcasts, newsprint, channels with full filmed hearings, posters of press headlines on telephone poles. There was no escaping the emotion and scale of the commission. No matter how people responded politically, it was a national site of massive (and, at times, contestational) recollection. In an innovative tide of response, creatively integrating these testimonies into political sentiments, another staging of African Spring flowed in the poems that crossed the color lines, such as those of Khulile Nxumalo, Antjie Krog, Seitlhamo Motsapi, and Ingrid de Kok.

Within this popular protest of past injustice and the ensuing poetic and press responses, how to imagine this democratic spring? Let's start by entering the town hall, decorated with signs of the commission, packed with audience members, mainly black South Africans, who wanted to see their history played out on this state stage. And that was not all: there were witnesses—perpetrators, survivors, family members of the dead—alongside translators, commissioners, and even specially hired comforters to console the traumatized. On the first day, when the appointed head of the commission, Desmond Tutu, introduced the first survivor, who was about to tell her story of human rights violation, he hoped that the commission could "unearth the truth about our dark past" so the people would not be haunted by these injustices, thus working toward the "healing of a traumatized and wounded people," especially since "all of us in South Africa are wounded people."[13]

Situating the commission as an emotional fulcrum, one of many popular stages to protest the crimes of the state, offers an alternative approach, extending other important analysis on the amount or types of truth-telling by critics like Sarah Nuttall and Carli Coetzee.[14] Even as the hearings began with chairman Tutu's opening remarks, it ended with a politically powerful response to the traumatic story of the survivor. Tutu broke down and wept, modeling a political emotion for this African Spring. These evocative actions, integrated into media, performance, and poems, became part of a media chain of political emotion, a mediation to frame a newly imagined space of democracy.

Mass media framed this emotional moment, a politically powerful journalism, turning the work of the commission into front-page news. *The Cape Argus* reported how Nomonde Calata cried relentlessly after detailing how she discovered her husband's death. The press reported that "her loud cry" produced a "palpable shock" amongst the four hundred people in the audience.[15] In my perusal of a hundred different articles that reported on the commission, as I buried myself for several months at a university library in Stellenbosch, I found the press circulated stories of suffering as a political force of powerful historical reportage. We read, continuing the article, that the speech of this witness overwhelmed an "overwrought chairman Tutu, who collapsed with his head on his hands and wept." The press highlighted how the commissioner's tears were part of an emotionally powerful, social witness. "I thought I was tough until today," Tutu said later. "I don't know if I'll survive." And this commissioner was not the only witness who responded with emotion: Tutu claimed that the commission did not let the "present generation" of South Africans learn slowly of injustices; in fact, many have "wept as we were confronted with its ugly truths."[16]

Other commissioners too responded with tears; so much so that reporters called the truth and reconciliation commission the "Kleenex Commission" because of the amount of weeping. Commissioner Mary Burton cried after witnessing a story of a youth killed by the police.

Afterward, she described a new South Africa, so that if your child was late returning from school, parents would know they are "not in danger."[17] As she proclaimed her hopes that this commission could assist in creating a "better society for our grandchildren," she started to cry. These responses to trauma were often reported, as in Joe Latakgoma's article in *The Daily News*, where overwrought "tears" responded to these "horrific tales of torture," and "anguish" poured from families, seeking out where their disappeared loved ones were buried, pensive while listening to perpetrator's testimonies.[18] These televised images and news broadcasts made a vast impression, according to the five-volume commission report: "images relayed to the nation" through the media were "probably the single most important factor in achieving a high public profile" for the commission. Loaded with "compelling images," commission-related news "formed up to one-third of the main evening news bulletins."[19] Newspaper headlines were even posted on street corners. The director of research at the commission, Charles Villa-Vicencio, claimed that the "images sent around the world were of people (mostly black, mainly women) weeping on stage."[20] Since 60 percent of the testimonies were by black women, at the heart of these images there was the mourning of women—of sisters, wives, mothers, and grandmothers alike.

While there is problematic language in labeling people as victims of human rights violation—instead of survivors—and while, perhaps, future commissions should allow survivors to approve (or write) their own abridged press statements to match their desired self-presentation, this testimonial stage of the commission was just one of many manifestations and identifications of the young democracy's African Spring.[21] As the journalist and poet Antjie Krog claimed, her purpose in writing on the commission was to "snatch" the survivors from the "death of forgetfulness," so that the "future inherits you."[22] The suffering documented time and time again constructed a common cultural site in the press, refuting postwar amnesia and denial. Were these testimonies, flowing in popular print, part of a larger vision of an "imagined community," as in Benedict Anderson's idea of nationalism? Or have we overrated narrative's power to consolidate vast factions?

Emotional landscapes, amid democratic contestation, were performed in the collective presence of witnesses, commissioners, and translators alike. To put this more strongly, tears are neither sentimental nor nostalgic; they are a form of evidence, an affective validation of past injustice. In many ways, the commissioners' responses not only acknowledged the injustice and oppression individuals' suffered, but their sentimental responses were also ocular proof of the power of memory, a validation of traumatic history. The African Spring that has been forgotten—germinating in the ethical and emotive response of audiences, the press, and poetry—formed a storm of disparate and drowning emotion that left no national citizen unaware of the commission's existence as a historical vehicle, a public mapping of political emotion.

The importance of Tutu's emotional reaction was stressed by the poet Ingrid de Kok. When the archbishop presided over his first session, she remembered how he placed his "grey head on the long table of papers and protocols and he wept." Her poem recorded how the media, national and international, filmed "his weeping, his misted glasses, his sobbing shoulders, the call for a recess."[23] Not just a portrait of compassion, this emotional response was the center of the commission, claimed this poet. And surely, the power of witnessing demands such an emotional response. To echo Sarah Ahmed and Peggy Phelan, emotional residues and audience moods are not extra, arbitrary, unimportant, or distractions from the rational forums of legislation; no, emotional responses, especially when they are repeated in diverse forms and inscribed on numerous bodies, become a political force, influencing collective mobilization and national subjectivities.[24] National witnessing is not a detached rationalization, for the commission is not a court of law, it is a place where communities watch the story of a student that they loved, who has been murdered, come to life again in the words of others. Cathartic for some, traumatic for others, moving for many, unbearable for quite a few—these words and responses of thousands of people in this public arena cultivated a contentious, emotional, powerful democratic voicing—an African Spring.

For some, a newly found nationalism through emotion and witnessing emerged, as in Antje Krog's poem, "Country of Grief and Grace."

While initially the poet felt shame because of her white origins, she later wept, hearing of past injustices. For "one brief shimmering moment," in the midst of tears, "this country" was also "truly mine."[25] Her response, her emotion, felt like a form of sentimental citizenship. Because of the witnesses, the nation was no longer about separation, claimed this poet; instead, citizenship resided in an emotional landscape as responsive listening created national belonging: an emotional form of national surrogation.

Many of these national claims gravitated toward collective stances. When Eunice Miya narrated the death of her son, now posted on the public website "Bones of Memory," she concluded with a collective statement about "our own children."[26] It started when she was watching the news. Peering at the screen, she saw a child on the TV, "who had a gun on his chest." Then she realized that it was her own son Jabulani! She found herself praying, please let the news "rewind" so that his death would not occur. After witnessing the shooting of her son on the news, she cried, "even a dog you don't kill" with that method. What made Miya weep at the commission was the inhumanity not just against her son, but also against all black South African children. "Even an ant, a small ant, you, you think you have feelings even for an ant. But now our own children they were not even taken as ants." Her loss was spoken of as a historical injury: she shifted from the first person to a political collective, from "my son" to our "people." Personal violations helped to further shape national collectivities, since after the outpouring of testimonies and tears, revisionists could hardly deny black suffering.

Emotional landscapes—profuse with devastated speech and images of injured bodies—when described as collective embodiments, redirect power. As in the poem of Gcina Mhlope, who described witnessing as a process to exhume as "the bones of memory"; the poetic metaphor is significant, given how thousands of South Africans disappeared. Mass graves were exhumed because of testimonies.[27] These physical injuries were reconceived in public poetry, as in "Body Parts," in which De Kok claimed that narrated injuries could redirect society toward social recovery. Unbearable images, such as the "maimed hand" planting crops and the "unfixable broken bone" of the dead, pointed out a new direction for the young democracy.[28] Moving from the individual "punctured ear" to the collective witnessing that would "give us new bearings," collectives are powerful images—what performance theorist Diana Taylor calls a national "transmission"—that do not privilege the individual claim of subjects as much as articulate a national presence for disempowered communities.[29]

Another powerful political protest, after the amnesty hearings, was fury. In Seitlhamo Motsapi's poem "andif," there is a collective future for "all of us," if certain conditions are met.[30] What must be remembered is not only the "lacerated earth" bleeding at "your feet," but also the past that "screams at us" (62). Memory was not just about individuals. The metaphors placed natural elements as the keepers of trauma—a significant choice given the forced removals from land during apartheid. Past trauma was still present in the current landscape. Recognition of this social injury, as the poet Malika Ndlovu suggested, was a prelude to democratic practices. Rejecting suggestions by authorities that the "time for rage has passed," Ndolvu brought these officials to mass cemeteries, reminding them of the numerous corpses, of beloved names. Only after remembering the injuries could there be healing, since national birth cannot occur "without blood," similar to the birth of a "baby."[31] Sentimental citizenship was not an easy emotional process. It raged. It renewed.

A similar shift from state violence toward democratic power was found in Monwa's story. After the racial violence of the apartheid regime, public spaces included black South Africans in a protest against injustice after the silencing act of torture. While stories of victimization can be problematic because they detail helplessness, stories of loss do have agency when performed as powerful collectivities: spoken as protest, armored in political and poetic images. When the commission recognized that many black women were speaking, not of their political experiences, but rather of the deaths that they witnessed, they formed a separate commission for women. Returning to my own work with guerrilla fighters, there were gendered differences in envisioning loss and empowering identifications.

While Monwa felt suicidal because of his anxiety that being tortured had stolen his ability to have children, the women of the group did not discuss torture. At one of our first performances of *Khumbulani*, one of the male leads in the opening scene with Monwa, still recovering from being tortured six years earlier, had to go to the doctor. Not certain of how we could do the play without his participation, I asked our group if they wanted to omit this part. But then a slender woman, about forty years old, gently smiled at me, placed her arm around me, and offered to take his place. I nodded with relief, but I did not see how this could be possible, given the story that she shared in our workshop about her community's battles with the police. There had not been any mention of imprisonment or torture. In the performance, however, she told the audience that she had been fighting for the resistance and had been beaten and placed in jail. But she spoke more of her resistance than of her torture. At that point, I realized that many of these women had been political prisoners who had probably been subjected to sexual violence. Given the social stigma and pain of rape, this was not the story that they chose to tell. This was not the history that they wanted to remember. So in terms of my work as a facilitator and as a scholar recording stories, I have always honored the injustice that people decided to present while never forgetting that the painful legacy of the past may have left as much unsaid as said. In fact, public expression—from the state forum to the stage—provided important venues for individuals, especially alternative venues where they could choose what parts of their memory to share. It was *empowering* to have control over one's narrative. Unlike the moment of torture, where their voices and bodies were stolen from them, the testimony was an action, an alternative body, a protest against injustice.[32] And the stories that these women wanted to tell in *Khumbulani* were heroic, gender-busting—tales of women with rifles, women with bombs, women in court, and of a woman who was a commanding officer.

At one of the *Khumbulani* workshops, one of the participants told a very painful story about her experience as a mother. At the beginning, I had no idea that she was a mother. In fact, this rather recalcitrant woman of few words seemed like the least likely participant to narrate a full story. Well on our way to practicing for our first performance, she was still repeating a few words about police brutality. Since it was the shortest testimonial scene in *Khumbulani's* record of memories, I tried a different approach to try to find out what was important to her. Describing to our small group of fourteen the idea of creating statues, I asked participants to freeze in active positions that they wanted to talk about, an approach adopted from *Theatre of the Oppressed*. Boal's strategy for the "oppressed" suggests that every participant "assumes the protagonist role, changes the dramatic action, tries out solutions, discuss plans for change."[33] I saw these embodied memories—similar to dances and songs—creating a physical practice, a challenge to habitual and obsessive traumatic thoughts, an active protest against past injustice. After I asked our group to select a stance to accompany their story, they explained their pose, and these embodied forms of memory assisted many members in telling their protests. Only then was this short speech about the police extended. As the police came into the township of Philippi, they tear gassed all the inhabitants. This mother fled to the hospital because her baby was sickened by the chemical gas. When the doctor asked her what was wrong, she was afraid that he would report her to the police for being in a tear-gas zone. She could be arrested as a terrorist; then no one would take care of her baby. Remaining silent, she returned on the bus. Looking around at her shanty dwelling, there was little left, since the police had burnt her house and many others down to the ground. Scavenging through her burnt possessions, she discovered a person's arm. Very shaken, she left this township ghetto. Not long afterward, her baby died. As she related her story, she cried. No, that's not quite accurate. Rather, she wailed as if she had lost her self, just as she had lost her child.

The body stance was not just a story pose. It released the memory, giving her courage as she held the unseen dead child. In terms of survivor's guilt—a force that can gnaw its way into the deepest cavities of the self—it shifted as group members nodded their heads, expressed their condolences, witnessed her mourning as one of many ways that the former regime had destroyed the soul and second generation of so many. She spoke of a fire in the past, which was not just recorded in memory, but also in a personal vision of shame, and which needed to be revised, as one of many examples of the state's oppression of its people. In terms of healing tactics, accessing another way of remembering healed the overworked, traumatized, cognitive frames of memory; physical forms of

8. South African township. Photograph by author.

recollection helped survivors tell their stories and released buried emotion—the corpses of the past still held tightly. After her narrative, this mother wept and wept, and the group circled her, holding onto her as she cradled herself. After protesting injustice and embracing grief, this public venue, this affective landscape, worked toward healing.

Even as these stories moved me, my sense of femininity, as a female facilitator, was challenged by the stories of women with weapons. One participant was an important commander of a military unit, fighting in contingent countries, since the regime had executed and arrested all major leaders within the nation. She was a commander in the army of the African National Congress—often called the spear of the nation. This group, branded by the United States as terrorists, was the militia of Nelson Mandela, but their historic revolt has been forgotten on the global screen. This particular military leader—a political dynamo—grabbed my arm, insisting that I join her in a dance. Swinging invisible rifles, singing "hey guerrilla, hey, hey, guerrilla man," I was asked to join in a revolt, a moving protest.

Protest—developed during the course of our rehearsals in public speeches—highlighted ways that group performance as a form of conflict resolution varied from working with a therapist. One difficult question a professional therapist would face is how much should a therapist urge a survivor to remember? But the group performance, because of improvisational testimonies, kept the control of the story in the individual's grasp. This conscious editing occurred for one woman who had fought the police. Fists forward, she described her protest; yet her powerful story did not fully emerge until the last few days of the workshop. Explaining that the police had chased after her, she returned to her house, which had been reduced to ashes. Continuing to run away, she was shot. When the police took her to prison, she witnessed a pregnant woman, beaten again and again and again—she miscarried her baby. Mentioning her own unspeakable sadness, she ended her protest with a dance and a song of resistance.

Controlling how much to tell, this participant did not deny the pain, but rather categorized the past as horrific. After labeling the horror, she began a resistance song and dance movement that released her emotion. While a Freudian approach might interrogate the repressed, in this case, survivors never questioned one another, but instead served as witnesses and comforted one another. Moreover, the professional therapist's role, guiding the patient to remember the past trauma to understand present unease, could be disrupted by the patient's knowledge that the experience of torture can never be fully understood by most therapists. Various barriers between therapists and their clients may exist—linguistic, cultural, experiential barriers. These barriers are also complicated by the secondary trauma that the therapist, as witness to the traumatic stories, might experience. Overall, while an individual's performance of the past in front of a therapist would be isolated, protesting as a collective body in public validated a larger social group.

The performance of the group became a community event. Staged in the township of Philippi, *Khumbulani* became a collective experience, since many Xhosa and Zulu residents knew the songs that transitioned between the scenes. Hundreds of people in the audience joined in the singing. As a result, the audience became both witness and participant with the survivors, who acted as cultural agents, performing personal memory and local history, protesting past injustice, current poverty, and democratic hopes.

Such cultural performances are vehicles that pass on second-generation memories after years of terror and tragedy. Survivors of atrocity were often individually silent about their past, so that their histories were not told to their children, according to one therapist at Cape Town's trauma center. If given a safe, public medium, however, then survivors would pass on their stories to their children. One *Khumbulani* member expressed concern about the omission of second-generation memories. If young people were not told of their protest heritage, they would become discouraged by present economic challenges, not persevere by recalling their revolutionary struggles; instead, they would seek altered identifications, joining gangs with American names. As the poet Khulile Nxumalo suggests, telling stories to the second-generation was essential for a democratic voicing, beyond the first vote.[34] If parent's stories of the past were not told, then the distinction between the ideal world and the harsh realities would be so discordant that they would bring despair. So while parents often cited the lack of order in their children's lives as a reason to resort not to stories but to rules, intergenerational histories would build the democratic future, proclaimed this poet. So even though the commission provided a forum for honoring the suffering during the former regime, the *Khumbulani* group emphasized that speaking of moments of heroism was an easier vehicle for passing on generational memory. While the commission aimed to find out about historical events, especially violations, the *Khumbulani* group wanted to talk more about heroic resistance in their communities. Only a few books described local heroes and protesting in Cape Town Townships. Untold histories of local heroes, not commemorated by the state forum, emerged in the play, to foster heroic identities necessary for individual healing, for community development.

Given what this protest accomplished, how it developed because of the courage of its participants—a commemoration of their heroism and suffering—I am not sure why I was so surprised by their choice of an ending. To maintain agency for group members, I invited their suggestions for the conclusion of the play. They asked me for staging options, so I gave the following possibilities: the group could ask the audience to remember the promises of reparation, light a candle, honoring those who have died, suggest a change hoped for in the township, tell the audience to remember a historical event. The options were translated into Xhosa, and after a long discussion, Monwa replied: "This play is about us. About our memories. Not about reparations." They did not want to focus on economic claims, but rather to light a candle to remember their loved ones who had died. After the ritual of lighting candles and naming their lost loved ones, they sang *Senzeni Na?*—a mournful chant that recaptured how they were brutalized. This song brought many group members to tears. If protest has a process, for this group, the first step was to speak of personal experiences of injustice, to gain control over paralyzing traumatic memories, to find renewed group identity in protest songs. These political laments made an emotional claim on this newly birthed democracy.

In one of our final sessions, I asked Monwa what he would change about the drama workshop. But he responded with a list of strengths and a personal reflection:

> We make decisions as a group. It is very good for us to remember together and to sing our songs. When I got out of prison, I didn't feel like living. I met my wife, and things are better. This play and meeting together helps us to feel strong again. When we sing, it reminds us what we fought for. It is important to tell our stories.

Furthermore, Monwa asked if we could repeat the same workshop with a second theme; this time emphasizing exile and the border war in Angola. "For a second play, I know many comrades who cannot speak of exile," Monwa emphasized. "No one knows what happened to us when we were sent to Angola. It was lonely and difficult." Hearing his words, I wondered how the truth and reconciliation commission could possibly capture so many different traumatic events. I remembered one case, where a soldier complained of being mistakenly identified as a spy, tortured by his own people while in Angola. Monwa looked resolved; he spoke once more, "We were fighting a war over there. People here don't understand that experience." In performing for one's community, there were varied experiences of violence, poverty, atrocity, exile—all a critical part of a voicing of political identifications in an open, democratic space.

After trauma, these individuals, living in makeshift houses with tin roofs, on land discarded by the state outside urban centers, were trying to weave the "broken threads of their lives."[35] Combined with control of personal stories, these activities reshaped their sense of self as public figures, speaking of past and current contexts. After listening to the group's response to the workshop, Monwa explained their feedback. One person mentioned, in this performance, "I became aware that if you speak to someone about your pain, you become free and heal." Feeling that the public setting brought about community healing, their protest recalled the injustice of the police and former regime, but also recalled Mandela's words, "we will forgive, but not forget." Thus, enacting injustices built reconciliation, many agreed, but forgiveness of the past, not related to any specific perpetrator, came through group enactment, collective bonding, and through commemoration of the dead. Common in cultural performances, commemoration and interpretation were forgiving because they sublimated terrorized fragments, accentuated strengthening elements. As the stories were extended, the fullness of their lives offered a coping strategy for loss, even though the poverty of the township remained a constant burden. The important words of Nelson Mandela were often repeated, but the release of emotion blossomed only from out of the aroma of consolation.

Imagine a global sphere where truth and reconciliation commissions were more commonly practiced after Arab and African Springs. State spaces of witnessing and innovative local sites, in this study, have suggested ways that violent memories are expressed in democratic voicing and popular protest. Commemorative protest as a collective healing and conflict resolution strategy shifted from the gravesite of horror to altered group identifications, a grassroots social bond. In this process, certain stories become sacred sites in national history; others are forgotten. Perhaps history should be remembered in populist terms, not just through the miracle of Mandela, but also through the courage of the man who lives in a shanty, my friend Monwa. While Mandela suffered over two decades of incarceration, his experience contrasted to that of these men and women who were tortured yet have returned to their shanties to raise their children in a challenging economic environment. Today, Monwa continues his public activities: he directs a choir of young men at his church, which he tells me will steer the youth clear from gangs, and he works in a performance group, this time as one of many actors telling their story about what it is like to have AIDS.

7 | 9/11 Media

Gendered Nationalism beyond Islamic/Jewish Borders

Since the New York incident [September 11], sales have really
gone down . . . I'm not saying it's your fault.
                                   —Nadia Davids, *At Her Feet*, 2006

Young democracies are often vulnerable to global tremors. Media
images trickle into global consciousness—war casualties broadcast on
al-Jazeera, demeaning images of the Prophet Mohammad, whose image,
flashed around the world, becomes virtual reality, and worldwide images
of 9/11; these images become forces of change. This chapter considers
protest and political identity through various responses to global images
of tortured or dead bodies in the decade before the Arab Spring. What
kind of fall-out does a traumatic image—broadcast on short waves or televised with telemetry—produce? For instance, watching the Twin Towers
fall, then seeing the rising edifice of U.S. and Israeli war machines in
Iraq, Afghanistan, and the Palestinian territories has had a global impact.
For two female playwrights, Nadia Davids and Yael Farber—whose
names reflect their separate Muslim and Jewish heritage—these images
have inspired their plays. While we expect Muslim and Jewish communities to respond to U.S. involvement in the Middle East, this chapter
shows a surprising response to media: in *At Her Feet* and *Molora*, both
of these plays focus on feminist-based nationalism. Through innovative
protests, these two women consider 9/11 and its aftermath from a distinct national angle—for both of these women are South African. In my

analysis of a feminist spring, I demonstrate how these two plays do not just replicate global media, but also show how national identities intertwine with international images and gendered locations—all part of this book's repertoire of traveling sites of public loss and democratic protest.

Nadia Davids, *At Her Feet*

Set in a Cape Muslim neighborhood, the play *At Her Feet* performs three mass media images: The first, the shadow of the Twin Towers falling, restaged as the shadow of incrimination by a white South African boss toward his Indian Muslim employee. The second, a magazine cover with the bloodied face of an Iraqi baby, arrests the attention of an expecting Muslim South African mother at the grocery store. The third, a Western documentary on a Jordanian woman's death, causes a political response from an Afro-Malay student, a self-described Islamic feminist. The images of loss—such as a newsflash of 9/11, or civilian deaths in Iraq, or like the photo of a bloodied child—circulate in this play, suggesting such images circulate as a global force.

After watching images of the dead and of 9/11, Nadia Davids, a South African playwright, reconsidered her ideas about historical, racial, and religious loyalties. Her identity "used to be very much a race issue," since she is classified as "coloured": a woman who is "not white and not black."[1] Yet her conception of her identity after September 11 was more about how she "positioned" herself as a "Muslim woman." In the urban communities of Cape Town, she began researching and interviewing other Muslim women, many of whom described their ideas of being Muslim South Africans as a communal bond, or as a "political subjectivity," or as a "spiritual link." Using these interviews and her experience, the playwright formed characters, composed through her research impressions. Connecting multiple female subjectivities in a one-woman play, *At Her Feet* performs the "fractured, creolized society" that she characterizes as Cape Muslims (68). And in the midst of these fragments, she imagines feminine connections and disconnections between South Africa and the Middle East.

The global connection of 9/11 is performed as an interaction between a white South African boss and his female employee. Abruptly, he begins reflecting on September 11, catching his employee Tahira by surprise. After this terrorist attack, "sales have really gone down at Talbot Travels." After a pause, he states, "I'm not saying it's your fault" (42). Later, the boss suggests that her head scarf has become associated with the violence of 9/11. Mr. Talbot ruminates that people are "scared to buy plane tickets" from a woman who chooses to wear a head scarf (43). Situating his religious attacks, he states that he has always "given you people the benefit of the doubt" (42). He reminds her that he is not an apartheid nationalist; in fact, he attended her wedding and complimented her mother on her Cape Malay food. Yet his self-posturing only heightens his dismissive attitude. Not only does he generalize "you people," he also disregards his relationship with Tahira, who has worked for him for ten years. His antiracist posturing, in the context of apartheid, has turned to blatant racism. How can she "keep wearing a scarf after all that," he demands (42). After 9/11, the media and events usher in a double racism. Thus it is that global fault lines—performed as hierarchical ethnicities and stereotypes of spiritual practices—are reenacted in the local arena.

The scarf becomes a symbol of controversy: a distorted measure of whether Tahira is extremist or devoted to her job. In a reactive tirade, the boss demands, "Do I cut off your ear because you spend hours on the phone to all of your relatives?" (43). And then assuming that travel sales are diminished because she wears a head scarf, he states, or cut off "your hand because you are costing me?" (43). Stereotypes of Islamic violence are reinscribed in this hate speech used against an employee. Mr. Talbot converts South Africa into an imaginary Islamic land, condemning his employee: "If you want to live in a country where the women are all closed up, you wouldn't even be able to work here" (43). Switching from economics to stereotypes, the boss uses language that suggests that his subtle racism against blacks from the Cape Malay region turned to a threatening racism against Muslims. Levels of racial assumption and control are played out in new ways after 9/11.

After 9/11, Tahira has to choose between economics and personal identity, between local vocation and global affiliations. The demand is that she take off her scarf or work at another job. But Tahira and her husband are living at her in-laws' house, so she values the work because they are saving for their own house. Taking off her scarf at work, she places it in her bag, so that she can wear it afterward. Having chosen to wear the scarf since she was sixteen, it is stressful to select between independence in her vocational space or independence in her living space. Expecting a child, she is overwhelmed by economic demands of the marketplace and antagonism faced at the grocery store. Besieged by a photo of a dead Iraqi baby in the grocery store stands—the baby resembles a "little doll, with tiny eyes squeezed shut"—she sees that the three-month-old child also wears a scarf, a small bandage "wrapped round her head" (57). It takes a moment for Tahira to register the shock of this photo—a delayed response that there is "something wrong" (57). And she loses her breath when she discovers that there is still a pacifier in the dead infant's mouth. She prays that the mother is not alive to see her dead child, and she fears bringing a Muslim child into this world. Thus, the invisible Iraqi mother and the expectant mother in South Africa become entangled. Imagined war zones, falling towers, shared publics, and economic spaces become "contact zones" charged with emotionally textured areas and reconceived identities.[2]

The post-9/11 image creates responses from the other customers as well, also waiting in the grocery line. But that's the "price you pay for terrorism!" says one man, justifying this death (57). "Does that baby look like a terrorist to you?" Tahira asks (57). Because of media, images of violence, antagonism, anxiety, and displacement fill the public square. In fact, the angst of a young Muslim mother turns to a prayer and provocative plea—a desperate hope that the Iraqi mother is dead. Her personal horror serves as a global index: a spiritual call to God in a moment of crisis, revulsion at the dead infant that is killed by Western military, and profound affection for her coming child. In all of these public confrontations—racial, religious, political—she clings to the umbilical cord of her communal identity.

To understand this protest against Islamic-rooted racism, we need to contextualize this work within its urban community. The playwright is part of a community whose language and creative traditions are distinct from that of other groups. Referred to as "coloured" to designate mixed race during apartheid, the city neighborhoods with their brightly painted houses in Cape Town often select various appellations as points of pride, such as Cape Malay. While some groups trace their identity back to Malaysian slaves, others have situated their lineage with the indigenous South African peoples, such as Khoi-San groups or the Griqua. Indeed, there is conflict over whether specific earlier ancestral lineage should be claimed, or a regional identity mapped on the coloured community, or whether only a national identity should be celebrated, or if a new term for this group is required.[3] Various markers of identity are claimed by this community through cultural locations: curry-rich restaurants of culinary distinctiveness, streets with people speaking the Afrikaans language, yearly performance festivals and music. And there are also public spaces that locate and memorialize their history of dispossession—like District Six and the Slave Lodge museums. But *At Her Feet* suggests a distinct entry point by Muslim Africans into a discourse of Islamic global affinity and national difference.

In a sense, 9/11 recontextualizes local racism. The play stages various vestiges of apartheid racism. When Tahira receives derogatory calls at work, the orientalist discourse about this Creole community is exposed. Answering the phone, Tahira follows protocol and states her agency and her name. The potential client inquires if her name is Arabic. The caller suggests that her name is exotic and wants to know what she is wearing. But Tahira resists these assaults, "Very exotic . . . to you," she says. "No, I've never been to India. Can I help you with something? What am I wearing? . . . You want me to what?" (40). Retorting that she wears the same uniform as the other employees and is married, she eventually hangs up the phone. The attack becomes another facet of racist, religious, and sexist assaults. But, unlike the memory frame of earlier violence against this community—not just racism against blacks in apartheid laws, but also much earlier forms of colonization and slavery—9/11 provides a new vantage point from which to consider local and global forms of power. This beginning point is a critical form of "social memory," to quote Paul Connerton's theory about the sequencing, struggle, and attempt to find "legitimacy" when there is a change in power.[4]

In this case, *At Her Feet*—performed ten years after democracy began in South Africa—struggles through the traumatic legacy of the past and present. Indeed, the play uses media images of Muslims in order to publicly stage an emergent identification that is distinctly "post"-apartheid. In the play, global images after 9/11 do not silence apartheid identifications, for the play shows agonizing forms of racial oppression that are continuing. But these excruciating events are critiqued from an altered lens, focusing on religious affiliations and communal ties that cross cultural and global terrain.

Not only does Tahira struggle against the violence of stereotypes, but she also participates in a racial discourse of exclusion. The scene of phone harassment precedes an example of Tahira's racist disregard of others. She dismisses Ayesha, a girl with hair that is "all out and bushy" (40), as a young woman who does not belong to "our community" (41). Racial profiling—in the aesthetics of beauty—becomes the standard for acceptance or dismissal for some members of this Islamic community. Having black skin or thick hair becomes an indicator of African versus coloured identity; it is a racism Tahira holds against another Muslim South African woman. Belonging in the Cape Malay community or in these public scenarios in urban South Africa, then, is characterized not just by Islamic faith, but also by multiple codes of ethnicity.

But it is not only a reaction to ethnicity; Tahira is aggrieved at Ayesha's practice of Islamic faith. She does not understand the political positions of Islamic feminism and black consciousness that inform Ayesha's identification as a young college student. Asked by Ayesha to sign a petition to protest the stoning of a Jordanian woman, Tahira states that it is not the right "time to be criticizing other Muslim people" (41). Both Tahira and Ayesha have an ardent sense of Islamic faith; however, one expresses it as a form of religious solidarity, the other as a protest voice for Islamic feminism. Significantly, these two characters are played by a single actress in this one-woman play, stressing the multiplicity and divergence of South African Muslim affiliations. Tahira could be regarded as more traditional and Ayesha the more radical Islamic feminist. But this play rejects these simplified divisions, since Tahira is the only one in the play who has a job and who seeks independence from her extended family. It is not her husband's choice that she works, but hers.

In contrast to Tahira, Ayesha's local subjectivity is informed by global icons—both religious and political. An early religious feminist icon is her namesake, for she is named after "a scholar, a warrior, a poet" (61). Ayesha was the Prophet Mohammad's wife and an early model of feminist power, riding to battle as a general of war. Also hoping for revolution, the South African Ayesha purchases iconic clothing—a shirt with the image of Che Guevara, a cap that pictures Malcolm X—not just because of her political ideals, but also because the clothing is "very sexy" (34). In contrast to Tahira—who wears designer outfits with her veil as a symbol of modernity and middle-class identity—Ayesha associates her own public vestments as a sign of a confident and sexy woman and as a symbol of political resistance to oppression. Ayesha also embraces the Islamic spiritual ideal of caring for the poor. The global icons of these three political figures—Malcolm, Che, and Ayesha—have a cultural aura and hybrid identifications. Black and coloured. Muslim and Feminist. African and Marxist.

Ayesha protests violence against women, but she also participates in racist stereotyping of others: for she is intolerant of Tahira and her friends who wear head scarves with expensive boots and designer wear. Watching these olive-skinned women, Ayesha views them as feigning a pure, Malaysian connection, disregarding the influence of their particular African location and ignoring the common Creole lineage. As Gabeba Baderoon suggests in the introduction to this play, these showy women circle, not the Kaaba, but rather the mall in search of Muslim boys to mate. Paradoxically, Ayesha also buys her Che shirt at this expensive mall, but only because it is a mass-produced item.

Despite her spiritual practice and political conviction, Ayesha still experiences bigotry in the Cape Muslim community. While dating Nazeem, for example, Ayesha realizes that her boyfriend does not want to introduce her to his mother, who is prejudiced against black Muslims. She asks if Nazeem would invite her to his family's house if she straightened her hair. The aesthetics of hair functioned as cultural markers of belonging and identity. When he assured her that straightening her hair would make her acceptable, she feels as if "emotional rocks" had been thrown at her (38)—a transnational parallel to the rocks thrown at the Jordanian woman viewed in a Western documentary. Deciding to go to his house in a blond wig, Ayesha stages her own Rapunzel act; then, after having tea with his mother—a stunned Auntie Kariema—she breaks up with her boyfriend.

In this reconstruction, however, both male and female are entrapped: one rejects the mores of beauty attached to cultural belonging, while the other remains in a close relationship with his mother, whom he will not confront about her racist views. Ayesha does not straighten her hair, but performs whiteness with a blonde wig, mocking the whitened identification that Auntie Kariema seeks. The racial hierarchy of apartheid—where "coloured" was defined as closer to white, so better than black—is exercised within the Creole community. It is a communal racism that repeats the oppression that was first constructed by segregation laws. This racism is analyzed by the scholar Zimitri Erasmus, who remembers both the oppressed history and complicit racism of her coloured community. Both contemporary racism and past racism must be confronted: an "ethical imperative" to mature coloured identity within a national palate.[5] Not just this hierarchical "complicity" but also, continues Erasmus, the complex "fluidity" of black identifications within histories of "cultural dispossession, borrowing, and transformation" deserves recognition.[6] Like Ayesha's African body, symbols of cultural division and communal affinity are traveling symbols, and the ambiguity of Islamic and African and Malaysian identifications tie together in circling motifs of gender aesthetics. Rapunzel's impossible locks are the scene of nuptial desire; Tamara's covered or uncovered hair is an economic locus; the bloodied scarf around the Iraqi baby's head uncovers the violence of war. Much in this way, the aftermath of 9/11 and apartheid become tangled in a mutual set of epistemological violence.

Racial hierarchies, still practiced by Auntie Kariema, are reified by considering who is acceptable, who is different, who fits in. This form of racism establishes a "disturbing distance" between the accepted black who is respectable and thus "different" from other blacks; what Homi Bhabha diagnoses as an insidious part of the "artifice" of white authority.[7] A "white mask" is placed on the black man who wants to fit into the dominating culture, claims one of the first black theorists, Frantz Fanon, in contrast to the "un-civilized" black other.[8] In effect, the exceptional position that apartheid constructed for the coloured community is a tenuous and fickle placement; while many whites selected this community for employment over "black" South Africans, the state never granted them citizenship, and coloured families also lost their land when apartheid cleared out what they termed the "black spots," like the neighborhood of District 6.

The play does not end with the racism of Auntie Kariema, and its protest strategy shows shifting identifications. Indeed, the media of 9/11 and its aftermath also change this character's self-reflections. Stirring her pungent curry dish on the stove, Auntie Kariema listens to her niece Sara, who is upset over a documentary about a Muslim woman who is stoned to death. The killing is "barbaric," Sara says. In response, Aunty Kariema suggests that there are "always two sides" (31). The girl was "breaking the rules, running off to see that boy." She surmises that the village received a radio, after which the girl began listening to Madonna, who influenced the girl's sense of sexual impiety. Clearly, the Aunt insinuates, the problem is Western secularization. When the niece counters that the Western music is in English, not Arabic, her Aunt retorts that the beat alone is enough to communicate "their sexy nonsense" (31). When asked how she knows about Western music, the Aunty retorts that she has TV or MTV on "24 hours a day" (32). Indeed, why should her husband pay "good money for satellite," if she doesn't keep it on all day? (32). When her niece challenges her to watch her own cultural programming, the Aunty rejects televised performances of the coloured community because it focuses on Indian South Africans, not Cape Malay, and she has had enough of henna prints and "Monsoon weddings" (32). Aunty upholds her own view of Islamic traditions, citing her own wealth and good life as a result of marrying a man that her father had approved. But she does not see her own hybridity, positioning her sacred identity alongside her adoration of secular infusions on television.

Yet the play reverses sentiments, selecting this bigoted Aunt as a sympathetic character. Aunty Kariema confesses that the global image of the dead girl does affect her own sense of gendered and religious history. Reflecting on her conversation with her niece, she wishes that her niece felt a kinship through cultural affinity. Sara calls herself "black" and "liberal" and "South African" (49), while the Aunt associates herself with Malay and her Scottish grandmother, who "turned" and became Muslim (49). The Aunt rejects Arab associations because they think they "own Islam" (50). At the same time, she distances herself from Malaysian women—veiling in public and a parade of "designer miniskirts" at home—hypocritical foreigners (50). After voicing her disappointment in the second generation's lack of cultural heritage, she then reflects on the dead girl in Jordan and her own dead mother.

Recounting her mother's death, Auntie recalls sitting at her mother's feet when she made pies. But Auntie's mother died when she was ten, wasting away with a disease that the doctor could not diagnose. After her mother's death, the young daughter could not bear to join the circle of women who gathered to wash the body. She wanted to walk with the men, but the Islamic tradition prohibited her from being part of this processional. Her father circled around and returned her to the kitchen, where the women were cooking "with their grief" (53). Recalling this crisis, the Aunt relates to the "Arab," to the young girl, to Azra. "I wanted to walk," Aunty says, "she wanted to talk" (53). The pathos of this scene lies in the pain placed in both the global and local site. And at this secret space of confession, the bigoted Auntie becomes the softened feminist. The confession occurs in a space that has no communal witness. This intimate space, where the woman finds her political voice, juxtaposes the media space of death, where the girl has no voice.

The play uses the image of the dead girl Azra as a collective bond between women; in fact, there are three references to mothers and daughters in this play. Tahira—who is expecting a little girl and has quit her job because of the stress of post-9/11 Islamophobia—faces the strain of living with her mother-in-law because they cannot afford their own house. Then, there is the invisible Iraqi mother and the image of her child saturated with blood that covers the newspapers in Cape Town, South Africa. And finally, there is the anonymous mother in Jordan, whose daughter Azra has been stoned to death. Rendered invisible by Western press, the mother is given a voice by the play, speaking back to violence. Mother-daughters infiltrate the play in overlapping embodiments by a single actress and media links between South Africa, Jordan, and Iraq—a globalization of images that suggests the power of media to cross international lines. At the same time, the play suggests that these images are localized, filtered through various African lenses.

At Her Feet circles not only between mothers and daughters but also in concentric circles from the Kaaba, to gender sites at the mall, to a circumference of dead women. The first death in this play is a patriarchal murder filmed in the Western documentary and restaged in the play by a ghost Azra who speaks of her own death. Describing herself as an "awkward zero," her life has been cancelled out (26). Azra's absent story in the documentary is replaced by her speaking spirit, who tells her own story in this play. Moreover, the play ends with Azra's mother, who takes the corpse and encircles it with a round embrace between mother, daughter, and God—no longer a zero, nor a nullified voice, she is now part of a "circle of gentleness" and an "embrace of blood" (64–65). As the play's final image of protest, the negotiation of a negated life is a simultaneous condemnation of violence, an embrace of mother-daughter communal bonds.

The mother is simultaneously a marker of compassion and a muse, the "mother of memory," who will "bear witness" (65). Unlike Auntie Kariema, distraught at the idea of washing her dead mother, the final image is of the mother giving her daughter to God for immersion in a place of transfiguring waters of "transparent sweetness" (65). While the mother bans the murderous fathers and patriarchs from the divine gates, the young woman enters heaven, a final birth in a play of anticipated deliveries. The ghostly girl, a connecting image throughout, had her speech taken from her, but in the play she regains her voice, part of a global harmony, a feminine protest.

These travelling sympathies cross between the Middle East and South Africa, a performance of diversified action within a feminine collectivity—a claiming of personal, social, and spiritual identities. As in the rap song of Ayesha, protests against injustice change into collective bonds, in a larger song for Muslim sisters from the slave history of South

Africa, from Afghanistan, Palestine, and Iraq—all attached in a common search for "routes to freedom that have not yet been built" (62). The importance of finding these liberation paths of feminine identity has generational implications for mothers and their children, small ones "at her feet" (62). So while globalization is often interpreted as a negative force that consumes local traditions, this performance suggests that global images can be used to invigorate local gender claims and create an altered national affinity. This collective voicing revises the color lines of segregation to embrace Islam as a type of global feminism and a multicolored nationalism.

Yael Farber, *Molora*

The media coverage of 9/11—an influence on a young Muslim playwright in Africa—also inspired a Jewish South African, who watched images of American violence in its aftermath. After watching the Twin Towers fall, as ash descended on New York, Yael Farber recorded the "particular" response of the United States as a technologically advanced and very "powerful" nation in contrast to the "spiritual" response and "sophistication" of everyday South Africans to violence.[9] She wrote her own rendition of the ashen effects of violence, selecting the Sesotho word for ash, *molora*.[10] While the ash that floated down from the American site led to political cries for wars, the ashes of the dead in this South African play are negotiated, mourned, and dispersed. At the heart of this play are two women: the torturer and the tortured. Thus the violent aftermath of the dead and wounded are staged, a protest that gives voice to the tortured other. But in this public staging, the play asks its audience to consider how democracies in any region can transition from violent regimes to political practices of justice.

In her protest against continuing violence, Farber weaves three separate stories about young democracies. A warning against revenge and an opening stage for democracy is alluded to through the classical tragedy *The Oresteia*. The second democracy is suggested by words of torture and pain, originally given at the truth and reconciliation commission, part of a political compromise to usher in elections in South Africa. And these allusions are both staged in ways that reframe contemporary images of torture after 9/11. In staging two central characters as female, women who enact torture, murder, and reconciliation, Yael Farber refuses the usual litany of male politicians, soldiers, and suicide bombers. Indeed, this fem-centric tale suggests how violence and reconciliation occur in both political and domestic sites—a creative, gendered subversion.

To understand this public protest, it is important to explain the classical story. To give a quick synopsis, there is a war, and King Agamemnon believes the sacrifice of his daughter (Iphigenia) will lead to victory. During this ten-year war, his wife takes Agamemnon's cousin (Aegisthus) as her lover. When Agamemnon returns from the war with his war prize, Cassandra, in tow, his drunken wife kills him, avenging her dead daughter. Learning of the king's death, the two remaining children—Electra and Orestes—vow revenge on their mother. Orestes kills his mother. Then a trial is held to decide whether to continue on this path of revenge and kill the son. Although the court is deadlocked, Athena breaks the vote, halting the cycle of vengeance, initiating the start of democracy. According to scholarship, this play was presented by Aeschylus after the "atrocities of extreme brutality" during the Peloponnesian War when revenge "demanded reexamination" and Athens had just created "final reforms" to create a "radical democracy."[11]

In Yael Farber's rendition, the mother Klytemnestra is the perpetrator: she takes an axe to her husband, tortures her daughter. Yet this play does not kill the mother. Rather, this female figure serves as an uneasy double for two democracies: a ghostly figure of present American and past Apartheid politics. In the segregated propaganda of apartheid, white women were presented as oppressed mothers—starved in concentration camps during the Anglo-Boer War. Often gender studies critique how women have frequently been held up as objects, the virgin territory of nationalism in need of a masculine protector. For instance, while colonization killed countless numbers of people, Victorian Brits imagined that all would be well since the angel of the homeland was an ethical mother who held the heartstrings of the country. Moreover, post-9/11 media focused on the body of the oppressed woman—a Muslim wrapped in a silencing black fabric. Or the female soldier next to a male victim at Abu Ghraib. In contrast to feminine models of victimization or military soldiers' power over a Muslim man, *Molora* stages the white mother as brutal agent. But Klytemnestra is not an angel, no protector of domestic virility nor of political honor; rather, she depicts an assassin.

What a contrast from the white mother in South Africa! The white mother is the figure of nationalism for apartheid identifications: during the Anglo-Boer War, the British army fought the Dutch settlers over property feuds and slavery. And in order to conquer the guerrilla fighters, the British militia arrested the slaves and the women and children of these protesting (largely Dutch) colonials. Thousands of blacks and whites died in the concentration camps of disease. The "humiliation" continued after the war because white English still held more economic power, according to Loren Kruger.[12] Historical pageants—like the settler celebration of the great trek—paraded statues of the white mother. In the elections of 1938, white men were celebrated as the "saviors of white women" from black men.[13] All forums are quite distinct from today's rhetoric of rescuing Islamic women, since the spectacle of suffering mothers or oppressed wives is subverted in this South African play. These two women—one white, one black—are political agents.

Let's begin with the white female torturer. Unlike the American scenario, Klytemnestra is not in the military. Nor is there any invocation of exceptional circumstances—a "bad apple." Not a war trophy, the women that the heroic males of Homer brought home, like Cassandra. Rather, the later dramatist Aeschylus imagined a different kind of woman: this woman is no mere object of exchange; the queen is a political power—rejecting an objectified role, she kills a king who had murdered her daughter and has taken a mistress—a warning against trespassing on women's rights during a time in Greece when women could not vote.[14]

Envisioned by Yael Farber, this female perpetrator can only speak of her own victimization, even after confessing to the murder of her husband. Her words echo former President DeKlerk in his testimony at the truth and reconciliation commission, wherein he emphasized the Anglo-Boer War and then ignored the ongoing bloodshed that unfolded for a century. "We were at war here," pronounces Klytemnestra. This allusion to war refers to commission statements by policeman, who claimed that the racist violence was but a cold war between white Christians and

9. White mother at Voortrekker Monument (Pretoria). Photograph by author.

black Communists. And it alludes to the Second Gulf War as well, when "war reached our shores on September eleventh," as claimed by President Bush, remembering a flight of political bandits, forgetting civilian deaths in wars. The past is only remembered with one reference point. Klytemnestra's mind is a grave in which the single corpse of Iphigenia takes up all the space. It is a haunting and dominating fiction. This consuming memory of perpetrators, as Hannah Arendt diagnoses, is a "banality of evil," a wall that blocks out other perspectives even while remaining strangely apocalyptic about its dire chances of survival.[15] Just as this selection of memories blocks out other voices, distorts reality itself, so too does Klytemnestra question, "What is guilt? What is memory?" (34). This singular vision is also the language of racial anxiety; even while attacking others, the state fears a "dark figure" hiding "beneath the bed" (51), in a racist economy that generates paranoia about the dark other.

The tortured body is not white. As the white mother tortures her black daughter, it is a stark reversal, for in many wealthy white homes in South Africa, the white and black woman alike are both at the heart of domestic roles. Instead, external places of domination are inscribed as familiar domestic spaces of oppression; what Anne McClintock analyzes as a power dynamic in a "cult of domesticity."[16] Domestic power, in the analysis of Mbembe, showed a mistress's "affection" for her African maid, but was limited to the points when the maid entered into the mistress's "world" and worked on her house, not as an important individual in her own right.[17] Not an affectionate mistress, this domestic liaison—often portrayed as a convivial relationship despite economic inequity—is rejected by *Molora*. The traditional inequality of maid and mistress is changed to a grisly display of racist power amidst women. This dominating white mother tortures her black servant, a woman that she cannot recognize as her kin. As the mother tortures her daughter Elektra for information about where her brother is hiding out, information about the enemy is not produced; rather, the mother's horrific brutalization of her daughter is evident. Enacting suffocation with a bag, the play confronts its audience with two parallels: a legacy of torture for both Abu Ghraib and apartheid.

When I saw the South African performance of *Molora* in 2007, the American photos of tortured bodies—especially the iconic pose of a hooded, dark figure—had made a global circuit. American military called this the "Vietnam" pose; the torture was practiced in Asia, and the British army, long familiar with the tactic, called it the "crucifixion." In South Africa these images also triggered their own history, for it was the South African police who first added electric voltage to the excruciating posture, just as the figure at Abu Ghraib was wired.[18] The suffocating sack covering the face of the victim, a relic of South Africa's past, was America's history as well.

But unlike a photo, which cannot speak, Elektra narrated her trauma. Unlike the tortured prisoners of 9/11, whose voices we do not hear, the voice of this black woman speaks to us: "one day you will face your God. And ask forgiveness for the things you did in those years" (48). Responding to these accusations, the mother protests that she was acting out of fear and had to strike first. In short, restaging the perpetrator as a white mother turns the violence against the marginalized into the common place—as widespread as each house in the suburb. Unlike torture in the midst of 9/11's war legacy, both the play and the space of the truth and reconciliation commission were public spaces, rejecting the hidden nature of past atrocities. They performed the hidden violence and loss in a second context, but this time we are the witnesses.

Inviting accountability, Farber avoided the stereotype of bad cops in well-meaning systems. The spotlight was not on military personalities, but rather on the rhetoric of terrorist-racist anxieties that were prevalent during apartheid and in the aftermath of 9/11. Its legacy of tortured bodies, the Western outrage at the homosexual acts and rape of male prisoners, Jasbir Puar contended, also solidified Western stereotypes of the perverse otherness of Muslims, doubly shamed because of their repressed sexuality and their accustomed sexual domination over women.[19] The publicized frozen body of an Iraqi victim was made "accessible": the tortured body is "available for comment, ridicule, shaming, scrutiny," Puar continued, even as dead American soldiers were protected by the press.[20] In contrast, Molora's torture performed on stage was not just a frozen shot of a violent spectacle, since the entire story of the survivor was shown in the play.

Unlike the frigid war trophies of maligned bodies, which distanced the viewer from the damage, because of the military lens, Molora's audience witnessed the white woman burning her daughter with cigarettes, beating her, stifling her, the daughter kicking with desperation. This "contact" should be "immediate and dynamic," Farber directed, so that the audience feels "complicit—experiencing the story as witnesses or participants," not as "voyeurs" (19). So close to these actors that I could almost touch them, I did not just witness this play; unable to intervene in this shocking torture scene, I felt like an accomplice. Closely following

Farber's mandate, Elektra's suffocation was performed beyond the audience's zone of comfort (48).

This suffocation also resembled a well-known moment at the truth and reconciliation commission when a former political prisoner, Tony Yengeni, asked his persecutor to model the torture he experienced. Captain Jeffrey Benzien demonstrated the wet-bag, which was filmed and photographed across the news networks. Not only did the tortured survivor want people to witness what he experienced, but he also insisted on an explanation. Yengeni cried, "What kind of man are you?" When there was no answer, Yengeni demanded, "I am talking about the man behind the wet-bag." After another pause, the police captain answered, "I ask myself the same question."[21] What kind of society tortures others? The play itself answered this question. Societies trapped in collective memories of their own persecution, blinded to the pain that they caused others, unable to see the global kinship around them. The play showed how torture has a global effect; military policies were not external affairs, they were present and palpable, as if in a family traumatized by abuse.

The survivor of torture, Elektra, has a voice, and she responds in two languages: English and Xhosa. In her cries of grief and rage, she speaks the language not of her mother but of her mother community, which allows white audience members outside of her native tongue to hear a requiem of unspeakable grief. Expecting English—in the performance in London in 2008, for instance—the audience is taken by surprise, disrupted. As Farber argues, the audience does not take the language or comprehension of speech "for granted"; rather, the audience recognizes that the actors are "reaching out" in a second language—a "generous act"—a bridge of reconciliation.[22] English is the language of the original British colonizers, but it can also be a counterforce to "reclaim yourself"—as in the largely white audiences in certain venues, what Farber sees as a recommissioning after oppression.[23] And in South Africa, a country with thirteen official languages, English serves as a bridge between multiple tongues. Veering between two historical presences, language scatters the ashes of colonization and segregation and tortured tongues onto the stage, shifting between two linguistic bodies.

As a figure of political protest, Elektra—who sleeps at night on the grave of her father—symbolizes a historical experience, reflected in the political testimony of Margaret Madlana. After her son was killed by the police, this mother too slept where her son was buried. But that is not all. She plotted revenge, imagining that she would find work as a nanny at a white suburban household, then "poison the white man's children. The way they killed my son hitting him against a rock," she declared, "I will never forgive."[24] But in her testimony at the commission, she detailed her plot—an imagined revenge—and also repented of her murderous thoughts, stating, "I would like to apologize before God." But Elektra has a different transformation of sorrow. Her vengeance subsides because she receives political recognition: no apology, but a transfiguration because of collective respect for her loss.[25] Seated in front of a desk like the commission, she says, "hear these words, carve them on your heart that we may never forget" (62). She rhythmically weaves lament through two languages, a mournful mosaic of languages.

The play does not end with witnessing the torture of dark-skinned bodies. Rather, the end of the play relies on the chorus, typical of classical drama but unique in its function as part of the action of the play. Indeed, unlike the masked observer in classical tragedy, these women took action: they were an event in democratic development; as witnesses to the tragic past, they interceded in the play, literally interrupting violence. In this South African rendition, the choral group was a Xhosa singing group called *Ngqoko*. In the opening of the play, this group of women emerged from the audience and walked to the stage, where they sat in chairs to watch Klytemnestra and Elektra tell their stories at the commission, their singing ushering in the two protagonists. They removed a piece of black plastic from the stage, showing the open grave that was at the heart of the performance. "Blood has been spilt here," they sing, "*Ho laphalal' igazi*" (23). Definitely an agent of power, the group of singing women invited the possibility of democratic advocacy.

Creating a validating and safe space for Elektra to express her desire for revenge, these women also took the axe away from Elektra when she tried to kill her white mother. Screaming at the feminine chorus, Elektra yells, "don't ask me to forget my hatred! There can be no forgiveness!"

(83). Pushing against these strong women—raging in the midst of their democratic forum—she then weeps, and they hold her like a child. Elektra "finally breaks down," Farber wrote, "weeping for every injustice of the past" (85). Whispering "encouragements," the women continued until Elektra found a sense of "stillness" (85). The chorus—a symbol of the presence of a community of witnesses at South Africa's commission—compassionately recognized the survivor's pain: relating to Elektra, they were a conduit of pathos and communal response.

The song of the chorus is a haunting, deep-throated singing, *umngqokolo*, accompanied by a calabash and other instruments; for many Xhosa, it is a lost art form. When Yael Farber went to the rural Transkei to seek out a chorus, she selected the musical group of women. After telling them the story of Orestes and Elektra, the women responded with shock at the characters' desire to kill their mother: it was like a witch hunt against women, blaming them for all the political evil. Agreeing to participate in the play, the chorus of female musicians responded to events on stage through song.

Often, if it thought of this commission at all, the truth and reconciliation commission was conceived of in the Western world as silent hearings or logical discourse. But at the hearings I attended, the audience had an extraordinary effect: through vocalized responses, they were a real, palpable presence. For instance, when the police chief discussed the so-called black threat or when the commission showed a police video of shooting young black men, the disbelieving laughter or the raucous wails of inconsolable mothers quite literally stopped the proceedings. Or at least the audience response discomfited the perpetrator. There was also power in the compassionate whispers to the bereft mother, who described how she found the body of her son on fire from a gasoline-filled tire—a horrific necklace.

What happened in public spaces when the perpetrator heard an edgy, communal laughter, or the survivor listened to a collective sigh and could not find the source? The impossibility of visually locating every speaker and the sounds that they made within a crowded room created a distracting presence.[26] As the mind wanders through an audience in the hope of locating sources, perhaps the sounds are associated with compassion or condemnation? To use the theory of Casey O'Callaghan, sounds them-selves are "events" in public spaces.[27] So even while the commission was characterized by discordant memories, audiences—often as many as four hundred people, largely black South Africans—also adjudicated the various claims by sounding out their sentiments. Research suggests that when noise is not random, but rather structured by other people and their speech, speakers are distracted, attempting to locate the sounds.[28] Since this interruption cannot be identified in any single face, multiple voices of an audience were hard to mask—a communal reverberation within public territory was a political stance.

Sounds of a community—critical interruptions and emotional noises of support—were also reflected in the South African play *Molora*. But in this case, the importance of audience participation was embodied by the Xhosa women. When Klytemnestra went outside, she was frightened by the drumming rhythm of the choir and by the collective presence of the women, who walked toward the edge of the stage to watch her. She called out, "Who's there?" and then retreated (55). In this manner, the chorus interrupted the confident, narcissistic position of a perpetrator. The music—guttural singing, drums, a mouth harp—sounded out eth-ics: judging the perpetrator, supporting the survivor. It was emotionally affective, following the research of L. L. Balkwill and W. F. Thompson, because even as music evokes culturally specific associations, tempo and complexity have "psycho-physical" qualities that cross cultural divides.[29] Beating out a traumatic legacy, the drums played by the chorus—not unlike audience voices at the commission—symbolized the presence of women in public, who are "inassimilable, interruptive and present"—to use Ranjanna Khanna's definition of emotional resistance to oppression— a resounding reminder that people have a "right not to be exploited."[30]

When the chorus brought out a basin of water, Klytemnestra bathed her child, a sign that "mother and daughter commit to the process of unearthing the past" (25). However, after the cleansing scene, the tes-timonies were enacted. Klytemnestra demonstrated how she killed Agamemnon by chopping at a table with an axe. This scene with the table symbolized the witness stand for the truth and reconciliation commis-sion, and the chorus sang loudly when actors were near the table. Their voices added emotional resonance to the few sparse objects in the play. With loud sounds associated with the site of murder and the site of testimony, symbolized by the table, political and public spaces merged. Sound becomes an actor in its own right, reminding us that public protests are not just visual events; it is the sound of a crowd.

Not just political signs, sound and objects were symbols of the commission. When Klytemnestra attempted to sleep on the table, instead of on a soft bed, the discomfiture of the perpetrator's body was fully revealed, tossing back and forth with night terrors.[31] Lying on the table, she dreamt that the violent acts she has given birth to return again in the form of a mamba snake, which will kill her. These tables, likewise, resemble the simple town halls, the meeting places of the commission set within witnessing communities, where perpetrators were met with hostility. But just as the commission gives birth to the dark angst of perpetrators, so, too, does Farber show how this process of creating uneasiness can, in the end, unchain the perpetrator, returning her to a human state. But this limited release was only after a painful birthing process, the labor of delivering into words her nefarious deeds. When the mother's nightmare of giving birth to a snake begins, the female community, depicting an audience of witnesses, also served as midwives, helping to deliver the serpent of the past. After poignant testimonies, various experiences became accessible and identities were destabilized—what Noelle McAfee terms a "transformative effect" on political communities within democracy.[32] The commission staged reversals of power.

The women of the chorus carried the table and literally transported the mother, who was drunk with uneasiness; figuratively, they carried her into the public spotlight, onto center stage. Thus, these women of the chorus were presented as the central force at the commission, for they wield power over Klytemnestra, over the perpetrator. Sounding out when objects were being visually lit on stage had a syncretic effect because, like emotional touchstones, objects hold memories. The longing and loss people transfer onto their possessions is a striking force, suggests Peter Schwenger.[33] Objects mark personal property and identity, producing an aura; they reflect on their "previous owner," to use Schwenger's terms.[34] In this play, all characters, in a web of violence, pick up the axe. After Klytemnestra killed Agamemnon, Elektra threatened Klytemnestra with the axe, and Orestes used the axe to kill the usurping King Ayesthus. Originally, the axe was buried in the body of the table— a symbol of feasting, foul murder, bloody history.[35] But the body of the dead Agamemnon, chopped up at the site of the table, changed to an economic site of a later abundant feast, celebrating the supposed death of the terrorist son. Expected to be a space where families gathered to eat, Klytemnestra's table never included her daughter—the economics of racial exclusion. The drunken mother, feasting at the table, recalled grisly confessions of apartheid police at the commission who burnt bodies while they grilled meat and drank beer. Bloody economics. Embodied tragedies. Continuing cycles of national grief.

But the public chorus offered an alternative as a political and spiritual presence in a democracy. They responded to the tortured Other, interrupting the spinning discourse of bloodshed. Speaking of the commission, Farber detailed how the "journey" into democracy was "neither simple nor easy." It was not based on a miracle of "forgiving." Instead, this outcome was based on the commitment by South Africans to "face their perpetrators across a table" (7). And this democratic spring was heralded with the political sounds of a public chorus. These women represent a form of political and spiritual leadership, for two of the women are prophetic diviners—known in Zulu as *sangomas*. While they do not use actual trances, their prayers to ancestors call for an "end to the cycle of violence" (13). Invoking the protection of ancestors and extorting Orestes to protect his sister, they also stage the rite of passage for a young democracy. After initiation, Orestes is an adult who has the power to act. Selecting vengeance, he kills Ayesthus, his mother's lover, and the women berate the young man in Xhosa: "My child! Why do you kill? Do you know that human blood will haunt you always? What you have done is terrible. Never kill again" (76). The figure of reprimand is also a prophetic voice, channeling an ancestral spirit, and Orestes, uncertain if she is "real or a vision," drops to his knees, "stunned" (76). The basics of heroics have evolved away from vengeance and he panics, "we are lost!" (77). When Elektra takes the axe to finish the vengeful legacy, the women once again intercede. While the commission itself did not include the authority of these local healers, their power, often exercised in rural communities, is reclaimed in the play.

Politically, spiritually, culturally—*Molora* performed healing. It began with a quote from the commission. If reconciliation is when "this perpetrator, this man who has killed my son, if it means he becomes human again," stated Cynthia Ngwenyu, "so that I, so that all of us, get our humanity back," she paused, "then I agree, then I support it all" (7). Adding the touching words of this mother to our post-9/11 world, when can we "get our humanity back"? What might truth and reconciliation look like after 9/11? "If the war is against terrorism," Judith Butler admonished, and if we perceive terrorism in "every questionable instance of global difficulty," then how can the war end; or is it, by definition, a war without end, given the lability of a war against our fears?[36] In South Africa, the world anticipated a civil war, wherein the "rage of generations shattered the apartheid regime"(7); however, witnessing connected survivors to their community, creating an important forum for democracy—what McAfee identified as a "space of political humanity."[37] Unlike the ashes of the Twin Towers that fell on prisons, wars, assassinations, and torture, in *Molora* the final ashes descended on both perpetrators and survivors, who reconceived their past in a present painful conversation. Contrasting the "peaceful transition into democracy" of South Africa to the Western offensive against Iraq, Farber charted out her vision of cultural reconciliation: the "shattered history of South Africa will take generations to heal"; yet, public spaces, like the commission, begin this voicing process (9). Articulation is directly linked to democratic agency, for Farber urged audiences to view "speaking and being heard" as a "modest but profound beginning" (9). After the first democratic elections, it was the citizens who faced their perpetrators, who found a "way forward for us all" (7). Not following the balding eagle of unending war, the final image of this homeland in *Molora* is that of a phoenix rising up from the ashes, recovering from the past, unfolding its democratic wings.

8 | Bewitched Democracies

A Ritual Spring for Youth Culture?

There is, indeed, some urgency in arriving at a closer understanding of this strange convergence of witchcraft and the
modern.

—Peter Geschiere, *Sorcery in the Black Atlantic*

Throughout this book, I have been discussing hurting and healing in
the breadth of single chapters. This chapter, focused on two South
African plays directed by Brett Bailey, also probes how historical injuries
are presented in mass media and in public spaces. But this chapter is a
challenge. Analyzing ritual drama in South Africa within the paradigm
of cultural spring enters divided turf and forbidden territory: for *Ipi
Zombi?* and *Mumbo Jumbo* expose how women heal with divinations
of history, even as women are the most frequent targets when accused
of sorcery. It is a challenge to cross cultural lines to explain these ritual
dramas. Perhaps I could describe how intelligent friends of mine have
sought out healers to speak of their collective histories, even though
my Western readers will be unable to relate to the healer—to the powerful black woman who throws bones on the floor. What language is
capable of explaining how these ritual dramas conceive of democracy,
money, healing, and witchcraft on a single stage? Perhaps I am bereft of
language that can speak to you—not the magical language of broom-
sticks, wands, and Harry Potter, not the ugly Halloween costume of a
despised Western woman with warts and knotty hair. Not at all. Seek,

rather, a language for rituals: communal expressions with vast numbers of participants.

While this chapter concentrates on two ritual dramas as a way to consider how African spiritual expression works toward healing in young democracies, my work cannot ignore how frustrations over economics in a young republic have also ignited spiritually clad forms of violence. But first, these ritual dramas require a hefty background to explain how some youth have associated the birth of democracy in South Africa not as the miracle of Mandela, but rather as the mystery of witchcraft. A year after the first democratic elections, one of the primary South African newspapers, *The Mail and Guardian*, recorded how a number of accused witches were murdered. The families of these "witches" had to flee into exile: "social outcasts in a region where superstition still reigns supreme."[1] But mass media—with its derisive label of superstition—only recorded part of this history. When the president publicized that it should be a human right for everyone to have a house—in a land emptied by white racist policies of forced removals—black South Africans felt frustrated after these elections when there was no apparent home or economic change in their lives. And one year after the first elections, after these brave words that democracy would usher in a human rights package that included economics, so, too, in 1995, did the witch hunts of Kokstad begin.[2]

During the dawn of democracy, youths visited villages and offered to exterminate witches, to eradicate "elements of tradition and superstition" that were blocking "political freedom" and democratic development.[3] This cascading violence of youths did not begin the year after elections; rather, it started escalating when the demise of the regime was evident yet the elections were not quite settled. During this four-year transitional period, several trials that prosecuted witchcraft killings documented 455 witchcraft cases, many of them involving the killing of elderly people.[4]

Modern witchcraft is associated not only with democratic opportunities, but also with material goods. When there is no development of the economy, when little wealth is to be had, witchcraft is viewed as the impediment; part of the "modernity" of these beliefs is their exposure of "socioeconomic" challenges or "changes," to echo Peter Geschiere's terms.[5] If you live in an area characterized by relative impoverishment and a neighbor accumulates great wealth, there is a sinking suspicion that blood has been spilt to acquire such disproportionate income. When attacked by a sudden disease after a neighbor seemed to give you the evil eye or cast a jealous look at your body or belongings, suspicions grow. In South Africa, where a small group of blacks and whites drive BMWs, there is a frustrated economic tension, for wealth within communities is supposed to be shared for the survival of all. These spiritual beliefs are adaptive, not fixed: so when Nelson Mandela promised more houses and jobs, the blame was fixed not on their beloved political leader, but instead transferred to local so-called witches, accursed forces against a youthful democratic spring.[6]

In a brave reenactment of these witch hunts only three short years after the killings, the South African director Brett Bailey worked with local diviners to perform a ritual invocation of this history, a play whose Xhosa title, *Ipi Zombi?*, questions the presence of witches and zombies.[7] Following the trail of Bailey's extraordinary ritual dramas—traveling to high-brow theaters, rural stages on outdoor veldts, and frequent enactments at the National Festival in South Africa over the past decade and a half—I have watched these dramas set the stage for an energetic political voicing of local healers and township actors. These ritual dramas suggest a spirited, alternative way of knowing—a communal structure outside of Western epistemologies, unhampered by the colonizing discourse of white reason—the recognition of a groundswell of *sangomas* and ensorcelled belief in a young democracy. In many ways, the plays express divided forms of spiritual healing and public violence as a sign of an excess of political emotion—not a simple cage of cognitive ideas about historical loss, but rather frustrated aspirations for democracy and economic opportunity. While Western media have paid attention to the killing of witches, there has been little in the press on the healers—the *sangomas* of South Africa. Derailing dismissive stereotypes of African mysticism, these dramas challenge Western notions of political spirit, especially when conceived on popular stages as a bewitched democracy in need of cultural healing—a *ritualized spring*.

Ipi Zombi? (Are There Zombies?)

In this first play, the drama unravels the angry response of a group of youth reacting to the deaths of their classmates, killed when their school bus crashed. Entering onto this theater space, young male actors vehemently protest, "do you see how we die like flies?" (74). In this play, these boys believe that a witch caused the accident and turned the dead youth into zombies. In this cosmology, witches steal the life from other people: they can turn others into zombies, who will accomplish their bidding, working without wages. Victims—forced to work as zombies—take on the identity of the witch's assistant, losing their sense of self. When I asked one of my friends to explain zombies, he said that in the Transkei, during the state of emergency in the eighties, hundreds of people changed personalities, stopped seeing their families, turned into zombies. Later that year in 1998, I watched a truth and reconciliation hearing, wherein the weeping perpetrator spoke of being kidnapped by the secret police, tortured, and forced to work for the state, never to see his family again. In effect, my friend was right. He diagnosed a traumatizing form of power—an accurate epistemology. However, people had been robbed of their identities because the nefarious force of the state had consumed them—not local witches.

But in *Ipi Zombi?* these youth protest not only the crash site of sorcery but also the "hunger of the mothers. Eating us alive" (74). Why would youth, angry about a school bus crash, be angry with their mothers? This incensed protest—voicing frustration with gender authority and their own sense of being socially consumed—coincided with research on witch hunts in contemporary South Africa. In the Western world, we often conceive of older women—those no longer adorned with external charms of youth, to whom you give your seat to on the bus—as powerless, in need of assistance. But this misconception is not present in South Africa, where women are powerful, especially when they are older, and they exert tremendous moral sway and control over economic and social capital—so much so that discontented youths imagine these women as a supernatural distortion, stealing communal resources while many men struggle to find work.

One example of how women and power are associated comes from Adam Ashforth's work, where he researches the "insecurity" of witchcraft in regard to a gang in Soweto.[8] He tells of a dangerous thug who terrorizes school children and is killed by mob justice—and then the mother is sought after, the witch who let this child have such dark power. In the center of this violence, extreme economic tensions exist with no easy release valve. Paradigms of poverty, gender, power, and democracy are not separate planes, but enmeshed, emotional vehicles. My own journey to understand these modern practices are through attending ritual dramas. And then there was my own experience—the time I was called a witch.

It happened several years ago, when a well-educated black psychologist—a twenty-something young man dedicated to his work—asked if he could attend one of my follow-up interviews with members of *Khumbulani* several years after I had facilitated those performances. Listening attentively to my questions, to the open responses by one of my participants, he then followed up with engaging questions about how I had structured the initial performance workshop. Later, he described his own important work with survivors and their children. So I was completely taken off guard afterward when he asked me if I was a witch. It was not a threat, for there was a trace of a jesting smile on his face. Yet the unswerving look in his eyes made it clear that he expected a response. Surprised, I glanced away from the therapist and over at Monwa, who had worked with me in the *Khumbulani* drama, with a questioning look, trying to gage how Monwa interpreted this question. In the township, I know what they do to women who exceed the bounds of power through unnatural means. From Monwa, however, there was no sign that he was nonplussed; after all it was a common-enough question—nothing dangerous. Then I looked back at the therapist. "What do you mean?" I asked. Continuing to smile, but watching me closely, he was curious how I had started an important performance that worked as group therapy to assist traumatized people in healing and built eight houses in a week in the urban squalor of Khayaleshia. No one else had done what I had accomplished, so he wanted to know how I had this kind of power. I quickly explained that every other year I brought college students to the township to work with Habitat for Humanity on a building project; there were many hands at work on these houses, including the family members. He was satisfied. But for me, it was the most threatening compliment I have ever received.

Watching *Ipi Zombi?*—a performance of witch hunts that questions if there are zombies—four years after the first democratic elections, I also felt unnerved. It was performed in an abandoned power plant, where the woman next to me cried during the last half of the show. Afterward, when I asked her if she was alright, she said that she knew one of the women who had been killed in Kokstad, so it was a very emotional experience for her. The terror of the woman killed—staged as a sympathetic death—was performed alongside the modern fury of youth who expressed violent angst about road blocks to their success in Mandela's promised land.

Anxious hopes about the young democracy emerged in the ritual drama of *Ipi Zombi?* The youth gang that killed older women imagined that these women were turning teenage boys into zombies, taking away their vital strength, controlling their actions, killing their potential and consuming their flesh. But the young are not the only political voice in this ritual drama. In fact, the director started this play by inviting women who were diviners to invoke the ancestors, consulting the elders of the past about these witch hunts. Their voices provoked a different image of spiritual hunger: the "country is struggling" in these "hungry times"; the "rich are eating the poor, the dead are eating the living!" (44). In effect, the play spoke of a second form of political appetite, the state of unfulfilled need in South Africa. There were divided cosmologies within the play: the female diviners were called in to render the past—emotive forms of releasing the pain of the past for their community—but their views on social problems did not accuse the women of witchcraft. Their perspective did not replicate those of the youth, who felt consumed by hard times, like this paradigm of living death—the child-zombie. To escape social dismay—feeling dominated by authority figures in an inescapable economic ghetto—the helplessness of poverty was repositioned as a powerful battle against spiritual forces.

The modality of these healers suggested a distinct kind of ethical system and healing. For these women, unlike Western views of humanity

with its solipsistic individual, wherein I think therefore I am, their practice of *ubuntu* conceived of ethical existence in community; I am human
because of my actions toward others. In many African belief systems,
the ancestors, when they were unhappy about the ethics of their living
progeny, returned as uneasy spirits. They haunted the dreams of their living ancestors. Ancestors warned their relatives of trouble, a voice of conscience, and they protected the living, a kind of guardian angel, but only
relatives. If one harmed others, injuring members of the community, bad
luck would befall, because there were no guardian spirits to intercede on
one's behalf. Thus, it was a mode of justice: not just a respectful model of
a moral grandfather, long dead, but rather a grinding stone for ethics, for
there were consequences for harming or betraying others.

When a client approached a healer, the diviner gave advice on contemporary problems by taking on the voice of a well-respected elder in a
trancelike evocation; it was advice from beloved relatives who have passed
away. So unlike Western psychoanalysis, where we will sit for hours with
counselors who do not know us, trying to assess the current problem and
how it was triggered by past experience, the modern diviner in a village
knows her client, as well as the client's relatives, some living, some dead.
Even as theorists from Sigmund Freud to Kai Erikson have examined
the ways traumatic events are based in earlier experiences or community
displacements—uncanny forms for individuals or social problems within
a community—*sangomas* use ritual to engage with a current crisis and
consider past associations of family. But they also give advice that considers the overall social health of their community.

I understand why Westerners struggle with local healers and their
alternative medicines, even though many of us will seek out Chinese herbs
and acupuncture when we are tired of our Western ways of cutting or pre-
scribing one more antibiotic. But can we truly rename cultural practices
as "postcolonial science," following Sandra Harding's corrective, after
centuries of dismissing the "knowledge systems" of non-Western cultures
as magical, "irrational," superstitious, and positively "pre-modern"?[9]
What happens when we follow local healers into this fraught modernity,
pursuing these women, not the modern state nor academic histories, as
our primary guides?

Perhaps it is easier to follow in the footsteps of an insightful anthropologist, Adam Ashforth, who called for justice, especially after a close friend, living in the urban sprawl and economically challenging site of Soweto, was accused of witchcraft. The stress of the accusation brought on a stroke, which killed her. The anthropologist diagnosed a problematic gulf between the judicial system of a modern state, arraigning through evidence as logical proof, and communal justice, prosecuting based on magical evidence that is unacceptable in any state court of law.[10] How can we follow *healers*—Harding's postcolonial scientists—alongside *witch-hunters*—Ashforth's postcolonial threat to democracy—in a single play, in a single search for democratic practices?

In *Ipi Zombi?* Brett Bailey asked local diviners to invoke the ancestors, to find out more about this unhealed site of witch killings. But this director has an unconventional approach to history and to theater, since he was not content to use professional actors, whom he considered elite, especially after growing up in the racially charged atmosphere of the state of emergency in South Africa. Instead, after his university training in theater, he apprenticed with a *sangoma* diviner, living in her small village, attending ritual initiations. He also studied masking rituals in Nigeria. For these two plays of *Miracle and Wonder*, Bailey selected Xhosa participants from remote villages or the urban ghettos of townships as the actors and agents. Through workshops, the group of diviners and local actors used ritual trance to invoke historical events. This process inspired the play—an extraordinary theater tactic, an experience-based protest of violence—a political identification outside of Western views.

But in his journal notes, which were published by a South African press alongside the scripts of *Miracle and Wonder*, there were also signs of Bailey's interpretation of community reactions, which suggest a measure of distance from supernatural belief. On route to a performance, their minibus slid off the road. One cast member, who played the role of an accused witch, yelled out. "This is a message from our ancestors about what we are doing!" (77). In response, Bailey rejoined, "No, this is the result of going around a sharp corner," especially traveling at high speed in the rain (77). The tension resided in the interpretations: two ways of looking at what happened in the past, both presented in the play.

But even before the director began his ritual-based workshops, he had interviewed members of the Kokstad community, unearthing their opinions about the killings. The initial event—the crash of the school bus that killed fifteen soccer players—had many interpreters. Some claimed the driver was drunk and fell asleep, but one young survivor stated that he had seen fifty witches on the side of the road, which fueled local hysteria, swelling through the ranks of young men, erupting in three murders. One of the slain was the mother of a young man in his twenties, who responded to the death: "My mother was not a witch. I never saw a snake or even a bird inside her room, there's no proof" (30). So while the son believed in witchcraft, he also believed his mother was innocent and cited the lack of magical objects as evidence. It is a hybrid stance: combining the language of evidence, similar to that of a modern trial system, alongside the language of mystical powers, where animals are "proof." Animals are not taken as indicators of nature's bounty, but as distorted signs of malevolence: an intriguing indicator given the ways that natural resources and land have been used in the apparatus of colonization and segregation—an era of exploitation, the equivalent of ethnic cleansing. For this young son, the unresolved loss of his mother created melancholy, for he continues to live in this community where his peers killed an important provider of income and a beloved member of his family.

Such volatile responses were as prolific as stars in the night sky—while a white farmer dismissed the incident as African nonsense, a frustrated youth saw his group as "moral guardians of a community" (32). Churches were also divided: some churches not believing in satanic embodiments; others including church diviners who cast out the demonic in the name of the Holy Spirit or even participated in the witch hunts. These hybrid churches were stunned at the "proliferation of witches" in the Bhongweni township of Kokstad. Other churches were aghast at the "community's plunge into paganism," for they did not believe in witches (33). Meanwhile, the courts charged eight young men with the murder of three women. Many of the youths, soon to be imprisoned for up to twenty-five years, reported to Bailey that they felt justified in their actions of communal cleansing: the Christians want to "bury those dead and just forget; the police they do nothing, they just drive around in their big cars, so who is going to stop these witches? We want a clean society" (32). So the authorities were divided in this: religious splits, generational divides, state police, and youth justice in a bewitched cosmology.

Democratic tensions were also suggested in an interview with the Kokstad police. When Bailey asked Sergeant Ndindwe if there were "ethical difficulties" in arrests and jail sentences—especially when the township felt "threatened by elements not acknowledged by law"—he scowled in response and did not answer allegations that police officers were part of the mob that killed the women (32). Then, after a pause, Sergeant Ndindwe stated that he was first and foremost bound to the "law of the land," and there must be "stiff penalties," especially when hooligans—so-called *tsotsis* who are full of social resentment—"fan the witch-fears to their advantage" (32). There were two reasons given here: First and foremost, the federal law of the democratic state must be followed. But an interesting second answer dissected the disrupted social order. Rebellious youth have become powerful agents over and above their elders. Women die. The old structure of village authority is killed—in effect, after the economic profits of South Africa were stolen by British colonizers (first), then by white Afrikaners during apartheid (second), then things fall apart.

Social disintegration, after racist economics, took an intergenerational form. Shortly after the death of these school children, a ten-year-old girl told other youth about her fears that she heard zombies locked in her grandmother's cupboards, and as the story traveled along, the crowd congregated and began to beat the old woman, Mrs. Magudu. The young girl was at the scene, and she related how her grandmother "just prayed to God, and said I don't know nothing" (31). Eventually the crowd killed her grandmother. "These witches must be killed because they will kill us all," said a key assailant, a young man named Senti, whom Bailey interviewed (32). The youth repeatedly spoke of being forced into a zombie state. The "insatiably hungry" witches referred to their desire to consume all resources, including living souls and dead corpses, as Ralph Austen postulates, to garner more power.[11] In this perspective, women were deemed "selfish individuals" because of their "dangerous appropriation of limited reproductive resources," and Austen connected this to a lack of tolerance to women's success and authority, which was seen as spiritually deviant in a "moral economy" that jealously hoarded scanty resources and opportunities for its men.[12] Women were eradicated, not just as a scapegoat, but also as a backlash, since the youth viewed their local authorities as decaying structures that have "closed [their] eyes to the actual source of the disorder destroying it"; this political protest against impotent structures had redefined these "guardians" of the black township (32)—a bloody spring of power at the cost of women's lives.

Increasingly frustrated while waiting for democratic elections, these young men have cast aside traditional responses. In the past, a rigid hierarchy of respected diviners and chiefs decided who the witches were and exiled them from the village, not necessarily killing them.[13] So these youth witch-hunters have defiled a vast social system of authority, creating their own political system—not exiling, but rather adjudicating and killing women whom they have deemed witches. It was a bloody political uprising, a popular protest against antiquated structures and hoped-for democratic change—a gendered upheaval. After a century and a half of racist legislation, deemed the official state system, these youth have constructed their own form of justice, their own structure of violent hope.[14]

In contrast to youth-led riots, the ritualized performance of *Ipi Zombi?*—concocted in a workshop with the local authority of *sangoma* women, actors from nearby townships, and the adventurous vision of the director—did not merely repeat the youth cry for political power and economic opportunity. The play critiqued political violence even as it affirmed the spiritual cosmology of ancestral wisdom. It was not a repeat of the traditional tale wherein witches enslaved people as zombies or killed people to brew black magical powers. Instead, the spirit of darkness that devoured the village was the spirit of social violence. A tragic history devoured its inhabitants. A hunger for violence emerged out of the dark "forest" and came into the "town to eat," and in "turning the people against each other, making children to kill their own mothers" (44). In the director's stage notes, he explained how theater "unravels conflict" (44), and how the main acting area was a "symbol of psyche" that fleshed out frustrations (42). This strategy uncovered discontent and deaths at the dawn of democracy.

The actors also saw this play as a form of collective hunger: they called the play a documentation of a time period of "sickness" during which no one knew "how to heal it" (73). A century of a racist regime's oppression and economic devastation had left their ancestors unappeased, which is why there were "hungry ghosts" (73). These starving phantoms—social symbols of colonization, segregation, and feudal hoarding of wealth—haunt current democratic structures. Given the history of racist economics and ghetto-like entrapment, these sentiments of hopelessness were invoked by the witch hunts. Disempowered youth found a sense of social agency. This is a "story of power!" the youth chant. "This is our power!" (73). In a scene of extraordinary emotion, a mother cried out to God before she was killed with an axe, while the teenagers chanted their anger: the frequency of death, the young swallowed alive "bones and all" (74). The powerless became spiritual chiefs. It was a furious spring.

Only a few feet in front of me, a woman in the audience screamed as the youth killed the mother, and I watched, one of many in a largely black audience, packed together, sitting on hay bales and informal bleachers. What struck me was the way that the dark forces of evil were presented; not as mere superstitions, but as real, so that the gangs acted the part of sincere agents against witchcraft. At the same time, in the death of the innocent mother was an injustice; the street justice of youth was dangerous, problematic. Such ritual drama created a charged atmosphere, which Bailey recorded in his journal of audience responses to the question and answer session after the play. "We know we are going to die," one audience member commented, "so why must you make a drama about it?" (82). Others also expressed anxiety about witchcraft: "Aren't you afraid of these things? They should be left alone" (82). At times, ritual drama drew unexpected responses—disconcerting laughter from one or two audience members during the violent killing of the mother. "Drama releases emotions," stated Bailey, and the laughter was a nervous anxiety amidst audience members who have witnessed so much violence (80).

Strident responses also emerged when the show traveled to rural areas: "Every weekend we bury children in this village," one spectator told a cast member. There are several "witches here" (77). In Bailey's journal, he recorded how one street corner performance had "shocked black spectators," to the point that the crowd "threatened violence" (78). They stopped the show. In another desolate venue, performing in front of the headlights of his pickup truck, Bailey felt uneasy about the crowd because the division between "reality and illusion" seemed different in this space, with this audience (77). Envisioning a crowd following the performance that moved toward an old woman's hut, prepared to kill the suspected witch, Bailey instructed his narrator to change the last line of the play from a general statement about evil to a specific judgment that this is a ghastly history that should "not be repeated" (77). In fact, later on, their Kokstad performances were cancelled because they received phone calls from relatives of "suspected witches" who were frightened that it would ignite a "reprisal of the killings" (77).

Reactions to the play ranged from nervous laughter to fear to African critics' praise of the play's social brilliance. Since spirituality in the play was never the object of mockery, but rather the lens through which to view the events, this approach has elicited both commendations and controversy. John Matshikiza, a young journalist working for an urban press, found the plays a "collective catharsis"—reaching into a subliminal space that touches the raw nerves [Bailey] is aiming at, to provoke us out of our lethargy"(7); an important performance for South African citizens, whose nation was in danger of breaking up on the "reefs of its own history at any moment."[15] While most black critics viewed the play in terms of its importance as a new theater strategy, other reviewers and audience members saw this ritualized theater as a presentation of African spirituality. In *The Sowetan*, Solomon Makgale claimed that the ritual drama is not "fictitious, but figurative, an authentic reflection of the power of African spirituality."[16] The belief system of the spectator influenced the interpretation: while some focused on spirituality, others labeled it a portrait of the social impact of superstition.[17] After attending one of the shows, the famous playwright and writer Zakes Mda adulated: *Ipi Zombi?* is a "work of genius that maps out a path to a new South African theatre that is highly innovative in its use of indigenous performance modes." Local beliefs and historical events are "redefined in a most creative manner that leaves one breathless."[18]

These responses to ritual-infused theater challenged mass media headlines with their archaic rhetoric of witch hunts. By performing the memories of a community in a drama of smoky ritual, raucous song, charged dialogue, the enactment had cast a portrait of a nascent democracy, ensorcelled by the effluvium of a violent history. After slaughtering a chicken, the diviners fell into trances in the first few minutes of the drama, invoking an emotional legacy. They summoned the emotive roots of history. Not the Western word, which we bind in book-weary form. And in this dramatic invocation of murder, I sat next to a woman who shook uncontrollably, weeping for her slaughtered friend. Stunned? No, bewitched. These *sangomas* transformed me into a witness of a community's unresolved loss. The play conjured a spell-binding form of democracy—still shaking free from the devilish history of colonization, land grabs, racist courts, and profiteering thefts.

Mumbo Jumbo

In the second play of Bailey's ritual-based series *Miracle and Wonder*, we were led into a different historical space. Translating the force of this drama, I try to imagine what would happen if one of our nation's central political leaders, perhaps George Washington, were defeated in battle— and then his body decapitated, his skull taken to another country as a war prize—which was what happened in South Africa. In 1836, the British murdered the Xhosa King Hintsa and took his head as a trophy to Britain. Two years after democratic elections, Chief Nicholas Gcaleka attempted to retrieve the skull from Britain. While mass media in South Africa were cynical of this quest to trace out the dead and mocked this journey, in contrast, Chief Gcaleka believed that the return of the skull would cure some of the current violence among the Xhosa, since the ghostly king's unhappy spirit was causing damage to the living. In short, the return of the skull was a spiritual and symbolic sign of the Xhosa taking back their identity, ancestry, and power from white dominators, traced all the way back to former British colonizers. But no one knew where the skull was. The unresolved loss of the king's head and this modern attempt at reclaiming a powerful collective identity were the subjects of the second ritual drama, *Mumbo Jumbo*.

In the play, we follow the path of a male *sangoma*, known as Chief Gcaleka, who admonished that black South Africans were losing their cultural identity. He claims that the diminished respect for local authority was leading to a careless and chaotic second generation—a lost youth culture. The only way to deal with the "dire state of social turmoil," Gcaleka contends, was to locate the skull of Hintsa and to return to "traditional values" (94). Chief Gcaleka's actual words, extracted from hours of recorded interviews, formulate the script, and the *sangoma's* spiritual beliefs, taken from these testimonial recordings, suggested that transformation in South Africa's modern democracy could occur only with the return to a cultural and spiritual basis of authority. This spiritual transformation would empower everyone, not just the Xhosa, because the ancestral spirits "want peace" (111). Having abandoned its spiritual and cultural roots, the modern state was a melancholic democracy.

The state history of defeat by the white colonizers, often written in textbooks, was revised by Gcaleka, and this revision was performed under Bailey's direction. The loss of the past was not because of the British, but because of the Xhosa. After one of the Xhosa kings drowned, the next historical King Khawutu did not request the Xhosa kingship back from the river spirits. According to Gcaleka, when the spirits began their rebellion against the people, this spiritual movement allowed the British to jail his son Hintsa, and then take King Hintsa's head (111). It was the fault of the Xhosa father, then; it was not the fault of the British, Gcaleka announces. Subverting Western history, the spiritual world took action not against the British, but against the Xhosa king (111). Instead of following history textbooks, which encapsulated that the more advanced weaponry, alongside a technological machinery of laws and imperial writing, allowed the British soldiers to subdue the Xhosa nation, it became a story of the Xhosa, who were the most powerful forces because of their ancestral connection. The Xhosa, in effect, fell because they did not follow their spiritual guides. In a parallel fashion, the modern problems of the state could be solved by returning to spiritual guidance and ancestral beliefs. This attempt to bring hope to contemporary South Africa was in the midst of "corruption, violence, poverty, AIDS, and dissatisfaction" (156). The modern ailment that this drama responded to in a form of neotribalism wove spiritual signs into amulets of political hope, collective loss, and rural melancholy.

South Africa was a dismal democracy, stated Gcaleka, because the modern state of justice advocated against black South African youth, without consulting local forums for discipline. For instance, when a teenage Xhosa boy raped an older woman, he was sentenced to fifteen years in prison. Instead of locking this teenager in a cell, Gcaleka wanted to reinstate local discipline based in a community of black elders: a spiritual inquiry, not a civic trial, to find out what was wrong with this young man's spirit, and to teach him about the ethics of the ancestors. The melancholy about democracy was that the federal government had taken over all authority, diminishing tribal authority. This disintegration of community ethics, according to this healer, was evident in high rates of gang rape; for sexual violence was a sign that elder and ancestral-based moral systems were no longer popular with the second generation.

So the skull became a sign of lost pride in national history. The play reenacted Gcaleka's trip to Scotland, where, based on his dream, he went to a farm and asked about a skull, which the Scottish family produced. Returning to South Africa, other Xhosa chiefs, perhaps concerned over Gcaleka's growing influence, handed the skull over to forensic specialists, who declared it was not Chief Hintsa's skull, but rather that of a Caucasian woman. The debate over the legitimacy of the skull became yet another form of loss—a local authority diminished. What was often regarded as hard science, with its nonemotive, noncommunal forms of knowing, took away the spiritual authority of the tribal heritage. As the play chastised, "Before you white people came with the professionals," the local healers were the professionals, and no one could "take that away!" (109). In this situation, when authority was solely grounded in imperial ideas of observation-based reasoning, other ways of knowing were discounted. In his performance notes, Bailey wrote that Gcaleka was responding to a deep need for "stability in uncertain times," and it reclaimed "power from the nation's colonial subjugators" (100). When the South African research hospital refused to return the skull, the domination became even more blatant; the white scientists and the hospital administration placed the skull on display as a curiosity. It was a second humiliating form of domination, another exposé of white power over local ways of understanding history and healing.

So the real tragedy of this play was not just King Hintsa's murder, or the subjugation of the Xhosa when diseases introduced by whites destroyed their cattle, leading to famine, or when almost all of their land was stolen in the ruthless Land Act of 1913, but rather the continual tragedy of the rejected authority of spiritual leaders and ancestral ethics for generations to come. "European expansion suppressed or destroyed—intentionally and unintentionally—competitive local knowledge systems," historicized Harding.[19] And it was this imperial domination over the diviner's postcolonial science that continued. The tragedy of this cultural collision, according to Bailey, was that the "sacred quest for self and national actualization" was demeaned by people in power, who overrate their importance and lack "imagination" (100). The relic recalled not only violence, since the ground zero of the past was the terrain of a skull, a symbol of ethical and political identifications, declared as sacred space.

What has become sacred space was also political, and this performance raised great debate. Although the popular reviewer Robert Greig praised the play for showing a "neglected way of seeing and experiencing" that appealed to the "powerless, the marginalized, the rural conservatives," he was troubled by the play's "attack on rationality in the South African state."[20] In contrast, Karen Makgamathe commented that these characters "tackle the evils in our society," which the play claims were caused by "people losing their roots, forgetting their ancestors and moving towards a western way of life."[21] The modern state, promising hope through reason, courts, and discipline, has run roughshod over the ancestral framework, where hope came through teaching the young about their culture and its core values.

But the tension was not a simple dichotomy between black urban and rural patterns of life, nor between local culture and the modern state; rather, there was real ambivalence about the mixture of cultural and scientific, African and external beliefs—contemporary hybridity. In a case study of forty-nine responses to a performance of *Mumbo Jumbo* conducted by several researchers with students from the University of the

Western Cape, tensions in interpreting the play showed identifications of "cultural insiders and outsiders."[22] Responses ranged from feeling connected to African culture in a "transformative" play to urban alienation felt because of the distinct culture (202). Many students thought the play validated local culture; they called it a great way of "educating others," for it was "cathartic and reconciliatory and healing" (202). Thus the play showed "alternative cultural knowledge," and responses revealed an ongoing negotiation of identity, concluded the researchers (193). Many university students—politically called "the rainbow nation"—struggled with cultural affiliations and hybrid spiritualties, especially as scientific reasoning also works as a relic of imperialism.

The play created discomfort for some viewers because the spiritual identifications acknowledged Xhosa ancestors, the hurricane spirit, and Jesus Christ. A few students who themselves were "straddling two cultural traditions" felt "embarrassed" (202) because the play displayed a merger of African spirituality and Christianity, set in contrast to Western science. But within these criticisms, some valorized the play as the "best" and most "real story I ever watched" (195). For others, the spiritual aspects were foremost: the setting was "transporting me or taking my soul to the deep Transkei," the area outside the formerly white apartheid-controlled cities, an area where "I belong, where my roots are waiting for me to come [home] from the world of science" (195). When Gcaleka divined the location of the skull, he claimed that Christ had shown him the way to this farm in Scotland. This hybrid belief contends that Jesus is the first ancestor, and one's own ancestors are also heavenly mediators.[23] But ancestors turn away if believers harm others in the community.[24] Unfortunately, some church denominations—claiming to be more "modern"—reject ancestral-based African Christianity. But this division places further strain on spiritually hybridized identities who have found a language of grace that embraces two ways of knowing.

This ritual drama suggested tension between local leaders, *sangomas*, and secular state authorities: a loss of centralized tribal authority after democratic federalism. Traditional leaders (like *amakhosi* chiefs) felt threatened by regional elections in rural areas like Transkei, Ciskei, and KwaZulu Natal. Research showed how their control over land allocation, fine collection in tribal courts, and decisions in structural development were challenged by the new democracy; many leaders urged their constituents not to register as voters. Such tension did the "inadequate definition of the future role of traditional leaders" in the new democracy cause that Nelson Mandela visited with various leaders and eventually promised to pay salaries to these leaders to "ensure political loyalty."[25] Nonetheless, this dismissal of tribal authority—first by colonization, then by apartheid, and once again by federal democracies—created multiple loyalties. However, neotribal identities, while melancholically gazing at the loss of former power, are still extremely modern; they are similar to Islamic modernists, who desire to "revive Islamic thought both by affirming continuity with the past" and integrating technology and western types of political organization.[26] In *Mumbo Jumbo*, rural modernists desired nostalgic associations in order to influence youth gangs: a contemporary hope for local jurisdiction, a branching out of democratic federalism, alongside acceptance of democracy and territorial lines of the larger nation-state.

So even though the play challenges spectators about the "paradoxes of South African modernity," Bailey's ritual performance validated cultural traditions, claims Linda Tini, a participant in the ritual drama.[27] Incorporating testimonials by community members, Bailey's investigation of traumatic events through workshops with *sangomas* is healing. Enacting the past, these healers applied their ritual to historical situations—a creative response, to use Margaret Thompson Drewal's theories of ritual.[28] As this ritual drama divulged multiple perspectives, hybrid beliefs, and a modern catharsis for communities, it functioned as a democratic forum for marginalized memories. While using rituals validated an African paradigm—what Temple Hauptfleisch described as hybrid theater—Bailey used different language.[29] Uniquely documenting rural histories in a distinctive space of controversy and ritualized epistemologies, these public sites, collecting emotion about past events, summon a regional "imagination" and a "collective unconscious."[30] These public spaces of theater offer alternative ways of knowing that could be adapted into democratic practice. Perhaps new democracies could invite alternative visions, for instance a female *sangoma* from rural Transkei, to participate in deciding which community problems need to be funded with government monies, inviting controversy and democratic debate, sharpening the usual white-coated thinking of solutions and concerns of varied communities.[31] The space of ritual recognizes communal tensions and historical conflicts that continue to define and haunt young democracies. Given the undertow of the Western world—unseen economic and epistemological riptides—the imperial streams that feed this groundswell are not easily parched. But this devastatingly deep well is also a replenishing current for political protest—waters for an *eternal spring*.

Conclusion

Looking for Fadwa

This spring is "widespread, it's sincere, and it cannot be put back in the bottle. . . . We just have to be realistic about time frames. I'm not saying it will take us 800 years, like it took you in the West, but at least we need more than a few months."
—Rami Khouri, Beirut Professor, 2011

More than a mere twitter on the global screen of Western media, the Arab and African Spring provides a window into democratic desire. Not just a sign-up sheet for protest, the Facebook pages and public stages personify a sentimental citizenship, a communal voicing. Often part of a youthful movement, these testimonial sites of desire pointedly redirect Western media, engaging us with multiple, creative permutations. Such political springs bloom in the massive participation of African township dwellers at the truth and reconciliation commission and in the Arab youth blogs that call for spring, even as they have protested injustices and advocated for economic opportunities. These alternative locations and innovative forms, alongside their widespread audiences, although not necessarily a recent phenomenon, have caught our attention. Changing our usual view of the Arab and African other as the object of our terror and terrorizing policies after 9/11, perhaps, after a decade of frosty imperialism, it may also be springtime for Western thought. Listening to these voices, we can celebrate global creativity: gendered landscapes of popular uprisings and political revolt.

194

This political tide is "widespread" and "cannot be put back in the bottle," claimed Rami Khouri, but we "have to be realistic about time frames."[1] Challenging assumptions about time and political transformations, *Performing Democracy* has questioned when we begin this drive toward democracy, whose voices we authorize, and what we expect. Protest is a living, moving, national monument—of varying sizes and clashing perspectives—suggesting transition out of autocracy and atrocity, curling around street corners, sung from stages and public squares, banking on blogs, performing in poetry; it is a working out of political identifications, part of an ever-shifting process, reminding us that healing processes and democratic transitions take time. Public protest works simultaneously as lament for a measure of healing and builds collective bonds after horrific suffering, even while performing current desire for political and economic options, all within a plethora of heterogeneous forms—a democratic voicing.

This book has further argued that Western media's ideas about the Arab Spring are often haunted (in terms of times of history) by popular sites of Anglo-American imagination—for instance, the horror of Iran, the miracle of South Africa—but much is forgotten. Such anxious media coverage of the Arab Spring relies on substitutions—what Western media presupposed about the post-9/11 decade of Iraq, and even earlier with Iran, or in newborn democracies like South Africa—transference to new locations.[2] These forgotten replacements have relied on misconceptions of ancient sectarianism, Islamic revolutions, gendered policing, oppressed women, and Western ideas of democracies; such concepts are not culturally located nor historically situated. To critique these undercurrents, these hidden epistemologies that frame democratic movements, I have followed, instead, Arab and African artists, who use syncretic forms to integrate technology or respond to mass media. In each chapter, we have sought out these intimate—and at times indignant—views, deeply knotted within dissension. These creative mediums with their gendered, political identities raise piercing cries about global and local injustices.

Given the democracy established in Kurdish Iraq in 1993, unrecognized by Western nations, or the democracy in Iran in 1953, overthrown in a coup by Western powers, claims within media that democracy may be incompatible with Islam strike me as particularly hollow. Furthermore, analysis of successful transitions, such as South Africa, reveal four years of violence and political debate between Nelson Mandela's release from prison and the formation of compromises, elections, and a constitution, suggesting the press is unrealistic with its expectations for democratic transitions. While the Western press was surprised by democratic desires in the Middle East and Africa, to most scholars of these regions, protest and democratic dreams were not especially new. But in terms of the uprising in 2011, some critics suggest patterns of continuous protest characterize places like Egypt and Morocco; others, like Hamid Dabashi, emphasize a new "revolutionary dispensation" not caused by, but rather first symbolized by, the Green Movement in Iran.[3] But what was unique, beginning in 2011, was the quick removal of dictators, followed by spreading revolts. Quite convincingly, Lynch has argued that media, such as al-Jazeera, modeling democratic debates and witnessing civilian deaths on issues like Iraq, spurred public debates.[4] So while Western media followed the American political administration, Arab media and creative forms showed a distinct portrait, a lament of the dead, a transnational protest on politics, which Lin Noueihed and Alex Warren argue were one of many factors in spurring on the 2011 Arab Spring.[5]

On the eve of the 2011 Arab Spring, more than 21 million people in the Arab world linked to Facebook, and a 2010 poll discovered that 85 percent of Arabs watch televised news and 78 percent cited al-Jazeera as one of their news sources, leading Noueihed and Warren to further argue that although these protests reflected economic and political anger and were not organized by virtual links, Internet use and media overall had a "democratizing effect" in authoritarian realms. These media not only spread activism and challenge the dictator's "barrier of fear," but also voice anger at rulers' silence or alliance on issues like Iraq; thus, once troops left Iraq and the rhetoric of war on terror died, this emergent tradition of virtual fury turned further toward regional frustration—both economic and political.[6] This book returns to this period and other forgotten springs, recording such voices of protest through blogs and public stages to reconsider this missed moment: the blindness of Western politics and media versus creative forms of local revolt.

10. Satellite dishes (Fez, Morocco). Photograph by author.

Within blogs and other public stages, we find new understandings, distinct from media spectacles. In my analysis of these public protests, I have paid attention to metaphors and media as types of national performatives; so too, within my detailed sketch of location and reception, I have provided an interpretation of gender within geographies. Replete with imprints of street life, of lived experience, of public protests, *Performing Democracy* is recorded on creative stages, war blogs, and memoirs. More explicitly, each case study in this book—unlike the stark image of a hidden woman or bearded extremism—depicts a wide range of national identifications. Feminine histories of grandmothers and daughters, generation gaps in national identities, transregional sites for Arab identities, and even gay patriotism inscribed next to Sunni feminism, provoke new ideas of gender and national expression. The list continues with diasporic nationalism, intergenerational spiritualties, African Marxist Muslims, Anfal survivors, and Kurdish globalism. And last, but not least, there is the final paradox of democratic witch hunts protested by female healers, who are in turn labeled within Hollywood's imagination as witch doctors. While all these creative expressions show national diversity, they also declare their own imagined communities, their democratic dreams.

To further consider this entanglement, I conclude with two final stories of protest, both of which end in fire. But unlike the witch hunts of gender policing from the previous chapter, these two twenty-somethings—a young man, a young woman—carve out public space. They strike the match, set their bodies ablaze. Let's begin with the young man who pushes his produce cart to earn a living. His name is Muhammad Al Bouazizi. He lives in Tunisia. After his cart is confiscated because he does not have a permit, he takes up a complaint at the governor's office. When the state official refuses to see him, he threatens to burn himself. And then, at the age of twenty-six, this young man goes in front of a government building on December 17, 2010 and lights himself on fire.

This event is reported one month later by CNN with the headline, "How a Fruit Seller Caused Revolution in Tunisia."[7] Afterward, according to the CNN report, many Tunisians in the area, especially unemployed twenty-somethings, protested in the streets against "living conditions and the economy." Within popular memory, then, Muhammad al-Bouazizi became a symbol of youth protest about an oppressive economic situation. But the article did not end there, noting that "thousands" of youth attempted to work in Europe, crossing illegally, seeking a "better life." These young women and men call themselves the burners— the *harraka*—because as soon as they reached Europe, they burned their passports to evade the police and avoid being sent back to North Africa. What the article further suggested was that quite a few Tunisians view al-Bouazizi as "*harraka*—but in his own way." The press did not merely name this death as a prelude to a national protest, it also inserted within this frame of death the widespread economic hunger alongside the ideal of Europe. Of the entangled histories of North Africa and Europe, not just Tunisia but also Egypt, Morocco, Algeria, there was no sign, just the economic frustration of youth. What was omitted was the violence of historical economics, such as Spain using chemical weapons in the Rif War that colonized Morocco, devastating crops, scorching the earth, impoverishing and terrorizing the populace, leading to an easy, cheap labor supply both for past recruitment in the Spanish Civil War and the current economy.

A careful search of this article suggests that the journalist was "not clear" about the exact reasons for al-Bouazizi's self-immolation. If we search beyond this Western frame showcased within popular media sites, the reasons for this outcry vary. Some, like the authors of a Wikipedia article, cite his unfinished education, his fury at police bribery and abuse, his gender outrage because a female police officer slapped him, and even his frustration with debt or desperation to support his mother and siblings. But what remains clear are the media time lines for democratic protest. Unlike scholars, press sources charted this particular death—this Tunisian *harraka*—as the beginning of Arab Spring, marking out the dawn of political protest. While Western media was enamored with this single death, surely this is not the beginning of democratic movements, as each country's protest reflected local situations, gendered perspectives, and international tensions. What is needed is a new framework.[8]

Performing Democracy has shown how Arabs and Africans have been identified in the media, especially in the 9/11 decade, and how they have been confined by politics, economics, and violence, as well as a history of colonization that was followed by select support given to regimes of privilege, as evident in policies from Iraq to Iran, from Egypt to Morocco, even from rural Transkei to urban ghettos. But this book presses beyond violence and victimization to contend that the populace has been resisting with cultural forms, protesting in songs that rise above despair, healing and forming communal groups, participating in variegated views—preludes to democratic movements. Indeed, while media have selected global images of protest, what is missing is the historical context, an understanding of why certain political ideals have become sacred turfs.

Although the reach of media has helped to fan the flames of protest to other regions, they have been selective about what sparks seize their attention. Indeed, the burning images of masculinity receive very different types of press coverage than those of femininity. In a blog post on "The Moroccan Mohamed Bouazizi," Laila Lalami detailed the death of a young woman that occurred shortly after the protest in Tunisia.[9] Just two months after Bouazizi's desperate act, Fadwa Laroui, only twenty-five years old, was not speaking for a political party but rather uttering cries of protest against the inequity that she experienced. Her protest was against the policies of the state, claimed Lalami in her February 27, 2011 blog: a widespread association of personal "despair" and hope for "change" within social and government-based policies.[10] Having first fought for rights in a corrupt social system and then within courts, her protests were against what Lalami called a two-tiered system of rich and poor, and a selective gender system for those who are married and those, like Fadwa, who are single mothers whose rights are often ignored by the state. But even though countless articles speak of Mohamed, as Lalami has noted, only a small column in Reuters press recorded Fadwa Laroui, whose protest ended in her fiery death, her self-immolation in front of a government building.

Despite the dearth of Western coverage, numerous Moroccan websites, as Lalami points out, have recorded the importance of Fadwa's protest. Several video clips showed the violence of her death as part of national resistance.[11] While being filmed on the street, probably from a cell phone, this twenty-five-year-old woman screamed for justice: "Who will look after my children!" Protesting in front of a government building, a place where we expect citizens to receive assistance, not neglect, she set herself ablaze; a nearby policeman did nothing to help her in the horrific inferno. Yet she was not alone. A young man tried to put out the fire, nearly burning himself, trying repeatedly to douse the flames with his jacket. But the gasoline fire is undeterred. In videos of this woman and this man, often posted on anonymous sites, the consuming flames and futile attempts at rescue seem endless. The only break in the filming of the violence is a picture: the symbol of a fist, rising above the flames, protests against dictatorship. In this clip, Fadwa is remembered as a national protest.

Looking for Fadwa, I found another video on a site called "Moroccans for Change," subtitled "For the Sake of Fadwa Laroui." There, an extraordinary recording by Nadir Bouhmouch shows an image of Fadwa, running down the street, crying in agony, covered with burning flames.[12]

But Nadir recorded other stories of protest against the corrupt dictator-ship as well. There was a young woman, with her megaphone, chanting her protest to a listening crowd. Another woman, leaning close to the camera, showing us her black eye, spoke of being beaten by the police. Equally disturbing, a middle-aged man with a long beard, dressed in tra-ditional garb, wept on camera, telling us of his friends who were killed in prison. Weeping with despair and shame, he spoke of police who sexually tortured him with a glass bottle. The video, made and narrated by a col-lege student, also described how Nadir's camera was taken by the police, his father forced to court for the "illegal" videotaping of protest, and how his family pressured him to remove the video from the web. Nadir at first consented, then took off to the beach to surf away his encounters with the police. While surfing the Moroccan waves, Nadir spoke with other surfers, some with half-broken boards, youth of the underclass. Considering the challenges of these youths, and after having filmed the sacrifices of Islamists who resisted state injustice and courageous mothers like Fadwa who died for political change, Nadir decided to keep the video posted. In this brave posting, amidst these images, then, the death of Fadwa was one of many protests: a multitude of ages with myriad gender roles, all declaring a lack of opportunities or national abuse.

Much later, there was another mention of Fadwa—a glancing ref-erence, no more than a sentence, in *The New York Times*. In contrast to locating Fadwa's death among the powerful depictions of local pro-test, Kristen McTighe cited her as a brief mention in an article on "Help for Unwed Mothers in Morocco."[13] The single line reads, having been rejected for "social housing because she was an unwed mother, Fadwa Laroui doused herself with flammable liquids and set herself on fire." McTighe's article describes Morocco as a country where "unmarried mothers are condemned as prostitutes," where families reject their young, where women are "ostracized by society even in case of rape." While such sexual politics do exist, there was no sense in this article of fam-ily members and communities with other beliefs—of the many Moroc-cans who regard Fadwa with compassion, cherishing her as a national symbol of protest. Instead, this article extols a women's center, depicted against a hopeless backdrop. The Western frame—the feminist rescue mission—feeds a larger Western mythos that we must save women from Islamic culture.

In contrast to this coverage, an American professor wrote an important article in *Foreign Policy* telling how six Moroccans have set themselves on fire. In her analysis, Rachel Newcomb detailed the protests, including the one by Fadwa Laroui, who was "unable to participate in a development project" because the wealthy with connections have "taken land intended for the poor."[14] In this academic analysis, the economic frustration in Morocco is central. Given this analysis, perhaps Fadwa's protest fed a larger discontent over economic fat cats in a country where many are hungry. Considering Fadwa's protest while traveling around Morocco in 2012, I asked my friends there about economic frustrations and was told of property deals, unemployment, elite networks, and widespread corruption. In Marrakesh, foreigners have purchased many of the hotels and choice houses. Spinning their wheels on the well-lit streets of Marrakesh, a number of BMWs and flash-red sports cars also suggested the showy wealth of the elite in Morocco. The protest of Fadwa—the mother crying against the elite taking over land designated for the poor—situates a political wail in the midst of Arab Spring.

The blog written for *The Nation* by Laila Lalami decried how Fadwa's protest, a fiery political act of suicide, has not drawn much press coverage, remaining widely "unnoticed." What if televised and political pressure had been placed on Morocco to bring more democratic change? Instead, foreign journalists were "confounded" by Morocco, Lalami writes in a different article on "Morocco's Moderate Revolution," because they cannot track the diverse views within the country.[15] Rather, the Western press pins Morocco as a country of polarization: as "modernity collides" against "religious" practices, writes Lalami, yet the "reform-minded" ruler Mohammad VI is viewed as a "liberal beacon."[16] Since the king has long been an ally, and was among the coalition of the willing in the invasion of Iraq, Morocco is seldom criticized in the West. When Lalami reflects on the media's polar views of modern versus backward, or on their idea of the hope in political reform alongside a dictatorship with a king, she labels these media comments as fragmented extremes: like "magnetic pieces" on a fridge door. The reforms of the king, and perhaps also of his father before him, through the truth and equity commission that brought to light torture and disappearances, offered some appeasement for the populace, but these measures were also strategies to maintain power.

After mass protests, King Mohammad VI quickly appointed a commission to draft a new constitution that dampened the flames. In response, the spotlight swung toward "bloodier" as well as more "chaotic uprisings" in other parts of North Africa.[17] These bloody uprisings "made for better television," Lalami noted. But the new constitution does not really confine the king's powers, since he can dissolve parliament, select regional governors, appoint heads of national companies, and direct military affairs. As a result, according to Lalami, the constitution has moved the country only imperceptibly from "autocracy to lighter autocracy." In Lalami's eyes, it is an unfinished revolution. The lack of press coverage on Morocco is one more example of a forgotten woman in a forgotten spring.

Looking for Fadwa, remembering the blog protests of River and Pax, I return to the forgotten spring of Baghdad, the youth cries amidst transitional violence. Identifying sectarian division with the violent occupation and economic upheaval, these blogs also wrote counterhistories: specific protests, such as that of Fallujah, devastated by uranium-tipped weapons that cause birth defects; banned chemical weapons, as in the phosphorous fires on civilian houses; and cluster bombs, targeting urban populations. Both blogs focus not on minority rights, but rather place the family and nation at the heart of their protests, destabilizing how broadcast media have customarily presented gendered and minority rights justifications of violence. These blogs—a creative self-positioning, a coming out for Iraqi nationalism—drastically revise Western genres of feminism and gay politics. While noting how Western media erase collective memories, perhaps we can also discover alternative histories through virtual and visual sites.

In seeking out these gendered spaces of self-declaration and political variety, I wonder why Western media ignore Fadwa's democratic dream? Seeking Fadwa, I travel to a site of protest in Morocco—not Fadwa's hometown of Rabat, but rather the sleepy town of Meknes. Thousands protested every Friday in the public square for a year during the Arab

Spring. Emerging from their shops, their homes, their universities, each person in the protesting crowd has had unique experiences, profound reasons for desiring a vote, a voice, a vocational opportunity. But then there was a change. As the crowd filled the square, week after week, there was a response. The public space of dissension was transformed into carnival. Quite literally, the amusement park, usually brought out for the public only on the birthday of the Prophet Mohammad, now became a regular—and free—space of opportunity. The young could ride; the young could forget; the young could play year round in this space. But not all forget. One of the most powerful groups continued to protest—the Islamists. A woman, Nadia Yassine, often led this charge. Are these Islamists extremists? Well, yes. Most want to overthrow the king, to force him out of power; they are done with the circus of rides, they want a change from the system of elite corruption, a turn to the ethical practice of good Muslims that care for the poor. But these Islamists, fighting for justice and charity, petitioning for democracy, do not support violence, since Nadia's group believes in Sufi practices of education, petitions, and nonviolent demonstrations.

Women's leadership and female protest take many political hues. It is a forgotten spring—one that sprouts throughout this book as I follow innovative, often autobiographical, protests to define political and social realms of feminine influence. Usually relegated to the personal, the experiential, the emotional, I have claimed creative forms in this book as indicators of complex terrains, political and contestational, even territorial. *Performing Democracy* offers an alternative cartography of "women's spaces of inclusion, exclusion, and containment," as two feminist geographers, Karen Morin and Jeanne Guelke, have articulated.[18] In cultural forms, this book notices the regulation of certain political or patriarchal confines in both public places and mass media spaces. But there is more to this terrain than gendered voices and violence, since there is often a negotiation of power, if not outright resistance. Spaces of empowerment can exist within restricted zones, including chances for women to "exercise their talents and skills" in religious spaces, as Guelke and Morin argue, augmenting "mobility for women."[19] Throughout this book, women express religious beliefs—varied sites of Arab practices of

Sunni and Shiite, and African practices of ancestors and Islam—but all narrate their spiritual locations within histories of female heroism. There is resistance, too, as women like Marjane Satrapi and Riverbend record their work or university life, and Heather Raffo and Nadia Davids, in their sketches of Islamic communities, select their modes of dress and gender roles, transgressing politics at certain locations.[20] This book has sought out emergent spaces for political feminisms, some claimed around modern spiritualties. What is needed, then, is a new map of gendered, political practice, one that includes belief. It is a fragile, even fractured, geography, since violence and its fallout of social loss are often negotiated at gendered sites. Nonetheless, positive inscriptions of female action and religious affiliations need to be represented, not as a simple war between the secular versus fanatic but rather as part of the contest, part of the perpetual debate, that is vital to the very life of democracy.

Continuing my search for Fadwa, I wander into a North African trance. The dark-skinned Gnawa, at the beginning of their singing, sound their metallic clappers, swing with rhythmic power, invoking the audience to join in their circle of rhythm. Pointing upward, these turbaned musicians invoke God. Not the Islam that the Western world has stereotyped, this motion declares that God is in charge of everything, that there is only God to balance all things, that God is mysteriously heavenly amidst this small room of dancers. Invited to dance, the sitting scholar joins the circle, becomes a swinging participant. But this is no Sunni spin toward meditative harmony. Invocations, filled with the spirits known as *jinns,* compel the divine gestures. The rhythm calls common believers to the divine, even as it declares their separate identity as black Moroccans. The cultural spirituality protests any singular Islamic or North African or Moroccan identity; this cultural crossroad, declared on an economic stage in a paid performance in front of tourists, dances its own political claim.

In this dance, my idea of Islam is contested, my thoughts of Arab Spring refined, my search for a dead mother channeled toward a famous spirit: Aisha Qandisha. Several people speak of this famous spirit who possesses women. Tales of resistance emerge. When a husband is murdered by the white colonizers, he is avenged by his wife, as she is possessed by the spirit of feminine power to take up the knife and slit the oppressor's throat. These spirits are believed to be all around, according to the research of anthropologist Deborah Kapchan, so that women must be "courageous," for if they become discontent and depressed, then they will be possessed by this spiritual form of power, Aisha, to enact change.[21] The African Spring, as in Fadwa's modern cry, throughout the Moroccan winter of colonization and dictatorship, has long held onto the spirit of women's protest.

Because it is challenging to find Fadwa, this book attempts to implode Western politics through a memorable collage of female freedom fighters, tortured heroes, and repentant torturers to rescript the legacy of 9/11. Given the bodies that litter our collective imagination after Iraq—the unseen caskets and unspeakable suicides of our soldiers, the refugees on the outskirts of our cities and borders, the selective tales of gender rescue, the tortured bodies in photos, and our own mistaken patriot acts, where the arrested are denied democratic rights—this unfinished mourning has become an ingested loss with painful consequences.[22] Such popular concepts cut equally across neoconservative desires to save the oppressed woman from a deadly religion to the liberal feminist longing to save the oppressed women themselves, on the assumption that all religious belief is oppressive. Not attentive to a wide range of politicized views (including hybrid combinations of gender, generation, class, culture, and religion), our views of Arab/African Springs remain haunted by the ghosts of our political past—what I refer to as the *9/11 syndrome*.

Let's return to the crash site with *New York Times* editor Bill Keller, who took a "hard look at why he wanted war," assessing media's "unfinished 9/11 business."[23] Keller contrasted the "hit-and-run democracy project" for Iraq with the "Arab Awakening" and its "powerful pride in its indigenous quality."[24] I hope that we have learned to recognize the democratic desires of others; yet, in an adjoining article, the press polarized the Arab Spring, as David Rieff claimed the Muslim Brotherhood are the "principal beneficiary," not "democrats," denying Islamists any democratic desires.[25] The writers reflected on American policies of assassinations and security systems, but then admitted that their post-9/11 discussion did not include the places and people "who were, by far, the most affected."

Not only does this book consider the people most affected, but it also asks us to take another look at why religious groups have great currency, since they often speak out against injustice and, as Mark Tessler and Marilyn Grobschmidt suggest, have economic relevance. Not just a means of "popular discontent," these groups signal a modern demand for an alternative form, especially when there is no "accountable government"; for these religious groups have often provided food and security, whereas the state has not.[26] As research shows, expectations in a democracy where all are given a voice are for not only an ethical spirit but also more monetary opportunity. While these powerful religious movements can create serious challenges for women, they are often economic protests, especially given the secular domination of the affluent class with its history of corruption in many regions.[27] While never an apologist for religious beliefs that police women's roles, this book does evoke positive spiritual frameworks of social justice or of economic concern as it traverses between the Arab and African Spring. *Performing Democracy* beckons to voices across religious and economic divides, encountering paradigms of politics that walk in the city and into the shanty.

Moreover, Islamist success in the election poles, as they quickly mobilized and are trusted to stand up to state militaries and Western pressure, are not the complete picture of these blooming democracies. After Boazizi first lit a match, a survey of Arab views toward democracy was conducted in 2011. Charting views in several countries, including 1,219 persons in Egypt, this survey reported an "overwhelming support" for democracy with the majority embracing democratic values of tolerance, a wide range of politicians and perspectives, and women in the workplace.[28] Using statistics from Egypt, for instance, free elections, the end of corruption, and economic possibilities were all key values. Moreover, nearly 80 percent thought religion was private, not a public matter; 86 percent thought "men of religion should not influence how people vote."[29] The majority believe that there is more than one interpretation of the Koran, allowing for a modern hybridity in views of spiritual ethics and politics:

72 percent thought laws should reflect the will of the people, even as many considered that laws should also reflect spiritual values. But unlike old-school Sharia, only 36 percent believe religious leaders should affect government.[30] These modern democrats do not see Islam and democracy as incompatible. Given the choice between the military's selected leader and the moderate Islamic leader, voters in Egypt chose a change; but given this 2011 survey (and the heterogeneous nature of Islamic groups), that does not mean that more leaders, more contestation, more possibilities will not happen in this young democracy.[31] Islam needs to be imagined as part of the "abundance of cultures that have, as value systems, been long giving shape to the collective identities" and "ethical goals" of multiple peoples, as Tariq Ramadan argues, not as a reductive tool to "justify oppression" of women.[32]

There is another reason that we miss Arab and African springtime: loss. Indeed, in contrast to Western media's forgotten corpses, Arab media, especially al-Jazeera, have beamed out to television sets around the world over one hundred thousand dead civilians in Iraq and the dead in Gaza and Syria. In Morocco, a young man in blue jeans explained to me how his father sits in front of the television, weeping as an Israeli soldier harasses an old man. These waves of sentiment in the media splashed into Internet forms such as blogs, and beneath the critique of post-9/11 violence and debate on political responses, discontent stirred because local dictators, following Lynch's views, were allied or silent during this decade of bloodshed.[33]

But transnational and local identifications of loss, such as the dead bodies in Iraq, Gaza, and Syria, have also triggered other associations in Arab/African communal and national memories, sometimes even changing political affiliations; for globalization of mass media does not create a single effect. At the edge of Africa's continent, *Molora's* 9/11 and the postwar fallout *At Her Feet* reverberate, an ionic impulse crossing national wires far beyond the small scope of New York's fallout site. Coming from an Islamic background, Nadia Davids stages the global fault lines of mass mediation: images of falling towers, a photo of an injured baby from Baghdad, or documentaries of honor killings in Jordan—all foster altered affinities. Indeed, the honor killing recorded by a Western documentary is given a voice of protest across the color line. Part of this fallout was an aftermath of racist responses sweeping from the television toward Muslim Malaysians and Islamic Indians at the tip of Africa. Not just racist sentiments, but also traveling sympathies and transnational affections evolve from this mediation. An Islamic feminism develops for an Afro-Muslim university student watching the news. These traveling images at first appear as simulators, creating shared publics, but these emotive zones can also reconceive cultural identifications, transfiguring into altered global affinities. Indeed, *At Her Feet* ends with a protest and evocative trumpet call for Islamic identity as a global feminism and multicolored nationalism.

And the horror of the past, in the 9/11 decade, is embodied in the scenes of *Molora*, staged as the unforgettable scene of a daughter tortured by her mother. But unlike the tortured victims of Abu Ghraib, whose stories are never told, locked away in military courts and jail cells, or transferred to prisons in Morocco, the tortured survivor of *Molora* tells her stories, speaks her history, rejecting the politics of imperial fear. And, contrasting 9/11's decade of media, *Persepolis* remembered the democracy displaced by a Western coup in the fifties and the ongoing protests for democracy in Iran.

What is of greatest concern about this American filter is how the consuming lens creates challenges for global witnessing. It becomes more difficult for women to speak of injustice when Western media, with its fanfaronade, subverts all stories of female oppression, converting them into evidence of backward foreign cultures or a part of its own displaced heroism. But even while Eastern media have created opportunities for democratic debate alongside Western media's challenge for women across the globe to speak such emergent testimonies, difficulties also breed resistance—both a crisis and a reconfiguration of global perceptions. From the start, Khawla and Marwa detail the effects of war, not just from experience, but as waves of telemetry beamed from television sets. Rejecting American sentiment, two youth bloggers remind us that their fight for democracy started ages ago and continues today. Even after genocide, songs and videos continue to rise up, declaring the survival of Kurdish identity in several times and places. And while Western media fear a religious spring—without contextualizing historical legacies that often generate changes in sacred sites of identity—creative media locate alternative sites of gendered hybridity and Islamic modernism. The political battle crosses continents as African Springs, fighting for economic opportunities, defy media accounts of violent tribalists. And Western media forget the histories of female fighters, not just Fadwa Laroui, who protested the corruption of the state and the violence of the police who destroyed the shack in which she lived with her children, but also women like Zakia Alkan, who lit herself on fire during the spring of New Roz as a protest against the Turkish ban against any Kurdish traditions in a country well-known for its human rights violations against Kurds. Indeed, her protesting figure, not tolerated on Turkish soil, has never been conceptualized by the Western press.

Western media marginalize diverse voices, but while marginalized voices are often imagined as uneducated villagers or feudal sheiks, the rural are not outside of modernity, and the urban reject any simplistic first- and third-world divides. While colonization and regimes have stripped local economies into dressings for their exports and benefit, local economies of support and syncretic beliefs continually emerge. These people are hybrid, existing in what V. Y. Mudimbe calls an "intermediate space," both global and cultural.[34] Truly off the map, these hybrids are not recognized by the West; as a result, Mudimbe asserts, they are in the most marginalized state.[35] Given this hybridity, a new map for the birthplace of young democracies is needed. Indeed, to create icons out of crowds, flash to violent spectacles, and politicize violence against women fails to note the *changing* street politics and gendered practices. Watch for syncretic beliefs, split practices, and feminized modules of community or of spiritual agency. While I cannot imagine two more different forums of gendered belief than River's inscription of Sunni healing and a South African performance of *sangoma systemics*, both describe female sites of authority as models of modernity that the Western media refuse to recognize. Not the individualism of Western feminisms, these communal affections evoke higher powers than the rippling purl of Western technologies. But when, at times, religious practices of women are loaded into the hierarchical carbine of scientific rationalism, then this

Western epistemology—this loaded gun—triggers problems. Instead, a focus on loss (past injustices and present struggles) and attention to cultural expressions of healing recognize a distinct form of democratic movement, an inspiring spring.

Highlighting my own strategies for diving into the wreck, I conclude by offering a simple yet provocative plea to recognize indigenous expressions of democratic desire. Indeed, conflict resolution—internal or across continental lines—can occur when we listen to cries of loss and songs of communal healing. Using this model, *Performing Democracy* extends beyond the media's focus on Egypt and slaughter in Syria to call attention to the exclusion of women's voices and marginalized groups—ranging across border lines. While very much a feminist and globalist approach, it is also a practitioner's lens with a desire to provide space for new voices and attention to places of healing. Initially, I suggested that we follow, not the channels of mass media, but by route of alternate archives and artistic guides, the protesting crowd. So perhaps some final thoughts are in order about new ways to chart out global protest, beginning with a definition of experiential mapping. For it makes a difference to follow not media spectacles but live bodies—performing stories on public stages or inscribing their street experiences in blogs.

Fadwa's burning body is a checkpoint that I cannot seem to cross. To conceive what new knowledge emerges in protests, we acknowledge that flesh, the body, is at times controlled with checkpoints or judged by a public glance. But it can also be transgressive, claiming identities outside of these public judgments. Thus, even as the physical body may be judged by the color of its skin, or the shape of its gender, it has the potential to be either socially regulated or performatively resistant. *Performing Democracy* is flush with these protests against the regulation of gender and ethnic identities. Most notably, one-woman performances show that identities are mutable: the Arab is an American, the African is Muslim. When performing protest, bodies are political. Such revolt is most effective, according to Bertolt Brecht's theories, when voices register contestation.[36] In the second chapter, two Shiite women spoke of distinct national affiliations, but they also related how their situations and identifications changed when they traveled from locales such as Baghdad to Seattle, and then back again, years later, this time to Babylon. These shifting identifications emerge from another two-decade sojourn as a Kurd redefines himself as an Iraqi nationalist, and then, finally, after the thaw in the 9/11 immigration freeze, as an American Kurd. Identifications of protest also shift, this time between urban and rural, state and local, stages, as Monwa travels to suburbia to kill his torturer, appeals for reparation at a state commission, and then protests on a local stage. Such Afro-nationalist and Afro-Islamic claims challenge the politics of identity. Finally, this book travels between city and country sites as Gcaleka demands ritual identifications and altered histories, blurring the false mapping of scientific urbanities and rural superstitions.

In contrast to protesting bodies, emotional overload directed around bodies is common in Western media. The August 2010 cover of *Time Magazine*, for instance, selected a traumatic image of a woman disfigured by the Taliban.[37] This narrative suggested that America must save her and must rescue Afghanistan. As in advertising, where bodies are depicted as potential sites of commodification, so too within mass media, bodies—both beautiful, like the iconic Afghan refugee girl on *National Geographic*, and horrific, like the Taliban victim on the cover of *Time Magazine*—are similarly located as political commodities. Powerful images of violence, showcased through images of bodies, sell magazines, and this same set of images also markets certain ideas about other locations. But bodies are more than their skin-drawn "materiality," they are also "a politicized site of struggle," suggest the editors of *Pleasure Zones*, who map out bodies, cities, homes, and sexual identities, and even the body language of "pleasure" and "pain."[38] In several chapters, I have mapped out bodies of suffering; yet, while these forgotten springs have provided a record of extraordinary loss across regions, I have sought to carefully situate these stories as ongoing protests—emblems of resistance, signs of lament, one of the budding tensions before the spring of 2011, creatively invoked within public and private sites of identity.

In my peculiar topography of protest, I have also paid attention to objects, evidence of oppression, and possessions that speaking agents use to mark their turf, suggest their identities, define their imagined country. While Western media have not shown thousands of dead, each chapter in this book has scrutinized objects of death and protest—the child's corpse dressed in clothing, flesh burned from chemical weapons, fixated on by River's blog; or the singular cake, a welcome dessert that declared national unity after the civil war in Iraq. Or the skull of the Xhosa chief, still searched for to bring contemporary conciliation. Within creative protests, unforgettable keepsakes and tactile forms of lament resist the detachment of Western media. When we lift up these objects and place them into theories of affect—like the ashes of the dead or a video that documents atrocity—Eve Kosofsky Sedgwick shows us that these objects touch a collective group of feelings. Imagine whether an object will be "safe or dangerous to grasp," whether this object is easy or challenging to hold; remember, she writes, that long before you, others have left their imprint on this object.[39] But such objects of lament, such props of identity, have crossed cultures within alternative media, as in the skulls, or the bag of bones carved out of a mass grave, or the photo of a tortured Arab. But cultural keepsakes, like the documentary pictures of River, of Huda, of Asad, can also commemorate, so that groups can relocate themselves with political affiliations after the fusillade of atrocity, since such communal embodiments dress painful wounds.

Stowed in objects or highlighted in the press, attachments of emotion suggest the political importance of sentiment. While stereotypes about feelings are often affixed as labels to women and non-Western cultures in order to show weakness or lack of rationality, this book has sought to reverse this trend. This book has followed sentiment—with its power and "cultural politics," to use Ahmed's language—to trace how emotion can show our "investments in social norms."[40] Feelings that respond to power can be difficult to trace out, states Ben Anderson, especially as political signs.[41] Not an easy trail to follow, I have tried to track patterns in print media, poetry, plays, television, songs, and blogs: hieroglyphs of democratic desire, signs of diverse identities, atlases of painful politicizations. These sentimental politics also emerged in song. In Morocco, as rap groups sing an ancient song for the poor, these sounds of protest rise from the lips of children, the airwaves of speakers, the discontent of a society. "Ash ta ta ta ta ta," pounds the rain on the fields, the staccato notes of the sound, the hope for water as Morocco suffers from drought and the poorest of the poor are hungry. As the young ask for bread, as the grandmother sings this song to little ones, as the hip-hop star rocks before a crowd, as a protest against Morocco as a "Kingdom of Doom" posts blog pictures of children along with this tune, the sounds of Arab Spring have not halted in Morocco. As in Fadwa's cries of protest, so too the emotive sounds pour through cultural venues.

These emotional tides, as in the Internet video of Fadwa, as in the angry lament of rap songs in Morocco, are forces of nationalism. In similar terms, this book has navigated another site of eager young democrats: thousands of people in a country far from northern Africa have rendered their traumatic experiences into testimony at the truth and reconciliation commission, on national television and newspapers, and finally in videotaped testimonial performances. During this transition to democracy in South Africa, compelling voices have testified; African women have been the most frequent witnesses to human rights violations at the commission. But their words were not the same as those of their male counterparts, despite similar roles as military commanders, guerrilla fighters, protesting parents. Women often avoided stories of political torture, especially of rape; instead, they have sought other memories that could be passed to their children—recollections of loss and heroics, to mourn, to cope, to heal.

This alternative mapping is critical because it records powerful forms of communal bonds unrecorded on the maps of mass media. These performances matter because attention to cultural studies—giving injustice a public forum—is crucial for understanding conflict. After atrocity, collective losses, part of the emotion about past events, discussed within communal relationships can saturate location and inform identities. Public forums for narrated memory hold an unusual role, as Paul Antze and Michael Lambek discuss in *Tense Past*: they ground our sense of self and our histories, especially after traumatic memory has disrupted our sense of what we are like.[42] Survivors are often consumed by traumatic events that have "no ending, attained no closure," that remain painfully present until the event is told to another and perceived as past, what Dori Laub calls an important public integration.[43] As violence decimates core values, trauma creates "shattered assumptions," to use the title and strident terms of the psychologist Ronnie Janoff-Bulman, and these shattered walls demand reconstruction of emotion and relationships.[44] Even though some individual memories of the past can never be completely resolved, these public stages of mourning establish roles in a group, offering the possibility of emotional stability, territorial naming, and even collective grounding. Cultural performances, protesting past and present injustices, assist participants in transitioning out of individual alienation into public expressions that solidify collective memory.

By closely studying spaces of cultural negotiation, this book does not hold with the misconception that character traits of Islamic or African communities are preventing the full development of democratic potential. *Performing Democracy* rejects the view that a few bad pomegranates—whether a handfuls of tribal zealots, a militarized youth league, or a specific terrorist group—are the central problem, but rather holds that the material, political, gender, and economic systems that inform these states are being challenged. Indeed, after the air bombings and mass graves of colonization and countless disappearances in dictatorships, cultural performances are ways of "re-inhabiting these spaces of terror," a social recovery expressed by Das and Kleinman.[45] It is a sign that the past and present are "undergoing negotiation," argues Tracy Davis, a display of how a "culture processes itself."[46] This "slowly shifting configuration" of cultural memory and public enactment within traditions, as Michael Kammen suggests, can be helpful as it "shapes a nation's ethos" and identifications.[47] As global protest shape ever-shifting ideals and ideas of identity within political groups and speak out for varying forums for the balance of power, there is controversy, marking protest as part of a democratic kiln.

Teaching one another to use such alternative views in the press, in the classroom, or on the streets demands geographies traced with bodies, politics as gendered affairs, and cultural forms replete with healing. But we need to begin by altering our own mythologies, including the archetypes of Western narratives. To defeat this marriage of empire and imperial typecasting, let's return to our own stories, embedded in Western history. Far from 9/11, there is an early wreckage of empire in the 1600s. On a public stage, Shakespeare depicted a European dictator who takes over an island, invoking the screens of his magical books. In this invasion, religion is an integral part of the regime of Prospero. By naming the mother of Caliban as a witch, he justifies taking over the island with a religious edict and gender clause that enslaves its civilians. And at times, such magical thinking about Arab and Africans as unable to govern themselves has continued—a modern tempest that forecasts more shipwrecks. But throughout, there has been resistance: not just Ariel's selective work to fight for her own liberation alongside Caliban's public protest and sexual politics and the protest of the spiritual mother who has been marginalized, but also within *The Tempest*, Prospero is advised by Ariel to forgive his past, to free his captives, to cease his torturous acts— all paths for revising archetypes of Western history, of remembering the import of cultural studies, of imagining global reconciliation.

Not just altered archetypes, but also altered ideas of healing are needed. For instance, across borders of place, of language, Khawla, coping with the disappearance and possible death of her husband, dared to voyage across the world and with words of translation and testimony to bring assistance to others, not just refugees but also student audiences. And Marwa traveled from Saudi Arabia to Seattle to Iraq, and from fury to small reconciliations, recalling the swapped houses of Shiite and Sunni families, or the respect exchanged between a Muslim woman and academic communities. These spaces of healing, both in the United States and across borders, are hopeful sites that return to our democratic roots.

Looking for new narratives, hearing Monwa speak of his torture, seeking Fadwa amidst the ashes, these voices beckon us toward public remembrance, awareness, perhaps even change. We must seek our freedom, not in the war zones that drone on and on, but rather in other perspectives in public spaces. We need a space for counterhistories sparked by the death of Fadwa, envisioned by bloggers across the transoceanic divide—a place to relocate terror into democratic ideals, perhaps a call for a truth and reconciliation of the American soul. As an American dream for an Arab woman, Raffo asks us to claim her story. In her collated memories, she gives us the advice of Huda; for in our Western soil, we must plant the revolution of democracy in forms that grow perennially, watered by voices of the past, tendered by its citizens that it might be rooted deeply. Seeking such public spaces of knowledge, we turn to models from other communities, such as the truth and reconciliation commission in South Africa, whose state forums usher in survivors to speak to us, so the path of political torture will not be repeated. Such spaces, sought by courageous individuals like Asad, who survived genocide, remind us of transnational hope. As we pay attention to voices from around the globe, we hear in these popular expressions a public healing that attends to unique voices of gender, generation, and location. Such expressions, such advocates for change, such gifts, can navigate our own democratic practice.

Cultural spring gives us a language to understand these popular expressions as democratic voicing—expressions of the past, hopes for the future. While we recognize that countries need ceremonies after political transitions, we often forget that we can learn from other communities, who have cultural expressions to assist us in recovering from our terrorized state, a social recovery that pulses with a verdant, healing spring. Such cultural blossoming—not just burning signs, but also blooming voices—offer us a fragrant reminder to remember democratic springs. By combining creative media with fulgent innovation, these jessant voices, these evocative Ariels—performing communal histories and trans-Atlantic protest—can offer models for conflict resolution, creating from out of the tempest of a violent past a paradigm to imagine the possibility of peace.

Appendix

Notes

References

Index

Appendix

These final notes—written for researchers interested in trekking into interdisciplinary fields of culture, gender, and the performance of political identity—suggest a trail to follow with texts that voice contestation within society. These central texts have all been recognized as important, long before I chose them, because they have been published, legitimated as sites of authority. Yet, unlike mass media, most of these publishers are seeking alternative voices not commonly heard within mainstream Western societies. These texts are sources for further reading, resources in classrooms, and deserve more scholarly attention. Listed below, they are annotated by chapter.

1. Hiner Saleem, *My Father's Rifle* (New York: Picador, 2004).

2. Sadek Mohammed, Soheil Najm, Haider Al-Kabi, Dan Veach, eds. *Flowers of Flame: Unheard Voices in Iraq* (East Lansing: Michigan State Univ. Press, 2008).

3. Heather Raffo, *9 Parts of Desire* (Chicago: Northwestern Univ. Press, 2006).

4. Riverbend, *Baghdad Burning: Girl Blog From Iraq* (New York: The Feminist Press at the City Univ. of New York, 2005). Salam Pax, *The Clandestine Diary of an Ordinary Iraqi* (New York: Grove Press, 2003).

5. Marjane Satrapi, *Persepolis I: The Story of a Childhood* (New York: Pantheon, 2003), and *Persepolis II: The Story of a Return* (New York: Pantheon, 2004).

6. Antjie Krog, *Down to My Last Skin* (Cape Town: Francolin, 2000). Gabeba Baderoon, *The Dream in the Next Body* (Cape Town: Kwela Books, 2005). Ingrid de Kok, *Terrestrial Things* (Cape Town: Kwela Books, 2002). Khulile Nxumalo, *Ten Flapping Elbows, Mama* (Grahamstown, South Africa: Deep South, 2004).

7. Nadia Davids, *At Her Feet* (Cape Town: Oshun Books, 2006). Yael Farber, *Molora* (London: Oberon Books, 2008).

8. Brett Bailey, *The Plays of Miracle and Wonder* (Cape Town: Double Storey, 2003).

These core texts—used in my courses that are accredited for global development, women's studies, reconciliation studies, and literature/theater—are useful for diverse venues. Since these primary texts are often interpreted against the backdrop of Western media, this book concludes with a brief sketch of a research path that is as apropos for politically minded studies of performance as it is for cultural geography.

Chapter 1: "Radio Songs, Kurdish Stories, Videos." While I could have focused only on the published text of *My Father's Rifle*, I decided that researchers should include their own experiences to show how they have selected their field and reached certain conclusions; in effect, I made myself a text, including my own first-person narrative, while living in Iraq during sanctions and the civil war. After promising Asad in 1993 that I would write about the Kurdish experience, I have met with him many times over the years and sent him my published article, which he thought was an important contribution to understanding the Kurds. There was only one "formal" interview with Asad, recording his answers to my specific questions on songs and stories, but I included a published interview with Asad from a newspaper and his online story from a Kurdish website.

Chapter 2: "Televised War, Poetry, and Shiite Women." I began gathering data about the refugee crisis through interviews with trauma center directors who I invited to speak at my university. To create a forum for witnessing, I asked therapists to help select participants who were ready for the public stage, and wrote a research grant that included stipends for the participants. Since Marwa requested a video copy of the performance, I arranged for the university to film the event, and I provided copies to Khawla and Marwa. The video was helpful for transcribing this performance of poetic witnessing. For data collection, I paid attention to unexpected moments, like diverse responses to the poetic representation of Iraq as a woman: how do they challenge the researcher's conceptions?

Chapter 3: "Sectarian Media, 9 Women, and the Stage." For data collection, I watched the performance live and gathered all print interviews, newspaper clippings, and live interviews from Al-Jazeera. I read the articles in *The New York Times* online database, key word "Iraq," from 2004 to 2007. My research question: What does this creative venue suggest that mass media does not? How does the time and place of multiple voices differ from the site of the news flash? How can you "conclude" a play that performs such extraordinary war trauma?

Chapter 4: "Baghdad Blogs and Gender Sites." Both of these blogs dealt with collective memories of al-Sadr and Fallujah. Why didn't I know about Fallujah? I did an online database search of "Fallujah" as the key word in *The New York Times*; then I used the Summit library database, linked to thirty-three libraries, in order to seek historical texts on Fallujah. After reading multiple histories and watching a home-video quality documentary on Fallujah, I decided to quote from several sources, including Nir Rosen's articles and his powerful book *Aftermath*.

Chapter 5: "Media and Iran's Forgotten Spring." Intrigued by two mass media references to Iran—NPR's "Revolutionary Road Trip" and Obama's speech in Cairo—I used these Western citations to contrast the depiction of Iran in Marjane Satrapi's war memoirs. For data collection, I limited my case study to NPR and listened to NPR's "Revolutionary Road Trip" online and printed the transcripts. Gathering published interviews with Marjane Satrapi, such as NPR's Fresh Air, I also watched Satrapi's commentaries on her film *Persepolis*, read several books of Iranian history, and contrasted Satrapi's feminism with Shahrnush Parsipur's Sufi feminism.

Chapter 6: "Guerrilla Fighters, Televised Testimonies." Two years of data collection inform this chapter. I read every article in three major newspapers on the Truth and Reconciliation Commission and South African Theater: *The Sunday Independent*, *The Cape Argus*, and *The Sowetan*. These articles were catalogued by research librarians at the University of Stellenbosch, and I am indebted to these librarians for their assistance. I attended several Truth and Reconciliation Commission hearings in Cape Town and Umtata. After reading history books on South Africa and living in South Africa, I studied the five-volume report on the Truth and Reconciliation Commission and the SABC disk of live testimonies. I have read almost every book of South African poetry that has been published since 1994. Given the extensive nature of this data, I carefully selected Monwa as the guide to this chapter, and over the years, I have met with Monwa periodically; this interview and *Khumbulani's* performance were recorded on videotape.

Chapter 7: "9/11 Media." While living in South Africa and returning for eight study abroad trips, I have attended uncountable numbers of theater performances at the Baxter and Market Theater, and on ten occasions I attended the National Arts Festival in Grahamstown. For data collection: I watched live performances of Farber and Davids, located the published scripts, gathered published interviews, and found South African reviews of the performances. There are two people, unmentioned in the chapter, who have influenced my interpretation of Cape Town and coloured townships. Liz Franklin and Desmond Daniels have both adopted me into their families, teaching me South African history from the inside. One was forced into exile for her protest against apartheid; the other for speaking of his family's dispossession from his home. Their stories inform my understanding of urban communities.

Chapter 8: "Bewitched Democracies." For data collection, I watched six live performances of ritual dramas directed by Brett Bailey over the past decade, gathered interviews and reviews from the National English Literary Museum in Grahamstown, attended Bailey's lecture at the theater festival, analyzed Bailey's journal and written notes on his plays, purchased sound recordings and play scripts, talked with Bailey after performances, discussed responses to the play with South African audience members, located a research study on student responses to Bailey's work, researched the South African histories that are recorded in the performance, and read theories of witchcraft and postcolonial science. While this book honors four extraordinary playwrights, I decided to cut out my chapter on Athol Fugard, instead attending important voices and creative media that have been largely forgotten. Also, I cut out two of Bailey's plays—*The Prophet* and *Orpheus*—to make this manuscript more approachable. More research needs to be done on these extraordinary performances of ritual drama.

Notes

Preface

1. From 1993 to 1995, most articles in *The New York Times* focus on Turkey's incursion into northern Iraq, where they were killing resistance fighters, Turkish Kurds. For instance, Alan Cowell, "War on Kurds Hurts Turks in U.S. Eyes," *New York Times*, November 17, 1994, http://www.nytimes.com/1994/11/17/world/war-on-kurds-hurts-turks-in-us-eyes.html?pagewanted=print. Or fear that Iraq would attack the Kurdish enclave: Chris Hedges, "Iraq Said to Prepare Attack on Kurds' Enclave in North," *New York Times*, May 24, 1993, http://www.nytimes.com/1993/05/24/world/iraq-said-to-prepare-attack-on-kurds-enclave-in-north.html?pagewanted=print&src=pm. There is one excellent article by Judith Miller on "Iraq Accused: A Case of Genocide," *New York Times*, January 3, 1993, http://www.nytimes.com/1993/01/03/magazine/iraq-accused-a-case-of-genocide.html?pagewanted=print&src=pm.

Introduction

1. See blog and report by Laila Lalami, "Fadoua Laroui: The Moroccan Mohamed Bouazizi," *The Nation*, February 27, 2011, http://www.thenation.com/blog/158878/fadoua-laroui-moroccan-mohamed-bouazizi.

2. Charles Krauthammer, "Syria and the New Axis of Evil," *Washington Post*, April 1, 2005, A27, http://www.washingtonpost.com/wp-dyn/articles/A17354-2005Mar31.html.

3. Gideon Rose, "Introduction," *The New Arab Revolt: What Happened, What It Means, and What Comes Next* (New York: Foreign Affairs, 2011), xiii.

4. Kelly Oliver, *Women as Weapons of War: Iraq, Sex, and the Media* (New York: Columbia Univ. Press, 2007), 2.

5. Ibid., 167.

6. W. Lance Bennett, Regina Lawrence, and Steven Livingston, *When the Press Fails: Political Power and the News Media from Iraq to Katrina* (Chicago: Univ. of Chicago Press, 2007), 8. Also see, Robert M. Entman, *Projections of Power: Framing News,*

Public Opinion, and U.S. Foreign Policy (Chicago: Univ. of Chicago Press, 2004). Entman argues that "cascading frames" describe the spread of post-9/11 media, since the "counter-frame" was not "culturally resonant" (16).

7. Paul Marshall, Lela Gilbert, and Roberta Green Ahmanson, eds., *Blind Spot: When Journalists Don't Get Religion* (Oxford: Oxford Univ. Press, 2009).

8. Michael Rubin, "Three Decades of Misreporting Iran and Iraq," in Marshall, Gilbert, and Ahmanson, *Blind Spot*, 47.

9. Thomas L. Friedman, "Hoping for Arab Mandelas," *New York Times*, March 26, 2011, http://www.nytimes.com/2011/03/27/opinion/27friedman.html?_r=1&pagewanted=print.

10. Roach coined the term "forgotten substitutions" to describe Mardi Gras and performed genealogies of identity and racial legacy. Joseph Roach, *Cities of the Dead: Circum-Atlantic Performance* (New York: Columbia Univ. Press, 1996), 5.

11. Riverbend, *Baghdad Burning: Girl Blog from Iraq* (New York: The Feminist Press at the City Univ. of New York, 2005), 84. Hereafter cited parenthetically in the text by page number.

12. Riverbend, *Baghdad Burning II: More Girl Blog from Iraq* (New York: The Feminist Press at the City Univ. of New York, 2006), 27. Hereafter cited parenthetically in the text as II and page number.

13. Jasbir K. Puar, *Terrorist Assemblages: Homonationalism in Queer Times* (Durham: Duke Univ. Press, 2007), 82.

14. This term "absent" expands on the rejection of the mind and body dichotomy, in Drew Leder, *The Absent Body* (Chicago: Univ. of Chicago Press, 1990).

15. Diana Taylor, *The Archive and the Repertoire: Performing Cultural Memory in the Americas* (Durham: Duke Univ. Press, 2003), xvi–xvii, 193.

16. For further discussion, see Laurence Kirmayer, "Landscapes of Memory: Trauma, Narrative, and Dissociation," in *Tense Past: Cultural Essays in Trauma and Memory*, ed. Paul Antze and Michael Lambek (New York: Routledge, 1996), 180.

17. Nouri Gana, *Signifying Loss: Towards a Poetics of Narrative Mourning* (Lewisburg: Bucknell Univ. Press, 2011), 141, 182.

18. Sigmund Freud, "Mourning and Melancholia," in *The Freud Reader*, ed. Peter Gay (New York: Norton, 1989), 586.

19. Ranjana Khanna, *Dark Continents: Psychoanalysis and Colonialism* (Durham: Duke Univ. Press, 2003), 22. Also see *The Nature of Melancholy: From Aristotle to Kristeva*, ed. Jennifer Radden (Oxford: Oxford Univ. Press, 2000).

20. Mohja Kahf, *Western Representations of the Muslim Woman* (Austin: Univ. of Texas Press, 1999), 4.

21. Caruth sees violent effects emerging in literature, like an unconscious repetition of PTSD. This repetition changes the reader into a "witness." Cathy Caruth, *Unclaimed Experience: Trauma, Narrative, and History* (Baltimore: Johns Hopkins Univ. Press,

1996). The psychoanalyst Ruth Leys challenges this idea that victims are doomed to repeat their initial experiences. Ruth Leys, *Trauma: A Genealogy* (Chicago: Univ. of Chicago Press, 2000), 268. In contrast, Khanna argues that oppressed characters that refuse to fit into the status quo, in effect, protest against the state (*Dark Continents*, 23).

22. Judith Butler, *Precarious Life: The Powers of Mourning and Violence* (London: Verso Press, 2004), 22.

23. Veena Das and Arthur Kleinman, "Introduction," in *Remaking a World: Violence, Social Suffering, and Recovery*, ed. Das and Kleinman (Berkeley and Los Angeles: Univ. of California Press, 2001), 4. Also, Judith Herman argues, "trauma forces the survivor to relive all her earlier struggles over autonomy, initiative, competence, identity, and intimacy," in Judith Herman, *Trauma and Recovery: The Aftermath of Violence* (New York: Basic Books, 1997), 52.

24. Kai Erikson, "Notes on Trauma and Community," in *Trauma: Explorations in Memory*, ed. Cathy Caruth (Baltimore: Johns Hopkins Univ. Press, 1995), 185.

25. Antonius C. G. M. Robben and Marcelo M. Suárez-Orozco, "Interdisciplinary Perspectives on Violence and Trauma," in *Cultures under Siege: Collective Violence and Trauma*, ed. Robben Suárez-Orozco (Cambridge: Cambridge Univ. Press, 2000), 3.

26. John Paul Lederach, *Preparing for Peace: Conflict Transformation across Cultures* (Syracuse: Syracuse Univ. Press, 1996), 32, 86.

27. Peggy Phelan, *Mourning Sex: Performing Public Memories* (London: Routledge, 1997), 5, 12.

28. See the literary theory of heteroglossia in M. M. Bakhtin, *The Dialogic Imagination: Four Essays*, ed. Michael Holquist, trans. Caryl Emerson and Michael Holquist (Austin: Univ. of Texas Press, 1981), 365.

29. My approach extends on Roach's views of Mardi Gras parades, a performance study of history traced on the streets. Roach, *Cities of the Dead*, 10.

30. Fatima Mernissi, *Sheherazade Goes West: Different Cultures, Different Harems* (New York: Washington Square Press, 2001), 21–22.

31. Chandra Talpade Mohanty, *Feminism without Borders: Decolonizing Theory, Practicing Solidarity* (Durham: Duke Univ. Press, 2003), 242, 244.

32. This "transformative" process, Flatley argues, speaks the depressing problem, to become "interesting," solicit community responses and bonds, draw political attention. Jonathan Flatley, *Affective Mapping: Melancholia and the Politics of Modernism* (Cambridge: Harvard Univ. Press, 2008), 4.

33. Augusto Boal, *Theatre of the Oppressed*, trans. Charles and Maria-Odilla McBride (New York: Theatre Communications Group, 1985), 10. Pierre Bourdieu, *The Field of Cultural Production: Essays on Art and Literature* (New York: Columbia Univ. Press, 1993).

34. I draw on the term "bloom space" for political emotion, in contrast to the social activity in Kathleen Steward's narrative, "Afterword: Worlding Refrains," in *The Affect*

Theory Reader, ed. Melissa Gregg and Gregory J. Seigworth (Durham: Duke Univ. Press, 2010), 342.

1. Radio Songs, Kurdish Stories, Videos: Politics of Healing after Ethnic Cleansing

1. Cited in Denise Natali, *The Kurds and the State: Evolving National Identity in Iraq, Turkey, and Iran* (Syracuse: Syracuse Univ. Press, 2005), 58–59. Research numbers of Anfal campaign from Middle East Watch 1993.

2. Tim Arango, "Kurds Prepare to Pursue More Autonomy in a Fallen Syria," *New York Times*, September 28, 2012, http://www.nytimes.com/2012/09/29/world/middle east/kurds-to-pursue-more-autonomy-in-a-fallen-syria.html?pagewanted=all. The following quotes continue from this article.

3. J. Michael Kennedy, "Kurds Remain on the Sideline of Syria's Uprising," *New York Times*, April 17, 2012, http://www.nytimes.com/2012/04/18/world/middleeast /kurds-remain-on-sideline-in-syrias-uprising.html?pagewanted=all&_r=0.

4. Liam Stack and Katherin Zoepf, "Syria Tries to Placate Sunnis and Kurds, *New York Times*, April 6, 2012, http://www.nytimes.com/2011/04/07/world/middleeast /07syria.html.

5. Dawn Chatty, *Displacement and Dispossession in the Modern Middle East* (Cambridge: Cambridge Univ. Press, 2010), 232.

6. Natali, *Kurds and the State*, xxx.

7. Ibid., xxiv.

8. For further discussion of Hiner Saleem's memoir, see Joan Dupont, "Making a Movie In and On Iraq," *New York Times*, May 13, 2005, http://www.nytimes .com/2005/05/12/arts/12iht-saleem.html?_r=0.

9. Hiner Saleem, *My Father's Rifle: A Childhood in Kurdistan*, trans. Catherine Temerson (New York: Picador, 2004), 3.

10. Christopher Houston, *Kurdistan: Crafting of National Selves* (Bloomington: Indiana Univ. Press, 2008), 6.

11. David McDowall, *A Modern History of the Kurds* (London: I. B. Tauris, 2004), 8. Chatty, *Displacement and Dispossession*, 233.

12. Also see Chatty, *Displacement and Dispossession*, 266. Kurdish historical claims have varied: some for "self-determination," others for "separatism" (26).

13. Ibid., 250.

14. Christiane Bird, *A Thousand Sighs, A Thousand Revolts: Journeys in Kurdistan* (New York: Ballantine Books, 2004), 70.

15. Asad Gozeh, "Images of Poison Gas Still Haunt People in Kurdistan," June 4, 2003, www.kurdishmedia.com.

16. Paul Connerton, *How Societies Remember* (Cambridge: Cambridge Univ. Press, 1989), 23.

17. William Forde Thompson, *Music, Thought, and Feeling: Understanding the Psychology of Music* (New York: Oxford Univ. Press, 2009), 253.

18. Ibid.

19. Choman Hardi, *Gendered Experiences of Genocide: Anfal Survivors in Kurdistan-Iraq* (Surrey: Ashgate, 2011), 163. Hereafter cited in the text by page number.

20. Kirmayer, "Landscapes of Memory," 180.

21. Some women attend public funerals to process their continued grief, claims Hardi in *Gendered Experiences of Genocide* (186).

22. Dieter Christensen, "On Variability in Kurdish Dance Songs," *Asian Music* 6, nos. 1/2 (1975): 2.

23. Thompson, *Music, Thought, and Feeling*, 193.

24. Author interview with Asad Gozeh, November 26, 2012.

25. Christine Allison, "Old and New Oral Traditions in Badinan," in *Kurdish Culture and Identity*, ed. Christine Allison and Philip Kreyenbroek (London: Zed Books, 1996), 43.

26. Pamela Constable, "Cloud over Halabja Begins to Dissipate," *The Washington Post*, August 7, 2003, A10.

27. Jonathan Steele, "Saddam Can't Be Blamed for Halabja's Latest Convulsions," *The Guardian*, March 2, 2007, http://www.guardian.co.uk/commentisfree/2007/mar/02/comment.iraq.

28. Natali, *Kurds and the State*, 49.

29. Nir Rosen, "Uncovering the Dead," May 28, 2003, www.kurdishmedia.com.

30. Paul Antze and Michael Lambek, "Introduction," in Antze and Lambek, *Tense Past*, xix.

31. Chatty, *Displacement and Dispossession*, 237.

32. Author interview with Asad Gozeh, November 26, 2012.

33. Antze and Lambek, "Introduction," xxi.

34. Shahin Sorekli, "Halabja: Another Sad Kurdish Song?" March 15, 2000, http://www.freewebs.com/mahabadassociation/shahinsorekli.html.

35. Mehrdad Izady, *The Kurds* (London: Crane Russak, 1992), 242.

36. Victor Turner, *The Anthropology of Performance* (New York: Performing Arts Journal, 1987), 24.

37. Lauren Gullion, "Family Finds Hope in America," *The Gazette*, Colorado Springs, July 4, 2002.

38. Ibid., 2.

39. Asad Gozeh, in conversation with author about this local journal article, December 1, 2012. The quotes in the next paragraph are also from this conversation.

40. Joan Dupont, "Making a Movie In and On Iraq," *New York Times*, May 13, 2005, http://www.nytimes.com/2005/05/12/arts/12iht-saleem.html?_r=0. All quotes in the paragraph are from this source.

41. Hoda Abdel Hamid, "Kurds Push for Future in Post-Assad Era," August 13, 2012, http://www.aljazeera.com/news/middleeast/2012/08/2012813123730538938 .html.

42. Giulio Petrocco, "Kurds in Syria Triumph over al-Assad Regime," November 20, 2012, http://www.aljazeera.com/indepth/inpictures/2012/11/201211191326526 03960.html.

2. Televised War, Poetry, and Shiite Women: A Case Study of Generation Gaps

1. James Deselow, "Iraq's Arab Spring: The Forgotten Frontier," *New Statesman*, July 15, 2011, http://www.newstatesman.com/blogs/the-staggers/2011/07/iraq-iran -largely-term-media.

2. Ibid.

3. On Arab identification and debate on mass graves (2), in Marc Lynch, *Voices of the New Arab Public: Iraq, Al-Jazeera, and Middle East Politics Today* (New York: Columbia Univ. Press, 2006), 11.

4. Lynch, *Voices of the New Arab Public*, 242. Protests against invasion of Iraq and civilian deaths, bombing of Palestinians, and bread riots as factors in Arab Spring, noted in Lin Noueihed and Alex Warren, *The Battle for Arab Spring: Revolution, Counter-Revolution, and the Making of a New Era* (New Haven: Yale Univ. Press, 2012), 52, 59.

5. Research on the attention to Iraq's elections in al-Jazeera in Lynch, *Voices of the New Arab Public*, 235.

6. Ibid., 27.

7. Charles Tripp, *A History of Iraq*, 3rd ed. (Cambridge: Cambridge Univ. Press, 2007), 1.

8. Ibid., 1.

9. Joseph Sassoon, *The Iraqi Refugees: The New Crisis in the Middle East* (New York: I. B. Tauris, 2009).

10. Yasir Suleiman, "Introduction," in *Literature and Nation in the Middle East*, ed. Yasir Suleiman and Ibrahim Muhawi (Edinburgh: Edinburgh Univ. Press, 2006), 5. For further discussion on national identities, see Benedict Anderson, *Imagined Communities* (New York: Verso, 1983; 1991).

11. Sara Ahmed, *The Cultural Politics of Emotion* (New York: Routledge, 2004), 11.

12. Flatley, *Affective Mapping*, 10.

13. Reported by Anne Garrels, "Baghdad Poets Find an Oasis from Violence," Morning Edition, NPR, October 19, 2006, http://www.npr.org/player/v2/media Player.html?action=1&t=1&islist=false&id=6286899&m=6301849.

14. Annia Ciezadlo, "From Street Bards to Saddam, Everyone's a Poet in Iraq," *Christian Science Monitor*, August 17, 2004, http://www.csmonitor.com/2004/0817 /p01s03-woiq.html.

15. Eric Davis, *Memories of State: Politics, History, and Collective Identity in Modern Iraq* (Berkeley and Los Angeles: Univ. of California Press, 2005), 283.

16. For instance, see introduction to Fadhil Al-Azzai's selected poems. Khaled Mattawa, "Introduction," in *Miracle Maker: Selected Poems of Fadhil Al-Azzawi*, ed. Khaled Mattawa (Rochester, NY: BOA Editions, 2003), 9–20.

17. Sadek Mohammed, Soheil Najm, Haider Al-Kabi, and Dan Veach, eds., *Flowers of Flame: Unheard Voices of Iraq* (East Lansing: Michigan State Univ. Press, 2008).

18. The poems were selected as responses to the 2003 American invasion, according to the anthology editor Dan Veach (ibid., vii).

19. Saadi Simawe, "Introduction," in *Iraqi Poetry Today*, ed. Saadi Simawe and Daniel Weissbort (London: Univ. of London Press, 2003), 7.

20. Haider Al-Kabi, "Bombardment," trans. Sadek Mohammed, in *Flowers of Flame*, 7.

21. Hashem Shafeeq, "The Needle," trans. Sadek Mohammed, in *Flowers of Flame*, 35.

22. Fadhil al-Azzawi, "The Last Iraq," trans. Khaled Mattawa, in Mattawa, *Miracle Maker*, 72.

23. Dunya Mikhail, "America," trans. Elizabeth Winslow, in *The War Works Hard*, ed. and introduction Saadi Simawe (New York: New Directions, 2005), 33–39.

24. Adam Hatem, "We Are Not Dead," trans. Haider Al-Kabi, in *Flowers of Flame*, 39.

25. Adil Abdullah, "A Country Out of Work," trans. Soheil Najm, in *Flowers of Flame*, 43. The entire population has a job to do: "kindling sunrise from the ash" that the foreigners have left, a hoped-for return to national leadership and prosperity.

26. Munthir Abdul-Hur, "We Are Not Dead," trans. Sadek Mohammed, in *Flowers of Flame*, 36.

27. Heather Raffo, *9 Parts of Desire* (Chicago: Northwestern Univ. Press, 2006), 37. Hereafter cited in text by page number.

28. Mahmud Al-Braikan, "Of Freedom," trans. Haider Al-Kabi, in *Flowers of Flame*. In images of civil strife, Iraq is imagined as a wounded animal, mistakenly attacked by its own kin. Eventually "shame will seize their souls"; these groups will realize "prey they feasted on last night was the flesh of their own children" (3).

29. Kareem Shugaidil, "Flour Below Zero," trans. Sadek Mohammed, in *Flowers of Flame*, 44–46.

30. Ahmed, *Cultural Politics of Emotion*, 80.

31. Davis, *Memories of State*, 283.

3. Sectarian Media, Nine Women, and the Stage: Transregional Identities

1. Heather Raffo, *9 Parts of Desire*, n.d., http://heatherraffo.com/projects/nine-parts-of-desire (accessed November 12, 2012).

2. David Gritten, "Long Path to Iraq's Sectarian Split," BBC News, February 25, 2006, http://news.bbc.co.uk/2/hi/4750320.stm.

3. Ibid., 3.

4. Thomas Friedman, "Hoping for Arab Mandelas," *New York Times*, March 26, 2011, http://www.nytimes.com/2011/03/27/opinion/27friedman.html.

5. Ibid. Also see Vali Nasr, *The Shia Revival: How Conflicts within Islam Will Shape the Future* (New York: Norton, 2007). Friedman praises Nasr's book, but misses Nasr's argument that "Sunni dominated Arab identity of old" is being rejected: a "convenient way of breaking apart the old order," to create a "new nationalism" (234).

6. Nir Rosen, *Aftermath: Following the Bloodshed of America's Wars in the Muslim World* (New York: Nation Books, 2010), 28.

7. Raffo, "Production Notes," *9 Parts of Desire*, 69.

8. Raffo, "Author's Note," *9 Parts of Desire*, x.

9. http://heatherraffo.com/projects/nine-parts-of-desire (accessed November 13, 2012).

10. Raffo, "Author's Note," x.

11. Ibid.

12. Eric Herring and Glen Rangwala, *Iraq in Fragments: The Occupation and Its Legacy* (New York: Cornell Univ. Press, 2006), 148.

13. Ibid., 148–49. Quoted from ICRSS and Gallup Polls, reported in State Department Office of Research, October 21, 2003, 6. In 2005, 70 percent polled that there should be "one unified Iraq with central government in Baghdad." In 2003, only "29 percent of Iraqis" thought that a leader needed to "represent my sect"; in 2004, only 4.5 percent considered "my religious group" important in a "political leader."

14. Ibid., 149.

15. See Nadje Al-Ali and Nicola Pratt, *What Kind of Liberation?: Women and the Occupation of Iraq* (Berkeley and Los Angeles: Univ. of California Press, 2009), 89.

16. Ibid., 80.

17. Toby Dodge, *Inventing Iraq: The Failure of Nation Building and a History Denied* (New York: Columbia Univ. Press, 2003), 163–64.

18. Ibid., 164.

19. Both the United States (post–Gulf War II) and the United Kingdom (after WWI) closed down newspapers and banned political parties (the U.K. during King Faisal's illness), or signed death warrants for a political leader (the U.S. eventually rescinded the order for Moqtad Al-Sadr).

20. Mernissi, *Scheherazade Goes West*, 2001. Also see Suha Sabbagh, *Arab Women: Between Defiance and Restraint* (New York: Olive Branch Press, 1996).

21. Brinda Mehta, *Rituals of Memory in Contemporary Arab Women's Writing* (Syracuse: Syracuse Univ. Press, 2007), 4.

22. She calls herself "half Iraqi, half American." Heather Raffo, interview by Riz Khan, "Women in Iraq War," al-Jazeera English, May 2, 2007, http://www.youtube.com/watch?v=LnqLMoHUStU.

23. Mernissi, *Scheherazade Goes West*, 46. Started as a "war between the sexes," it became a "political upheaval, with bereaved fathers rebelling against the King" (46).

24. Bakhtin, *Dialogic Imagination*, 360.

25. Raffo, interview by Riz Khan, "Women in Iraq War."

26. James Clifford, *The Predicament of Culture: Twentieth-Century Ethnography, Literature, and Art* (Boston: Harvard Univ. Press, 2002), 23.

27. The Gulf War singer's name is Ilham al Madfa'I (75).

28. Marvin Carlson, *Speaking in Tongues: Languages at Play in the Theater* (Ann Arbor: Univ. of Michigan Press, 2006), 64.

29. Al-Ali and Pratt, *What Kind of Liberation?*, 41.

30. Leila Ahmed, *Women and Gender in Islam: Historical Roots of a Modern Debate* (New Haven: Yale Univ. Press, 1992), 237.

31. Ibid., 5.

32. Erikson, "Notes on Trauma and Community," 190.

33. Re-presenting history could simply mirror violence, without resisting events, argues Della Pollock in "Introduction: Making History Go," in *Exceptional Spaces: Essays in Performance and History*, ed. Della Pollock (Chapel Hill: Univ. of North Carolina Press, 1998), 11.

34. From the Iraqi song "Che Mali Wali," trans. Salaam Yousif, in Raffo, *9 Parts of Desire*, 75.

4. Baghdad Blogs and Gender Sites: An Iraqi Spring for Youth Culture?

1. As of 2011, little research exists on these two blogs. On Pax's "auto-blog-ography," see the chapter "Arablish: The Baghdad Blogger," in Gillian Whitlock, *Soft Weapons: Autobiography in Transit* (Chicago: Univ. of Chicago Press, 2007), 24–44.

2. Ben Anderson, "Modulating the Excess of Affect: Morale in a State of 'Total War,'" in Gregg and Seigworth, *Affect Theory Reader*, 173. Anderson uses morale to conceptualize the "terror effect" of the "shock and awe campaign" (181).

3. Salam Pax, *The Clandestine Diary of an Ordinary Iraqi* (New York: Grove Press, 2003; Chicago: Northwestern Univ. Press, 2006), 5. Hereafter cited in text by page number.

4. Whitlock, *Soft Weapons*, 1, 24.

5. Ibid., 11. Pax receives various Internet responses from readers, some encouraging, others homophobic.

6. For work on terror and location, see Allen Feldman, *Formations of Violence: The Narrative of the Body and Political Terror in Northern Ireland* (Chicago: Univ. of Chicago

Press, 1991); Michael Taussig, *Shamanism, Colonialism, and the Wild Man: A Study in Terror and Healing* (Chicago: Univ. of Chicago Press, 1987).

7. Frederic Schaffer, *Democracy in Translation: Understanding Politics in an Unfamiliar Culture* (Ithaca: Cornell Univ. Press, 1998), 7.

8. This blog is published in two volumes (see "Introduction," notes 13 and 14). All parenthetical page number citations refer to volume 1, unless marked as "II."

9. Under Paul Bremer's jurisdiction, he allowed for a new constitution that denied women property rights, guaranteed under the former Iraqi constitution.

10. Chandra Talpade Mohanty, "Feminist Scholarship, Colonial Discourses," in *The Postcolonial Studies Reader*, ed. Bill Ashcroft, Gareth Griffiths, and Helen Tiffin (London: Routledge, 1995), 261.

11. Amal Amireh, "Writing the Difference: Feminists' Invention of the 'Arab Woman,'" in *Interventions: Feminist Dialogues on Third World Women's Literature and Film*, ed. Bishnupriya Ghosh and Brinda Bose (New York: Garland, 1997), 185, 203.

12. Al-Ali and Pratt, *What Kind of Liberation?*, 45. For example, the Women's Union of Kurdistan assisted women after the Anfal and "promoted women's rights."

13. Puar, *Terrorist Assemblages*, 83.

14. Valentine Moghadam, "Women, Citizenship, and Civil Rights in the Arab World," in *Human Rights in the Arab World: Independent Voices*, ed. Anthony Chase and Amr Hamzawy (Philadelphia: Univ. of Pennsylvania Press, 2006), 104. Eyad El Sarraj, "Justice in Heaven," in Chase and Hamzawy, *Human Rights in the Arab World*, 133.

15. Nawar Al-Hassan Golley, *Reading Arab Women's Autobiographies: Shahrazad Tells Her Story* (Austin: Univ. of Texas Press, 2003), 33–34. Similarly, Cooke chooses to speak of Arab "feminism," because the term, despite its genealogical context of Western white women, elicits a political sharpness, distinct from more moderate terms, like "womanism." Miriam Cooke, *Women Claim Islam: Creating Islamic Feminism through Literature* (New York: Routledge, 2001), ix.

16. Nicola Pratt, "Human Rights NGOs and the Foreign Funding Debate in Egypt," in Chase and Hamzawy, *Human Rights in the Arab World*, 125. Also see: Nicola Pratt, *Democracy and Authoritarianism in the Arab World* (Boulder, CO: Lynne Rienner, 2007).

17. R. Marie Griffith, *God's Daughters: Evangelical Women and the Power of Submission* (Berkeley and Los Angeles: Univ. of California Press, 1997), 1.

18. Kelly H. Chong, *Deliverance and Submission: Evangelical Women and the Negotiation of Patriarchy in South Korea* (Cambridge: Harvard Univ. Press, 2008), 196.

19. Cooke, *Women Claim Islam*, 60.

20. Judith Butler, *Gender Trouble: Feminism and the Subversion of Identity* (New York: Routledge, 1999), 181.

21. River contrasts Mark Kimmet, who announced how seven hundred insurgents died as if "it was a proud day," with Iraqi street knowledge of civilians shot because they were male and seen as insurgents (254).

22. Lynch, *Voices of the New Arab Public*, 24, 27.

23. For further information, see *The Control Room*, DVD, directed by Jehane Noujaim (Lion's Gate, October 26, 2004).

24. James Ridgeway, "April through September 2004," in Riverbend, *Baghdad Burning*, 237.

25. Ibid., 238.

26. Jeremy Scahill, *Blackwater: The Rise of the World's Most Powerful Mercenary Army* (New York: Avalon, 2007), xii.

27. Ibid.

28. Bing West, *No True Glory: A Frontline Account of the Battle for Fallujah* (New York: Bantam, 2005), 7.

29. Aaron Glantz, *How America Lost Iraq* (New York: Penguin, 2005). After closing the newspaper *al-Hawza*, writes Glantz, "all hell broke loose"; the U.S. military lost all public support and went to war with almost all of "Iraq's Arab population" (164).

30. See Nir Rosen, "Home Rule," *The New Yorker*, July 5, 2004, www.newyorker.com/archive/2004/07/05/040705fa_fact (accessed November 18, 2012). See also, "What Really Happened: The History the Government Hopes You DON'T Learn," "List of Iraqi civilian martyrs killed in Fallujah by chemical weapons used by the Americans in their assault on the city in April 2004," by the Babel Centre for Studies and Media and the People's Struggle Movement in Iraq, n.d.: 749 deaths with signs of chemical weapons injury, "580 of which are males and 169 are females, and among them were large numbers of children and elderly," http://whatreallyhappened.com/WRHARTICLES/Fallujahvictims.html?q= Fallujahvictims.html (accessed November 18, 2012). Also see River's account.

31. Ridgeway, in Riverbend, *Baghdad Burning*, 238.

32. Glantz, *How America Lost Iraq*, 193.

33. Jean Baudrillard, *Simulacra and Simulation*, trans. Sheila Faria Glaser (Ann Arbor: Univ. of Michigan Press, 2008), 30, 34.

34. Arjun Appadurai, "Grassroots Globalization and the Research Imagination," in *Globalization*, ed. Appadurai (Durham: Duke Univ. Press, 2001), 4. Global discourse has "emancipatory politics," imagining human rights, new options, and elections; at the same time, the "global flow of arms" violently suppresses any change (6).

35. Ibid., 6.

36. Baudrillard, *Simulacra and Simulation*, 3. Illness when believed can also be produced, as with a psychosomatic, Baudrillard argues; simulation partially produces itself.

37. Riverbend, comment on "Baghdad Burning," October 22, 2007, http://riverbendblog.blogspot.com/.

38. While Pax's published blog ends June 28, 2003, his last posted blog, "Where Is Raed?," ends almost a year later, April 10, 2004.

39. Rosen, *Aftermath*, 73.

40. Deborah Campbell, "Exodus: Where Will Iraq Go Next?," March 31, 2008, http://www.democracynow.org/2008/3/31/exodus_where_will_iraq_go_next. Nir Rosen, "The Flight from Iraq," *New York Times*, May 13, 2007, http://www.nytimes.com/2007/05/13/magazine/13refugees-t.html.

41. Riverbend, comment on "Baghdad Burning," October 22, 2007, http://riverbendblog.blogspot.com/, and in ensuing quotes.

42. See Liisa H. Malkki, *Purity and Exile* (Chicago: Univ. of Chicago Press, 1995).

43. Rosen, *Aftermath*, 557.

5. Media and Iran's Forgotten Spring: Intergenerational Politics in *Persepolis*

1. Marjane Satrapi, *Persepolis: The Story of a Childhood* (New York: Pantheon, 2003). Hereafter cited in text by page number. *Persepolis II: The Story of a Return* (New York: Pantheon, 2004). Hereafter cited in text as II and page number.

2. Eleanor Beadsley, "Some Taboos Vanish in Tusisia, Replaced by Others," June 4, 2012, NPR, http://www.npr.org/2012/06/04/154149524/some-taboos-vanish-in-tunisia-replaced-by-others (accessed September 11, 2012).

3. Satrapi, "Introduction," *Persepolis.*

4. Beadsley, "Some Taboos."

5. Mark Tessler, Amaney Jamal, and Michael Robbins, "New Findings on Arabs and Democracy," *Journal of Democracy* 23, no. 4 (2012): 102.

6. Soraya Sarhaddi Nelson, "Presidential Hopefuls Use Fear Campaigns in Egypt," NPR, June 12, 2012, http://www.npr.org/2012/06/12/154872724/presidential-hopefuls-use-fear-campaigns-in-egypt.

7. Barak Obama, "Remarks by the President on a New Beginning," June 4, 2009, Cairo, Egypt, Office of the Press Secretary http://www.whitehouse.gov/the-press-office/remarks-president-cairo-university-6-04-09.

8. See Massoud Karshenas, *Oil, State, and Industrialization in Iran* (Cambridge: Cambridge Univ. Press, 1990).

9. Edward Said, "Revised Introduction," in *Covering Islam* (New York: Vintage, 1997), xxxiii.

10. For background on graphic novels as illustrated narratives, see Scott McCloud, *Understanding Comics: The Invisible Art* (New York: Harper, 1993).

11. Peter Homans, ed., *Symbolic Loss: The Ambiguity of Mourning and Memory at Century's End* (Charlottesville: Univ. of Virginia Press, 2000), 20.

12. Erikson, "Notes on Trauma and Community," 194.

13. Butler, *Precarious Life*, 23.

14. Marjane Satrapi, interview by Terry Gross, Fresh Air, NPR, June 2, 2003, www.npr.org/templates/story/story.php?storyId=1283520.

15. Freud, "Mourning and Melancholia," 586.

16. Anne Anlin Cheng, *The Melancholy of Race: Psychoanalysis, Assimilation, and Hidden Grief* (New York: Oxford Univ. Press, 2001), 19.

17. Marjane Satrapi, interview with Dave Weich, Powell's Books, Portland, Oregon, September 17, 2004, http://www.powells.com/blog/interviews/marjane-satrapi -returns-by-dave/.

18. Maurice Halbwach, *On Collective Memory*, trans. Lewis A. Coser (Chicago: Univ. of Chicago Press, 1992), 175.

19. Erikson, "Notes on Trauma and Community," 190.

20. Mansoor Moaddel, *Class, Politics, Ideology in the Iranian Revolution* (New York: Columbia Univ. Press, 1993), 5.

6. Guerrilla Fighters, Televised Testimonies: Democratic Miracle or African Spring?

1. Thomas L. Friedman, "Hoping for Arab Mandelas," *New York Times*, March 26, 2011, http://www.nytimes.com/2011/03/27/opinion/27friedman.html?_r=1&page wanted=print.

2. For further discussion, see Sarah Nuttall and Carli Coetzee, eds. *Negotiating the Past: The Making of Memory in South Africa* (Cape Town: Oxford Univ. Press, 1998). Also see Martha Minow, *Between Vengeance and Forgiveness* (Boston: Beacon Press, 1998); Terry Bell, *Unfinished Business* (Muizenberg, South Africa: Red Works, 2001); Wilmot James and Linda van de Vijver, eds., *After the TRC: Reflections on Truth and Reconciliation in South Africa* (Athens: Ohio Univ. Press and Swallow Press, 2001); Anthea Jeffreys, *The Truth about the Truth Commission* (Johannesburg: Institute for Race Relations, 1999); *Truth and Reconciliation Commission of South Africa Report*, 4 vols. (Cape Town: TRC, 1998); and Desmond Tutu, *No Future without Forgiveness* (Johannesburg: Rider, 1999).

3. Loren Kruger, *Post-Imperial Brecht: Politics and Performance, East and South* (Cambridge: Cambridge Univ. Press, 2004), 346, 344.

4. The TRC in South Africa deviated from other previous commissions, not only because the conditional amnesty prevented the blanket pardon that leaders often grant perpetrators of crimes, but also because any survivor of a human rights violation could tell his or her story, and twenty-one thousand people came forward. From these records, a number of witnesses were selected to speak in their communities (two thousand public hearings). Select amnesty was granted for full testimonies about post-1960 acts associated with political objectives—eight thousand perpetrators applied.

5. Catherine Cole, *Performing South Africa's Truth Commission: Stages of Transition* (Indianapolis: Indiana Univ. Press, 2010), xv.

6. Pamela Sethunya Dube, "The Story of Thandi Shezi," in *Commissioning the Past: Understanding South Africa's Truth and Reconciliaiton Commission,*" ed. Deborah Posel

and Grame Simpson (Johannesburg: Witwatersrand Univ. Press, 2002), 129. Hereafter cited in the text by page number.

7. For further discussion, see Robert J. Landy, *Persona and Performance: The Meaning of Role in Drama, Therapy, and Everyday Life* (New York: Guilford Press, 1993); Robert Grainger, *Drama and Healing: The Roots of Drama Therapy* (Bristol, PA: Jessica Kingsley, 1990); Michael White and David Epston, *Narrative Means to Therapeutic Ends* (New York: W. W. Norton, 1990).

8. Veit Erlmann, *Nightsong: Performance, Power, and Practice in South Africa* (Chicago: Univ. of Chicago Press, 1996), 211.

9. Elaine Scarry, *The Body in Pain: The Making and Unmaking of the World* (New York: Oxford Univ. Press, 1985), 18, 36.

10. Teresa Godwin Phelps, *Shattered Voices: Language, Violence, and the Work of Truth Commissions* (Philadelphia: Univ. of Pennsylvania Press, 2004), 4.

11. Ibid., 5.

12. Hilde Lindemann Nelson, *Damaged Identities, Narrative Repair* (Ithaca: Cornell Univ. Press, 2001), xi. Mary Duggan and Roger Grainger, *Imagination, Identification, and Catharsis in Theater and Therapy* (London, PA: Jessica Kingsley, 1997), 52. Also see Renee Emunah, *Acting for Real: Drama Therapy Process, Technique, and Performance* (New York: Brunner/Mazel, 1994).

13. Desmond Tutu, "Opening Remarks," in *South Africa's Human Spirit: An Oral Memory of the Truth and Reconciliation*, produced by Angie Kapelianis and Darren Taylor, online posting, April 13, 2000, SABC, http://www.sabctruth.co.za/bones.htm (accessed November 18, 2012).

14. Nuttall and Coetzee, *Negotiating the Past*, 1–6.

15. Anonymous editorial, "A Harsh Cry: A Wife Grieves," *Cape Argus*, October 27, 1998, 12.

16. *Truth and Reconciliation Commission Report*, vol. 1.

17. Mary Burton, "Bones of Memory," in Kapelianis and Taylor, *South Africa's Human Spirit.*

18. "We have had to endure the pain" while "reliving the horrors," and the raw "wounds" amidst moments of "forgiveness" still "bring a lump to the throat." Joe Latakgomo, "Treading Truth's Fine Line," *The Daily News*, November 3, 1998, 10.

19. *Truth and Reconciliation Commission Report*, 1:358.

20. Charles Villa-Vicencio, "On the Limitations of Academic History: The Quest for Truth Demands Both More and Less," in James and van de Vijver, *After the TRC*, 25.

21. For instance, see Yazir Henry, "Where Healing Begins," in *Looking Back, Reaching Forward: Reflections on the Truth and Reconciliation Commission of South Africa*, ed. Charles Villa-Vicencio and Wilhelm Verwoerd (Cape Town: Univ. of Cape Town Press and Zed Books, 2000), 167.

22. Antjie Krog, *Country of My Skull* (Johannesburg: Random House, 1998), 27.

23. Ingrid de Kok, "The Archbishop Chairs the First Session," in *Terrestrial Things* (Roggebaai, South Africa: Kwela Books, 2002), 22.

24. For further discussion, see Eve Kosofsky Sedgwick, *Touching Feeling: Affect, Pedagogy, Performativity* (Durham: Duke Univ. Press, 2004).

25. Antjie Krog, *Down to My Last Skin* (Johannesburg: Random House, 2000), 97.

26. This testimony of Eunice Miya is from http://www.sabctruth.co.za/bones.htm.

27. Gcina Mhlope, "The Bones of Memory, South Africa's Human Spirit," SABC Recording, vol. 1, Johannesburg, September 1, 1999.

28. De Kok, "Body Parts," in *Terrestial Things*, 37.

29. Taylor, *Archive and the Repertoire*, 21.

30. Seitlhamo Motsapi, *Earthstepper/The Ocean is Very Shallow* (Grahamstown, South Africa: Deep South, 2003). Hereafter cited in the text by page number.

31. Malika Lueen Ndlovu, *Born in Africa, But* (Cape Town: Educall, Harrington House, 2000), 67, 68.

32. A key role of society is to stabilize pain, this "most elementary sign"; see Scarry, *Body in Pain*, 13.

33. Boal, *Theater of the Oppressed*, 135, 122.

34. Khulile Nxumalo, "Xstacy" and "Into the Whistle's Nostrils," in *Ten Flapping Elbows, Mama* (Grahamstown, South Africa: Deep South, 2004).

35. Jacob Lindy and Robert Lifton, eds., *Beyond Invisible Walls: The Psychological Legacy of Soviet Trauma* (New York: Brunner-Routledge, 2001), 3.

7. 9/11 Media: Gendered Nationalism beyond Islamic/Jewish Borders

1. Nadia Davids, *At Her Feet* (Cape Town: Oshun Books, 2006), 68. Hereafter cited in text by page number.

2. I am indebted here to the idea of the "contact zone" between cultures to Mary Louise Pratt, *Imperial Eyes: Travel Writing and Transculturation* (London: Routledge, 1992).

3. Zimitri Erasmus, "Re-imagining Coloured Identities in Post-Apartheid South Africa," in *Coloured by History, Shaped by Place: New Perspectives on Coloured Identities in Cape Town*, ed. Zimitri Erasmus (Cape Town: Kwela Books, 2001), 1–28.

4. Connerton, *How Societies Remember*, 7.

5. Erasmus, "Re-imagining Coloured Identities," 16.

6. Ibid., 25, 21. Black political identities are also "constructions," writes Erasmus, for there is no singular or "authentic black self" (25).

7. Homi Bhabha, "Remembering Fanon: Self, Psyche, and the Colonial Condition," in *Colonial Discourse and Postcolonial Theory*, ed. Patrick Williams and Laura Chrisman (New York: Columbia Univ. Press, 1994), 117.

8. Ibid.

9. Interview with Yael Farber by Nadia Neophytou, "Why New York Needs to See MoLoRa," July 5, 2011, http://www.youtube.com/watch?v=kEMJyWWLCcU.

10. Yael Farber, "Foreword," in *Molora: Based on the "Oresteia" by Aeschylus* (London: Oberon Books, 2008). Hereafter cited in text by page number.

11. Josh Beer, *Sophocles and the Tragedy of Athenian Democracy* (Westport, CT: Praeger, 2004), 118.

12. Loren Kruger, *The Drama of South Africa: Plays, Pageants, and Publics since 1910* (London: Routledge, 1999), 39.

13. Leslie Witz, *Apartheid's Festival: Contesting South Africa's National Pasts* (Indianapolis: Indiana Univ. Press, 2003), 122.

14. Beer, *Sophocles*, 4.

15. Hannah Arendt, *Eichmann in Jerusalem: A Report on the Banality of Evil* (New York: Penguin Books, 1994), 276.

16. Anne McClintock, *Imperial Leather: Race, Gender, and Sexuality* (New York: Routledge, 1995), 16, 156.

17. Achille Mbembe, *On the Postcolony* (Berkeley and Los Angeles: Univ. of California Press, 2001), 27.

18. Puar, *Terrorist Assemblages*, 102.

19. Ibid., 82.

20. Ibid., 108.

21. Cape Town amnesty hearings, quoted in Ingrid de Kok's poem "What Kind of Man," in *Terrestrial Things*, 25.

22. Farber, interview, in *Theatre as Witness: Three Testimonial Plays from South Africa*. London: Oberon Books, 2008, 26.

23. Ibid., 25.

24. Ingrid de Kok, "Revenge of the Imagination," in *Terrestial Things*, 28.

25. In *Molora*, it is the survivor, not perpetrator, who details the perpetrator's nightmares. At the TRC, some victims expressed outrage that perpetrators spoke of their murderous action alongside their PTSD, when so many black South Africans had been murdered; yet it is a reversal to hear of the formerly powerful now speak of psychological anxiety.

26. Richard Wright and Lawrence Ward, *Orienting of Attention* (Oxford: Oxford Univ. Press, 2008), 53.

27. Casey O'Callaghan, *Sounds: A Philosophical Theory* (Oxford: Oxford Univ. Press, 2007), 57.

28. C. J. Darwin, "Listening to Speech in the Presence of Other Sounds," in *The Perception of Speech: From Sound to Meaning*, ed. Brian Moore, Lorraine Tyler, William Marslen-Wilson (Oxford: Oxford Univ. Press, 2009), 157, 164.

29. L. L. Balkwill and W. F. Thompson, "A Cross-Cultural Investigation of the Perception of Emotion in Music: Psychophysical and Cultural Cues," *Music Perception* 17 (1999): 43–64. L. L. Balkwill, W. F. Thompson, and R. Matsunaga, "Recognition of Emotion in Japanese, Western, and Hindustani Music by Japanese Listeners," *Japanese*

Psychological Research 46, no.4 (2004): 33–49. Also see Thompson, *Music, Thought, and Feeling*, 148.

30. Khanna, *Dark Continents*, 24.

31. If perpetrators do not apply for amnesty, they could be placed on trial at a later date. If they lie, their amnesty application will be denied.

32. Noelle McAfee, *Democracy and the Political Unconscious* (New York: Columbia Univ. Press, 2008), 104.

33. Peter Schwenger, *The Tears of Things: Melancholy and Physical Objects* (Minneapolis: Univ. of Minnesota Press, 2006), 3.

34. Ibid., 80.

35. See Robert Fagles and W. B. Stanford, *The Oresteia* (New York: Penguin, 1977).

36. Butler, *Precarious Life*, 79.

37. McAfee, *Democracy and the Political Unconscious*, 85.

8. Bewitched Democracies: A Ritual Spring for Youth Culture?

1. "Outcasts of the Witch Village of the North," *Mail and Guardian*, November 3, 1995, http://mg.co.za/article/1995-11-03-outcasts-of-the-witch-village-of-the-north.

2. "Between 1985 and 1995 the courts prosecuted 109 (52 percent) of the 209 persons accused of involvement in witch-killings." In Isak Niehaus, "Witchcraft in the New South Africa: From Colonial Superstition to Postcolonial Reality?," in *Magical Interpretations, Material Realities: Modernity, Witchcraft, and the Occult in Postcolonial Africa*, ed. Henrietta L. Moore and Todd Sanders (London: Routledge, 2001), 189.

3. Anthony Minnaar, Marie Wentzel, and Catherine Payze, "Witch Killing with Specific Reference to the Northern Province of South Africa," in *Violence in South Africa*, ed. Elirea Bornman, Rene van Eeden, Marie Wentzel (Pretoria: HSRC, 1998), 188.

4. Ibid., 174. Era of 1990–1995.

5. Peter Geschiere, *The Modernity of Witchcraft: Politics and the Occult in Postcolonial Africa* (Charlottesville: Univ. Press of Virginia, 1997), 118–19.

6. Minaar, Wentzel, and Payze, "Witch Killing," 189–90.

7. The plays *Ipi Zombi!* and *Mumbo Jumbo* are published in Brett Bailey, *The Plays of Miracle and Wonder* (Cape Town: Double Storey Books, 2003). Hereafter cited in text by page number.

8. Adam Ashforth, *Witchcraft, Violence, and Democracy* (Chicago: Univ. of Chicago Press, 2005), 247. Ashforth argues that there is no "moral distinction" made between the gang member's violence and his mother, who is viewed as the black magic provider; both are considered "equally wrong" and killed, a horrific problem for secular justice, which demands evidence (247).

9. Sandra Harding, *Science and Social Inequality: Feminist and Postcolonial Issues* (Chicago: Univ. of Illinois Press, 2006), 5.

10. Ashforth, *Witchcraft, Violence, and Democracy*, 247, 265.

11. Ralph Austen, "The Moral Economy of Witchcraft," in *Modernity and Its Malcontents: Ritual and Power in Postcolonial Africa*, ed. Jean Comaroff and John Comaroff (Chicago: Univ. of Chicago Press, 1993), 91.

12. Ibid., 92.

13. Minnaar, Wentzel, and Payze, "Witch Killing," 184.

14. Mbembe, *On the Postcolony*, 25. As Mbemebe pronounced, the native was never an equal and could only be "wrong." Colonization's "virtually infinite permutations between what was just or unjust," this flexibility about what could be "punished," continually flaunted domination and diminished local "power"(26).

15. John Matshikiza, "The Politics of Performance," *Mail and Guardian*, May 7–13, 1999, 2–3.

16. Solomon Makgale, "Bailey's Calling Up the Spirits to Stay," *Sowetan*, July 15, 1998, 18. Also see popular reviews by Karen Makgamathe, "Xhosa Play Tackles the Evils of Westernization," *Cue*, July 6, 1997, 10.

17. Fred Khumalo, "A Glimpse into South Africa's Dark Soul That's Worthy of Tarantino," *Sunday Times*, July 5, 1998, 3.

18. Zakes Mda, "Zombi Magic Triumphs," *Cue*, July 4, 1998, 6.

19. Sandra Harding, "Is Modern Science an Ethnoscience?: Rethinking Epistemological Assumptions," in *Postcolonial African Philosophy*, ed. Emmanuel Chukwudi Eze (Lewisburg, PA: Blackwell, 1997), 60, 63.

20. Robert Greig, "Genre-Bending Operas Breach Fresh Frontier," *Sunday Independent*, July 4, 1999, 12.

21. Karen Makgamathe, "Xhosa Play Tackles the Evils of Westernization," *Cue*, July 6, 1997, 10.

22. Mikki Flockemann, Gino Fransman, Linda Tini, Ignatius Ticha, "Furiously Enthused?: Performing Identities, Encounter *IMumbo-Jumbo*: A UWC Case Study," *South African Theatre Journal* 19, no. 1 (2005): 191. Hereafter cited in text by page number.

23. For a discussion of African Christ figures, see Diane B. Stinton, *Jesus of Africa: Voices of Contemporary African Christology* (Maryknoll, NY: Orbis Books, 2004).

24. For further research on religion and trauma, see Debra Kaminer and Gillian Eagle, *Traumatic Stress in South Africa* (Johannesburg: Wits Univ. Press, 2010). In their examples, there were several worldviews: "trauma was due to random chance or bad luck," was part of "God's plan," caused by "other people using witchcraft," or caused by "ancestors because of something I did or did not do" (64).

25. Anthony Minaar, Sam Pretorius, and Marie Wentzel, "Political Conflict and Other Manifestations of Violence in South Africa," in Bornman, van Eeden, and Wentzel, *Violence in South Africa*, 30.

26. Michaelle L. Browers, *Democracy and Civil Society in Arab Political Thought: Transcultural Possibilities* (Syracuse: Syracuse Univ. Press, 2006), 35.

27. In Flockemann, "Furiously Enthused," 197.

28. Margaret Thompson Drewal, *Yoruba Ritual: Performers, Play, Agency* (Bloomington: Indiana Univ. Press, 1992), xix.

29. Temple Hauptfleisch, *Theatre and Society in South Africa* (South Africa: Van Schaik, 1997). For further discussion of South African theater, see David Coplan, *Township Tonight!: South Africa's Black City Music and Theatre* (South Africa: Ravan, 1996); and Catherine Knox, "The Story of Our Times," *Mail and Guardian*, June 12–18, 1998, 2.

30. Brett Bailey, "Performing So the Spirit May Speak," *South African Theatre Journal* 12, no. 1 (1998): 192.

31. For further discussion on health practices and knowledge as potentially undemocratic, see the excellent text by Sandra Harding, *Science and Social Inequality*.

Conclusion: Looking for Fadwa

1. Rami Khouri, American University of Beirut, Lebanon, quoted in Liz Sly, "Reversals Challenge Hope of Arab Spring," *The Washington Post*, May 12, 2011, http://www.washingtonpost.com/world/middle-east/reversals-challenge-hope-of-arab-spring/2011/05/12/AFkgcV1G_story_1.html.

2. See Roach, *Cities of the Dead*, 5.

3. Hamid Dabashi, *The Arab Spring: The End of Postcolonialism* (London: Zed Books, 2012), 14.

4. Lynch, *Voices of the New Arab Public*, 28.

5. Noueihed and Warren, *Battle for Arab Spring*, 52.

6. Ibid., 54, 50.

7. Nick Hunt and Mustafa al-Arab, "How a Fruit Seller Caused Revolution in Tunisia," January 16, 2011, http://articles.cnn.com/2011-01-16/world/tunisia.fruit.seller.bouazizi_1_tunisian-history-street-vendor-police-officer?_s=PM:WORLD.

8. I chart protest and democratic practice to Iraqi Kurdistan, two decades past, in what I call "the forgotten spring." Chapters 1 and 6 were first published in a slightly different form in *Comparative Studies of South Asia, Africa, and the Middle East* 25, no. 1 (2005): 138–51, stating how protest songs shifted ideas about time, suggesting the terror of the past has passed, an important collective voicing and political process that takes time.

9. While I have taught Laila Lalami's fiction for many years in African women's studies and study abroad courses in Morocco, and had already studied blogs, I want to thank Nouri Gana for drawing my attention to this blog that contains Lalami's idea of Morocco's Bouazizi in our conversation at the MLA in January 2012. The research and gender focus of this analysis, connecting Fadwa to the forgotten spring, is, of course, mine, with all its potential faults.

10. Laila Lalami, "Fadoua Laroui: The Moroccan Mohamed Bouazizi," February 27, 2011, http://www.thenation.com/blog/158878/fadoua-laroui-moroccan-mohamed-bouazizi.

11. "Fadwa Laroui Story till Martyrdom," February 26, 2011, www.youtube.com /watch?v=4dYWCfY40tI.

12. Nadir Bouhmouch "My Makhzen and Me," 2011, http://www.mymakhzen andme.com/.

13. Kristen McTighe, "Help for Unwed Mothers in Morocco," *New York Times*, June 9, 2011, http://www.nytimes.com/2011/06/02/world/middleeast/02iht-M02 -MOROCCO-HAMMAM.html?_r=1&pagewanted=all.

14. Rachel Newcomb, "The Young and the Restless, *Foreign Policy*, March 25, 2011.

15. Laila Lalami, "Morocco's Moderate Revolution," *Foreign Policy*, February 21, 2011, excerpted in her blog, http://lailalalami.com/2011/moroccos-moderate -revolution/.

16. Lalami, "Morocco's Moderate Revolution," http://www.foreignpolicy.com /articles/2011/02/21/moroccos_moderate_revolution.

17. Laila Lalami, "Revolution in the Arab World," *The Guardian*, January 13, 2012, http://www.guardian.co.uk/books/2012/jan/13/arab-spring-one-year-on.

18. Karen M. Morin and Jeanne Kay Guelke, "Introduction: Women, Religion, and Space—Making the Connections," in *Women, Religion, and Space: Global Perspectives on Gender and Faith*, ed. Morin and Guelke (Syracuse: Syracuse Univ. Press, 2007), xix.

19. Jeanne Kay Guelke and Karen M. Morin, "Missionary Women in Early America," in Morin and Guelke, *Women, Religion, and Space*, 114.

20. For further discussion on transgressive spaces, see Tim Cresswell, *In Place/Out of Place: Geography, Ideology, and Transgression* (Minneapolis: Univ. of Minnesota Press, 1996).

21. Deborah Kapchan, *Traveling Spirit Masters: Moroccan Gnawa Trance and the Music in the Global Marketplace* (Middletown: Wesleyan Univ. Press, 2007), 78.

22. Butler, *Precarious Life*, 53–57.

23. Bill Keller, "A Liberal Hawk Recants," *New York Times Magazine*, September 11, 2011, 36.

24. Ibid., 37.

25. Scott Malcomson, "A Free-for-All on a Decade of War: From *Times Magazine*, a Post-9/11 Debate on What Has Been Learned and Where Our Conclusions Might Take Us," *New York Times Magazine*, September 7, 2011, http://www.nytimes .com/2011/09/11/us/sept-11-reckoning/roundtable.html?_r=2ref=magazine&. Round table: Michael Ignatieff, David Rieff, James Traub, Ian Buruma, and Paul Berman.

26. Mark Tessler and Marilyn Grobschmidt, "Democracy in the Arab World and the Arab-Israeli Conflict," in *Democracy, War, and Peace in the Middle East*, ed. David Garnham and Mark Tessler (Bloomington: Indiana Univ. Press, 1995), 153. As research studies show, the "level of economic development" influences the "probability that democracy will survive" (153).

27. Adam Przeworski, Michael Alvarez, Jose Cheibub, and Fernando Limongi, "What Makes Democracies Endure?" in *Global Divergence of Democracies*, ed. Larry Diamond and Marc Plattner (Baltimore: Johns Hopkins Univ. Press, 2001), 168–69. And the research of Tessler and Grobschmidt in "Democracy in the Arab World" suggests Islamist politicians can step down when they do not win, and will not be re-elected if they do not produce satisfying results (153, 159). Muslim groups are heterogeneous; their movements can reflect democratic divergence and opportunities (159).

28. Tessler, Jamal, and Robbins, "New Findings on Arabs and Democracy," 90.

29. Ibid., 96.

30. Ibid.

31. Marc Lynch sees as an important democratic development the fact that Salafis "who spent decades denouncing democracy as an affront to God's law now race to form political parties" (209). Also in Egypt, the Muslim Brotherhood is joined by a "rainbow of new Islamist parties" (210), and splintering between the Brotherhood and its many youth supporters has begun, because "they identified more with the restless impatience of their secular peers than with their cautious organization" (212). In Marc Lynch, *The Arab Uprising: The Unfinished Revolutions of the New Middle East* (New York: Public Affairs, 2012).

32. Tariq Ramadan, *Islam and the Arab Awakening* (Oxford: Oxford Univ. Press, 2012), 143.

33. Lynch, *Voices of the New Arab Public*, 28. Noueihed and Warren, *Battle for Arab Spring*, 52.

34. V. Y. Mudimbe, *The Invention of Africa: Gnosis, Philosophy, and the Order of Knowledge* (Bloomington: Indiana Univ. Press, 1988), 4–5.

35. "Marginality designates the intermediate space between . . . tradition and the projected modernity of colonialism . . . an urbanized space . . . syncretic" (ibid., 5).

36. "Qualities" of the character should "contradict one another" to create critical thinking in the audience. Bertolt Brecht, *Brecht on Theatre (1898–1956): The Development of an Aesthetic*, ed. and trans. John Willett (New York: Hill and Wang, 1964), 196.

37. *Time Magazine*, August 2010. The photograph of Aisha Bibi, taken by Jodi Bieber, was awarded the World Press Photo of the Year in 2010. The photo shows the disfiguration, the cut off nose, of a young woman who fled her marriage.

38. Jon Binnie, Robyn Longhurst, and Robin Peace, "Upstairs/Downstairs—Place Matters, Bodies Matter," in *Pleasure Zones: Bodies, Cities, Spaces*, ed. Binnie, Longhurst, and Peace (Syracuse: Syracuse Univ. Press, 2001), vii–viii.

39. Sedgwick, *Touching Feeling*, 14.

40. Ahmed, *Cultural Politics of Emotion*, 4, 196, 33.

41. Anderson, "Modulating the Excess of Affect," 164.

42. Antze and Lambek, "Introduction," xii.

43. Dori Laub and Shoshana Felman, *Testimony: Crisis of Witnessing in Literature, Psychoanalysis, and History* (New York: Routledge, 1991), 69.

44. Ronnie Janoff-Bulman, *Shattered Assumptions: Towards a New Psychology of Trauma* (New York: Free Press, 1992).

45. Das and Kleinman, *Remaking a World*, 8.

46. Tracy Davis, *Cambridge Companion to Performance Studies* (New York: Cambridge Univ. Press, 2008), 5.

47. Michael Kammen, *Mystic Chords of Memory: The Transformation of Tradition in American Culture* (New York: Alfred Knopf, 1991), 13.

References

Adams, Paul C. *The Boundless Self: Communication in Physical and Virtual Spaces*. Syracuse: Syracuse Univ. Press, 2005.

Ahmed, Leila. *Women and Gender in Islam: Historical Roots of a Modern Debate*. New Haven: Yale Univ. Press, 1992.

Ahmed, Sara. *The Cultural Politics of Emotion*. New York: Routledge, 2004.

Al-Ali, Nadje, and Nicola Pratt. *What Kind of Liberation?: Women and the Occupation of Iraq*. Berkeley and Los Angeles: Univ. of California Press, 2009.

Allison, Christine. "Old and New Oral Traditions in Badinan." In *Kurdish Culture and Identity*, edited by Christine Allison and Philip Kreyenbroek, 29–47. London: Zed Books, 1996.

Amireh, Amal. "Writing the Difference: Feminists' Invention of the 'Arab Woman.'" In Ghosh and Bose, *Interventions*, 185–212.

Anderson, Ben. "Modulating the Excess of Affect: Morale in a State of 'Total War.'" In Gregg and Seigworth, *Affect Theory Reader*, 61–185.

Anderson, Benedict. *Imagined Communities*. New York: Verso, 1983; 1991.

Antze, Paul, and Michael Lambek, eds. "Introduction: Forecasting Memory." In *Tense Past: Cultural Essays in Trauma and Memory*, edited by Antze and Lambek, xi–xxxviii. New York: Routledge, 1996.

Appadurai, Arjun. *Modernity at Large: Cultural Dimensions of Globalization*. Minneapolis: Univ. of Minnesota Press, 1996.

——, ed. *Globalization*. Durham: Duke Univ. Press, 2001.

——. "Grassroots Globalization and the Research Imagination." In Appadurai, *Globalization*, 1–21.

Arendt, Hannah. *Eichmann in Jerusalem: A Report on the Banality of Evil*. New York: Penguin Books, 1994.

Asad, Talal. *On Suicide Bombing*. New York: Columbia Univ. Press, 2007.

Ashforth, Adam. *Witchcraft, Violence, and Democracy*. Chicago: Univ. of Chicago Press, 2005.

Austen, Ralph. "The Moral Economy of Witchcraft." In *Modernity and Its Malcontents: Ritual and Power in Postcolonial Africa*, edited by Jean Comaroff and John Comaroff, 89–110. Chicago: Univ. of Chicago Press, 1993.

Bailey, Brett. "Performing So the Spirit May Speak," *South African Theatre Journal* 12, no. 1 (1998): 191–202.

———. *The Plays of Miracle and Wonder*. Cape Town: Double Storey Books, 2003.

Bakhtin, M. M. *The Dialogic Imagination: Four Essays*. Edited by Michael Holquist. Translated by Caryl Emerson and Michael Holquist. Austin: Univ. of Texas Press, 1981.

Balkwill, L. L., and Thompson, W. F. "A Cross-Cultural Investigation of the Perception of Emotion in Music: Psychophysical and Cultural Cues." *Music Perception* 17 (1999): 43–64.

Balkwill, L. L., and R. Matsunaga. "Recognition of Emotion in Japanese, Western, and Hindustani Music by Japanese Listeners." *Japanese Psychological Research* 46, no. 4 (2004): 337–49.

Baudrillard, Jean. *Simulacra and Simulation*. Translated by Sheila Faria Glaser. Ann Arbor: Univ. of Michigan Press, 2008.

Beer, Josh. *Sophocles and the Tragedy of Athenian Democracy*. Westport, CT: Praeger, 2004.

Bell, Terry. *Unfinished Business*. Muizenberg, South Africa: Red Works, 2001.

Bennett, W. Lance, Regina Lawrence, and Steven Livingston. *When the Press Fails: Political Power and the News Media from Iraq to Katrina*. Chicago: Univ. of Chicago Press, 2007.

Bhabha, Homi. "Remembering Fanon: Self, Psyche, and the Colonial Condition." In *Colonial Discourse and Postcolonial Theory*, edited by Patrick Williams and Laura Chrisman, 112–24. New York: Columbia Univ. Press, 1994.

Binnie, Jon, Robyn Longhurst, and Robin Peace. "Upstairs/Downstairs—Place Matters, Bodies Matter." In *Pleasure Zones: Bodies, Cities, Spaces*, edited by Binnie, Longhurst, and Peace, vii–xiv. Syracuse: Syracuse Univ. Press, 2001.

Bird, Christiane. *A Thousand Sighs, A Thousand Revolts: Journeys in Kurdistan*. New York: Ballantine Books, 2004.

Boal, Augusto. *Theatre of the Oppressed*. Translated by Charles McBride and Maria-Odilia McBride. New York: Theatre Communications Group, 1985.

Bornman, Elirea, Rene van Eeden, and Marie Wentzel, eds. *Violence in South Africa*. Pretoria: HSRC, 1998.

Bourdieu, Pierre. *The Field of Cultural Production: Essays on Art and Literature*. Columbia Univ. Press, 1993.

Brecht, Bertolt. *Brecht on Theatre (1898-1956): The Development of an Aesthetic*. Edited and Translated by John Willett. New York: Hill and Wang, 1964.

Browers, Michaelle L. *Democracy and Civil Society in Arab Political Thought: Transcultural Possibilities*. Syracuse: Syracuse Univ. Press, 2006.

Butler, Judith. *Gender Trouble: Feminism and the Subversion of Identity*. New York: Routledge, 1999.

———. *Precarious Life: The Powers of Mourning and Violence*. London: Verso Press, 2004.

Carlson, Marvin. *Speaking in Tongues: Languages at Play in the Theatre*. Ann Arbor: Univ. of Michigan Press, 2006.

Caruth, Cathy, ed. *Trauma: Explorations in Memory*. Baltimore: Johns Hopkins Univ. Press, 1995.

———. *Unclaimed Experience: Trauma, Narrative, and History*. Baltimore: Johns Hopkins Univ. Press, 1996.

Chase, Anthony, and Amr Hamzawy, eds. *Human Rights in the Arab World: Independent Voices*. Philadelphia: Univ. of Pennsylvania Press, 2006.

Chatty, Dawn. *Displacement and Dispossession in the Modern Middle East*. Cambridge: Cambridge Univ. Press, 2010.

Cheng, Anne Anlin. *The Melancholy of Race: Psychoanalysis, Assimilation, and Hidden Grief*. New York: Oxford Univ. Press, 2001.

Chong, Kelly H. *Deliverance and Submission: Evangelical Women and the Negotiation of Patriarchy in South Korea*. Cambridge: Harvard Univ. Press, 2008.

Christensen, Dieter. "On Variability in Kurdish Dance Songs." *Asian Music* 6, nos. 1/2 (1975): 1–6.

Clifford, James. "Introduction: Partial Truths." In *Writing Culture: The Poetics and Politics of Ethnography*, edited by James Clifford and George Marcus, 1–26. Berkeley and Los Angeles: Univ. of California, 1986.

———. *The Predicament of Culture: Twentieth-Century Ethnography, Literature, and Art*. Boston: Harvard Univ. Press, 2002.

Cole, Catherine. *Performing South Africa's Truth Commission: Stages of Transition*. Indianapolis: Indiana Univ. Press, 2010.

Connerton, Paul. *How Societies Remember*. Cambridge: Cambridge Univ. Press, 1989.

Cooke, Miriam. *Women Claim Islam: Creating Islamic Feminism through Literature.* New York: Routledge, 2001.

Coplan, David. *Township Tonight!: South Africa's Black City Music and Theatre.* South Africa: Ravan, 1996.

Cresswell, Tim. *In Place/Out of Place: Geography, Ideology, and Transgression.* Minneapolis: Univ. of Minnesota Press, 1996.

Cubilie, Anne. *Women Witnessing Terror.* New York: Fordham Univ. Press, 2005.

Dabashi, Hamid. *The Arab Spring: The End of Postcolonialism.* London: Zed Books, 2012.

Darwin, C. J. "Listening to Speech in the Presence of Other Sounds." In *The Perception of Speech: From Sound to Meaning,*" edited by Brian Moore, Lorraine Tyler, and William Marslen-Wilson, 151–70. Oxford: Oxford Univ. Press, 2009.

Das, Veena, and Arthur Kleinman, eds. "Introduction." In *Remaking a World: Violence, Social Suffering, and Recovery,* edited by Veena and Kleinman. Berkeley and Los Angeles: Univ. of California Press, 2001.

Davids, Nadia. *At Her Feet.* Cape Town: Oshun Books, 2006.

Davis, Eric. *Memories of State: Politics, History, and Collective Identity in Modern Iraq.* Berkeley and Los Angeles: Univ. of California Press, 2005.

Davis, Tracy. *Cambridge Companion to Performance Studies.* New York: Cambridge Univ. Press, 2008.

De Kok, Ingrid. *Terrestial Things.* Roggebai, South Africa: Kwela, 2002.

Dodge, Toby. *Inventing Iraq: The Failure of Nation Building and a History Denied.* New York: Columbia Univ. Press, 2003.

Drewal, Margaret Thompson. *Yoruba Ritual: Performers, Play, Agency.* Bloomington: Indiana Univ. Press, 1992.

Dube, Pamela Sethunya. "The Story of Thandi Shezi." In *Commissioning the Past: Understanding South Africa's Truth and Reconciliation Commission,*" edited by Deborah Posel and Grame Simpson, 117–30. Johannesburg: Witwatersrand Univ. Press, 2002.

Duggan, Mary, and Roger Grainger. *Imagination, Identification, and Catharsis in Theatre and Therapy.* London, PA: Jessica Kingsley, 1997.

Emunah, Renee. *Acting for Real: Drama Therapy Process, Technique, and Performance.* New York: Brunner/Mazel, 1994.

Entman, Robert M. *Projections of Power: Framing News, Public Opinion, and U.S. Foreign Policy.* Chicago: Univ. of Chicago Press, 2004.

Erasmus, Zimitri. "Re-imagining Coloured Identities in Post-Apartheid South Africa." In *Coloured by History, Shaped by Place: New Perspectives on Coloured Identities in Cape Town*, ed. Zimitri Erasmus, 1-28. Cape Town: Kwela Books, 2001.

Erikson, Kai. "Notes on Trauma and Community." In Caruth, *Trauma*, 183–99.

Erlmann, Veit. *Nightsong: Performance, Power, and Practice in South Africa.* Chicago: Univ. of Chicago Press, 1996.

Fagles, Robert, and W. B. Stanford. *The Oresteia.* New York: Penguin, 1977.

Farber, Yael. *Molora: Based on the "Oresteia" by Aeschylus.* London: Oberon Books, 2008.

———. *Theatre as Witness: Three Testimonial Plays from South Africa.* London: Oberon Books, 2008.

Feldman, Allen. *Formations of Violence: The Narrative of the Body and Political Terror in Northern Ireland.* Chicago: Univ. of Chicago Press, 1991.

Flatley, Jonathan. *Affective Mapping: Melancholia and the Politics of Modernism.* Cambridge: Harvard Univ. Press, 2008.

Flockemann, Mikki, Gino Fransman, Linda Tini, and Ignatius Ticha. "Furiously Enthused?: Performing Identities, Encountering *IMumbo-Jumbo*: A UWC Case Study." *South African Theatre Journal* 19, no. 1 (2005): 191-207.

Freud, Sigmund. *The Freud Reader.* Edited by Peter Gay. New York: Norton, 1989.

Gana, Nouri. *Signifying Loss: Towards a Poetics of Narrative Mourning.* Lewisburg: Bucknell Univ. Press, 2011.

Geschiere, Peter. *The Modernity of Witchcraft: Politics and the Occult in Postcolonial Africa.* Charlottesville: Univ. Press of Virginia, 1997.

Ghosh, Bishnupriya, and Brinda Bose, eds. *Interventions: Feminist Dialogues on Third World Women's Literature and Film.* New York: Garland, 1997.

Glantz, Aaron. *How America Lost Iraq.* New York: Penguin, 2005.

Golley, Nawar Al-Hassan. *Reading Arab Women's Autobiographies: Shahrazad Tells Her Story.* Austin: Univ. of Texas Press, 2003.

Grainger, Robert. *Drama and Healing: The Roots of Drama Therapy.* Bristol, PA: Jessica Kingsley, 1990.

Gregg, Melissa, and Gregory J. Seigworth, eds. *The Affect Theory Reader.* Durham: Duke Univ. Press, 2010.

Griffith, R. Marie. *God's Daughters: Evangelical Women and the Power of Submission.* Berkeley and Los Angeles: Univ. of California Press, 1997.

Halbwach, Maurice. *On Collective Memory.* Translated by Lewis A. Coser. Chicago: Univ. of Chicago Press, 1992.

Hardi, Choman. *Gendered Experiences of Genocide: Anfal Survivors in Kurdistan-Iraq.* Surrey: Ashgate, 2011.

Harding, Sandra. "Is Modern Science an Ethnoscience?: Rethinking Epistemological Assumptions." In *Postcolonial African Philosophy*, edited by Emmanuel Chukwudi Eze, 45-70. Lewisburg, PA: Blackwell, 1997.

———. *Science and Social Inequality: Feminist and Postcolonial Issues.* Chicago: Univ. of Illinois Press, 2006.

Hauptfleisch, Temple. *Theatre and Society in South Africa.* South Africa: Van Schaik, 1997.

Henry, Yazir. "Where Healing Begins." In Villa-Vicencio and Verwoerd, *Looking Back, Reaching Forward*, 166–73.

Herman, Judith. *Trauma and Recovery: The Aftermath of Violence.* New York: Basic Books, 1997.

Herring, Eric, and Glen Rangwala. *Iraq in Fragments: The Occupation and Its Legacy.* New York: Cornell Univ. Press, 2006.

Homans, Peter, ed. *Symbolic Loss: The Ambiguity of Mourning and Memory at Century's End.* Charlottesville: Univ. of Virginia Press, 2000.

Houston, Christopher. *Kurdistan: Crafting of National Selves.* Bloomington: Indiana Univ. Press, 2008.

Huyssen, Andreas. "Present Pasts: Media, Politics, Amnesia." In Appadurai, *Globalization*, 57-77.

Izady, Mehrdad. *The Kurds.* London: Crane Russak, 1992.

James, Wilmot, and Linda van de Vijver, eds. *After the TRC: Reflections on Truth and Reconciliation in South Africa.* Athens: Ohio Univ. Press and Swallow Press, 2001.

Janoff-Bulman, Ronnie. *Shattered Assumptions: Towards a New Psychology of Trauma.* New York: Free Press, 1992.

Jeffreys, Anthea. *The Truth about the Truth Commission.* Johannesburg: Institute for Race Relations, 1999.

Kahf, Mohja. *Western Representations of the Muslim Woman.* Austin: Univ. of Texas Press, 1999.

Kaminer, Debra, and Gillian Eagle. *Traumatic Stress in South Africa.* Johannesburg: Wits Univ. Press, 2010.

Kammen, Michael. *Mystic Chords of Memory: The Transformation of Tradition in American Culture.* New York: Alfred Knopf, 1991.

Kapchan, Deborah. *Traveling Spirit Masters: Moroccan Gnawa Trance and Music in the Global Marketplace*. Middletown: Wesleyan Univ. Press, 2007.

Karshenas, Massoud. *Oil, State, and Industrialization in Iran*. Cambridge: Cambridge Univ. Press, 1990.

Khanna, Ranjana. *Dark Continents: Psychoanalysis and Colonialism*. Durham: Duke Univ. Press, 2003.

Kirmayer, Laurence. "Landscapes of Memory: Trauma, Narrative, and Dissociation." In Antze and Lambek, *Tense Past*, 173–98.

Krog, Antjie. *Country of My Skull*. Johannesburg: Random House, 1998.

———. *Down to My Last Skin*. Johannesburg: Random House, 2000.

Kruger, Loren. *The Drama of South Africa: Plays, Pageants, and Publics since 1910* London: Routledge, 1999.

———. *Post-Imperial Brecht: Politics and Performance, East and South*. Cambridge: Cambridge Univ. Press, 2004.

Landy, Robert J. *Persona and Performance: The Meaning of Role in Drama, Therapy, and Everyday Life*. New York: Guilford Press, 1993.

Laub, Dori, and Shoshana Felman. *Testimony: Crisis of Witnessing in Literature, Psychoanalysis, and History*. New York: Routledge, 1991.

Leder, Drew. *The Absent Body*. Chicago: Univ. of Chicago Press, 1990.

Lederach, John Paul. *Preparing for Peace: Conflict Transformation across Cultures*. Syracuse: Syracuse Univ. Press, 1996.

Leys, Ruth. *Trauma: A Geneology*. Chicago: Univ. of Chicago Press, 2000.

Lindy, Jacob, and Robert Lifton, eds. *Beyond Invisible Walls: The Psychological Legacy of Soviet Trauma*. New York: Brunner-Routledge, 2001.

Lynch, Marc. *The Arab Uprising: The Unfinished Revolutions of the New Middle East*. New York: Public Affairs, 2012.

———. *Voices of the New Arab Public: Iraq, Al-Jazeera, and Middle East Politics Today*. New York: Columbia Univ. Press, 2006.

Malkki, Liisa H. *Purity and Exile*. Chicago: Univ. of Chicago Press, 1995.

Marshall, Paul, Lela Gilbert, and Roberta Green Ahmanson, eds. *Blind Spot: When Journalists Don't Get Religion*. Oxford: Oxford Univ. Press, 2009.

Mattawa, Khaled, ed. *Miracle Maker: Selected Poems of Fadhil Al-Azzawi*. Rochester, NY: BOA Editions, 2003.

Mbembe, Achille. *On the Postcolony*. Berkeley and Los Angeles: Univ. of California Press, 2001.

McAfee, Noelle. *Democracy and the Political Unconscious*. New York: Columbia Univ. Press, 2008.

McClintock, Anne. *Imperial Leather: Race, Gender, and Sexuality.* New York: Routledge, 1995.

McDowall, David. *A Modern History of the Kurds.* London: I. B. Tauris, 2004.

Mehta, Brinda. *Rituals of Memory in Contemporary Arab Women's Writing.* Syracuse: Syracuse Univ. Press, 2007.

Mernissi, Fatima. *Sheherazade Goes West: Different Cultures, Different Harems.* New York: Washington Square Press, 2001.

Mikhail, Dunya. "America." In *The War Works Hard,* edited and introduction by Saadi Simawe, translated by Elizabeth Winslow, 33-39. New York: New Directions, 2005.

Minnaar, Anthony, Marie Wentzel, and Catherine Payze. "Witch Killing with Specific Reference to the Northern Province of South Africa." In Bornman, van Eeden, and Wentzel, *Violence in South Africa,* 175-200.

Minnaar, Anthony, Sam Pretorius, and Marie Wentzel. "Political Conflict and Other Manifestations of Violence in South Africa." In Bornman, van Eeden, and Wentzel, *Violence in South Africa,* 13-56.

Minow, Martha. *Between Vengeance and Forgiveness.* Boston: Beacon Press, 1998.

Moaddel, Mansoor. *Class, Politics, Ideology in the Iranian Revolution.* New York: Columbia Univ. Press, 1993.

Moghadam, Valentine. "Women, Citizenship, and Civil Rights in the Arab World." In Chase and Hamzawy, *Human Rights in the Arab World,* 89–106.

Mohammed, Sadek, Soheil Najm, Haider Al-Kabi, and Dan Veach, eds. *Flowers of Flame: Unheard Voices of Iraq.* East Lansing: Michigan State Univ. Press, 2008.

Mohanty, Chandra Talpade. "Feminist Scholarship, Colonial Discourses." In *The Postcolonial Studies Reader,* edited by Bill Ashcroft, Gareth Griffiths, and Helen Tiffin, 259–64. London: Routledge, 1995.

———. *Feminism without Borders: Decolonizing Theory, Practicing Solidarity.* Durham: Duke Univ. Press, 2003.

Morin, Karen, and Jeanne Kay Guelke. "Introduction: Women, Religion, and Space—Making the Connections." In Morin and Guelke, *Women, Religion, and Space,* xix-xxiv.

———. "Missionary Women in Early America." In Morin and Guelke, *Women, Religion, and Space,* 105–26.

———, eds. *Women, Religion, and Space: Global Perspectives on Gender and Faith.* Syracuse: Syracuse Univ. Press, 2007.

Motsapi, Seitlhamo. *Earthstepper/The Ocean Is Very Shallow*. Grahamstown, South Africa: Deep South, 2003.

Mudimbe, V. Y. *The Invention of Africa: Gnosis, Philosophy, and the Order of Knowledge*. Bloomington: Indiana Univ. Press, 1988.

Nasr, Vali. *The Shia Revival: How Conflicts within Islam Will Shape the Future*. New York: Norton, 2007.

Natali, Denise. *The Kurds and the State: Evolving National Identity in Iraq, Turkey, and Iran*. Syracuse: Syracuse Univ. Press, 2005.

Ndlovu, Malika Lueen. *Born in Africa, But*. Cape Town: Educall, Harrington House, 2000.

Nelson, Hilde Lindemann. *Damaged Identities, Narrative Repair*. Ithaca: Cornell Univ. Press, 2001.

Niehaus, Isak. "Witchcraft in the New South Africa: From Colonial Superstition to Postcolonial Reality?" In *Magical Interpretations, Material Realities: Modernity, Witchcraft, and the Occult in Postcolonial Africa*, edited by Henrietta L. Moore and Todd Sanders, 184-205. London: Routledge, 2001.

Noueihed, Lin, and Alex Warren. *The Battle for Arab Spring: Revolution, Counter-Revolution, and the Making of a New Era*. New Haven: Yale Univ. Press, 2012.

Nuttall, Sarah, and Carli Coetzee, eds. *Negotiating the Past: The Making of Memory in South Africa*. Cape Town: Oxford Univ. Press, 1998.

Nxumalo, Khulile. *Ten Flapping Elbows, Mama*. Grahamstown, South Africa: Deep South, 2004.

O'Callaghan, Casey. *Sounds: A Philosophical Theory*. Oxford: Oxford Univ. Press, 2007.

Oliver, Kelly. *Women as Weapons of War: Iraq, Sex, and the Media*. New York: Columbia Univ. Press, 2007.

Pax, Salam. *The Clandestine Diary of an Ordinary Iraq*. New York: Grove Press, 2003.

Phelan, Peggy. *Mourning Sex: Performing Public Memories*. London: Routledge, 1997.

Phelps, Teresa Godwin. *Shattered Voices: Language, Violence, and the Work of Truth Commissions*. Philadelphia: Univ. of Pennsylvania Press, 2004.

Pollock, Della. "Introduction: Making History Go." In *Exceptional Spaces: Essays in Performance and History*, edited by Della Pollock, 1-48. Chapel Hill: Univ. of North Carolina Press, 1998.

Pratt, Mary Louise. *Imperial Eyes: Travel Writing and Transculturation.* London: Routledge, 1992.

Pratt, Nicola. *Democracy and Authoritarianism in the Arab World.* Boulder, CO: Lynne Rienner, 2007.

———. "Human Rights NGOs and the Foreign Funding Debate in Egypt." In Chase and Hamzawy, *Human Rights in the Arab World,* 114–26.

Przeworski, Adam, Michael Alvarez, Jose Cheibub, and Fernando Limongi. "What Makes Democracies Endure?" In *Global Divergence of Democracies,* edited by Larry Diamond and Marc Plattner, 167–84. Baltimore: Johns Hopkins Univ. Press, 2001.

Puar, Jasbir K. *Terrorist Assemblages: Homonationalism in Queer Times.* Durham: Duke Univ. Press, 2007.

Radden, Jennifer, ed. *The Nature of Melancholy: From Aristotle to Kristeva.* Oxford: Oxford Univ. Press, 2000.

Raffo, Heather. *9 Parts of Desire.* Chicago: Northwestern Univ. Press, 2006.

Ramadan, Tariq. *Islam and the Arab Awakening.* Oxford: Oxford Univ. Press, 2012.

Ridgeway, James. "April through September 2004." In Riverbend, *Baghdad Burning,* xi-xxiii.

Riverbend. *Baghdad Burning: Girl Blog From Iraq.* New York: The Feminist Press at the City Univ. of New York, 2005.

———. *Baghdad Burning II: More Girl Blog from Iraq.* New York: The Feminist Press at the City Univ. of New York, 2006.

Roach, Joseph. *Cities of the Dead: Circum-Atlantic Performance.* New York: Columbia Univ. Press, 1996.

Robben, Antonius C. G. M., and Marcelo M. Suárez-Orozco, eds. *Cultures under Siege: Collective Violence and Trauma.* Cambridge: Cambridge Univ. Press, 2000.

Rose, Gideon. "Introduction." In *The New Arab Revolt: What Happened, What It Means, and What Comes Next,* edited by Rose Gideon, xii–xvi. New York: Foreign Affairs, 2011.

Rosen, Nir. *Aftermath: Following the Bloodshed of America's Wars in the Muslim World.* New York: Nation Books, 2010.

Rubin, Michael. "Three Decades of Misreporting Iran and Iraq." In Marshall, Gilbert, and Ahmanson, *Blind Spot,* 47-64.

Sabbagh, Suha. *Arab Women: Between Difference and Restraint.* New York: Olive Branch Press, 1996.

Said, Edward. "Revised Introduction." In *Covering Islam: How the Media and the Experts Determine How We See the Rest of the World*. New York: Vintage, 1997.

Saleem, Hiner. *My Father's Rifle: A Childhood in Kurdistan*. Translated by Catherine Temerson. New York: Picador, 2004.

Santner, Eric. *Stranded Objects: Mourning, Memory, and Film in Postwar Germany*. Ithaca: Cornell Univ. Press, 1990.

El Sarraj, Eyad. "Justice in Heaven." In Chase and Hamzawy, *Human Rights in the Arab World*, 127–36.

Sassoon, Joseph. *The Iraqi Refugees: The New Crisis in the Middle East*. New York: I. B. Tauris, 2009.

Satrapi, Marjane. *Persepolis: The Story of a Childhood*. New York: Pantheon, 2003.

———. *Persepolis 2: The Story of a Return*. New York: Pantheon, 2004.

Scahill, Jeremy. *Blackwater: The Rise of the World's Most Powerful Mercenary Army*. New York: Avalon, 2007.

Scarry, Elaine. *The Body in Pain: The Making and Unmaking of the World*. New York: Oxford Univ. Press, 1985.

Schaffer, Frederic. *Democracy in Translation: Understanding Politics in an Unfamiliar Culture*. Ithaca: Cornell Univ. Press, 1998.

Schwenger, Peter. *The Tears of Things: Melancholy and Physical Objects*. Minneapolis: Univ. of Minnesota Press, 2006.

Sedgwick, Eve Kosofsky. *Touching Feeling: Affect, Pedagogy, Performativity*. Durham: Duke Univ. Press, 2004.

Shayegan, Daryush. *Cultural Schizophrenia: Islamic Societies Confronting the West*. Translated by John Howe. Syracuse: Syracuse Univ. Press, 1997.

Simawe, Saadi. "Introduction." In *Iraqi Poetry Today*, edited by Saadi Simawe and Daniel Weissbort, 1-5. London: Univ. of London Press, 2003.

Steward, Kathleen. "Afterword: Worlding Refrains." In Gregg and Seigworth, *Affect Theory Reader*, 339-53.

Stinton, Diane B. *Jesus of Africa: Voices of Contemporary African Christology*. Maryknoll, NY: Orbis Books, 2004.

Suleiman, Yasir, and Ibrahim Muhawi, eds. *Literature and Nation in the Middle East*. Edinburgh: Edinburgh Univ. Press, 2006.

Taussig, Michael. *Shamanism, Colonialism, and the Wild Man: A Study in Terror and Healing*. Chicago: Univ. of Chicago Press, 1987.

Taylor, Diana. *The Archive and the Repertoire: Performing Cultural Memory in the Americas*. Durham: Duke Univ. Press, 2003.

Tessler, Mark, and Marilyn Grobschmidt. "Democracy in the Arab World and the Arab-Israeli Conflict." In *Democracy, War, and Peace in the Middle East*, edited by David Garnham and Mark Tessler, 135–69. Bloomington: Indiana Univ. Press, 1995.

Tessler, Mark, Amaney Jamal, and Michael Robbins. "New Findings on Arabs and Democracy." *Journal of Democracy* 23, no. 4 (2012): 89–103.

Thompson, William Forde. *Music, Thought, and Feeling: Understanding the Psychology of Music*. New York: Oxford Univ. Press, 2009.

Tripp, Charles. *A History of Iraq*. 3rd ed. Cambridge: Cambridge Univ. Press, 2007.

Truth and Reconciliation Commission of South Africa Report. Vols. 1–4. Cape Town: TRC, 1998.

Turner, Victor. *The Anthropology of Performance*. New York: Performing Arts Journal, 1987.

Tutu, Desmond. *No Future without Forgiveness*. Johannesburg: Rider, 1999.

Villa-Vicencio, Charles. "On the Limitations of Academic History: The Quest for Truth Demands Both More and Less." In James and Van de Vivjer, *After the TRC*, 21–31.

———, and Wilhelm Verwoerd, eds. *Looking Back, Reaching Forward: Reflections on the Truth and Reconciliation Commission of South Africa*. Cape Town: Univ. of Cape Town Press and Zed Books, 2000.

West, Bing. *No True Glory: A Frontline Account of the Battle for Fallujah*. New York: Bantam, 2005.

White, Michael, and David Epston. *Narrative Means to Therapeutic Ends*. New York: W. W. Norton, 1990.

Whitlock, Gillian. *Soft Weapons: Autobiography in Transit*. Chicago: Univ. of Chicago Press, 2007.

Witz, Leslie. *Apartheid's Festival: Contesting South Africa's National Pasts*. Indianapolis: Indiana Univ. Press, 2003.

Wright, Richard, and Lawrence Ward. *Orienting of Attention*. Oxford: Oxford Univ. Press, 2008.

Index

Italic page number denotes illustration.